PHP

There is no shortage of websites that use the PHP programming language in some or other capacity. PHP (Hypertext Preprocessor) is a server-side scripting language that allows you to create dynamically-generated web pages. Rasmus Lerdorf created PHP in 1994.

PHP works in the backend of a website because it is a server-side technology. This is the part of a website that no one sees. This means that PHP is frequently used to run server-side programs such as data collection and processing and database management. The fact that PHP is a simple language is one of the key reasons why learning it is a wise investment. PHP was created with the goal of speeding up web development; therefore, it features a basic syntax that is ideal for beginners. Furthermore, because PHP is a dynamically typed language, there are less restrictions to follow while creating features. The PHP programming language offers a wide range of applications and features, such as authentication, payments, user administration, and other "dynamic" aspects of a website.

Efficiency, syntax compatibility, platform independence, error detection, and encryption are just a few of the interesting properties of PHP.

Why should you learn PHP? PHP developers work with the PHP programming language to create websites, applications, and programs. As a PHP developer, you'll usually be working in IT companies (all over the world), but there are also a lot of opportunities in design and business. A PHP developer, like any other programming/scripting language developer, should be able to work with many languages and ideally have some knowledge of database, web design, or some page formatting language.

This book offers:

- A step-by-step approach to problem solving and skill development
- A quick run-through of the basic concepts, in the form of a "Crash Course"

- Advanced, hands-on core concepts, with a focus on real-world problems

- Industry-level coding paradigms and a practice-oriented explanatory approach

- Special emphasis on writing clean and optimized code, with additional chapters focused on coding methodology

PHP
The Ultimate Guide

Sufyan bin Uzayr

CRC Press
Taylor & Francis Group
Boca Raton London New York

CRC Press is an imprint of the
Taylor & Francis Group, an **informa** business

First edition published 2023
by CRC Press
6000 Broken Sound Parkway NW, Suite 300, Boca Raton, FL 33487-2742

and by CRC Press
4 Park Square, Milton Park, Abingdon, Oxon, OX14 4RN

CRC Press is an imprint of Taylor & Francis Group, LLC

Library of Congress Cataloging-in-Publication Data

Names: Bin Uzayr, Sufyan, author.
Title: PHP : the ultimate guide / Sufyan bin Uzayr.
Description: First edition. | Boca Raton : CRC Press, 2023. | Includes
bibliographical references and index.
Identifiers: LCCN 2022025685 (print) | LCCN 2022025686 (ebook) |
ISBN 9781032312224 (hardback) | ISBN 9781032311784 (paperback) |
ISBN 9781003308669 (ebook)
Subjects: LCSH: PHP (Computer program language) | Web site development.
Classification: LCC QA76.73.P224 B56 2023 (print) | LCC QA76.73.P224 (ebook) |
DDC 005.2/762--dc23/eng/20220919
LC record available at https://lccn.loc.gov/2022025685
LC ebook record available at https://lccn.loc.gov/2022025686

ISBN: 9781032312224 (hbk)
ISBN: 9781032311784 (pbk)
ISBN: 9781003308669 (ebk)

DOI: 10.1201/9781003308669

Typeset in Minion
by KnowledgeWorks Global Ltd.

Contents

Acknowledgments

There are many people who deserve to be on this page; this book would not have come into existence without their support. That said, some names deserve a special mention, and I am genuinely grateful to:

- My parents, for everything they have done for me.

- My siblings, for helping with things back home.

- The Parakozm team, especially Divya Sachdeva, Jaskiran Kaur, and Vartika, for offering great amounts of help and assistance during the book-writing process.

- The CRC team, especially Sean Connelly and Danielle Zarfati, for ensuring that the book's content, layout, formatting, and everything else remains perfect throughout.

- Reviewers of this book for going through the manuscript and providing their insight and feedback.

- Typesetters, cover designers, printers, and all related roles for their part in the development of this book.

- All the folks associated with Zeba Academy, either directly or indirectly, for their help and support.

- The programming community in general, and the web development community in particular, for all their hard work and efforts.

Sufyan bin Uzayr

About the Author

Sufyan bin Uzayr is a writer, coder, and entrepreneur with over a decade of experience in the industry. He has authored several books in the past, pertaining to a diverse range of topics, ranging from History to Computers/IT.

Sufyan is the Director of Parakozm, a multinational IT company specializing in EdTech solutions. He also runs Zeba Academy, an online learning and teaching vertical with a focus on STEM fields.

Sufyan specializes in a wide variety of technologies such as JavaScript, Dart, WordPress, Drupal, Linux, and Python. He holds multiple degrees, including ones in Management, IT, Literature, and Political Science.

Sufyan is a digital nomad, dividing his time between four countries. He has lived and taught in universities and educational institutions around the globe. Sufyan takes a keen interest in technology, politics, literature, history, and sports, and in his spare time, he enjoys teaching coding and English to young students.

Learn more at sufyanism.com.

CHAPTER 1

Introduction to PHP

IN THIS CHAPTER

➢ Introduction to PHP

➢ Installation of PHP

➢ PHP basics

➢ HTML and CSS

➢ Data types

Several people learn PHP for many reasons. All languages have a bit of a learning curve. If you want to build a simple blog or as advanced as a vast online e-commerce site or e-learning site with thousands of stuff, it is tough to know where to start getting the needed things or knowledge if you are looking for a way to grow fast in order to make sure that you have come to the right place! This book's main motive is to get you to start on your journey to PHP and MySQL. It will tell you the essential stuff you need to know to get started quickly as the fresher or beginner in either PHP or MySQL, so you get to do some useful stuff as quickly as possible. This is not a full-fledged guidebook to PHP and MySQL, but will cover all the aspects of both these languages and will provide a crash course that gives you a practical guide on how to perform really cool basic stuff with PHP and MySQL, both individually and together. They both can get advanced, but with the knowledge in this PHP book, you should be able to know that prototype is up and running as you handle the more advanced topics.

We will start with a basic knowledge of HTML, and CSS will be provided because PHP is working as a back-end (client-side) language that managed to produce web pages, and its final output is HTML. We will be going to cover the basics of PHP and MySQL and finally put it all together and build a simple website where you will be able to store a record of your favorite artists using the dynamic duo. The basics are all you need to get going in this, and this book, of course, is all you need.

HISTORY

PHP stands for Personal Home Page. It was created by Rasmus Lerdorf in 1994. Lerdorf first used it for his personal page to track visitors. It has a lot of additional functions added to it. However, it took many years for it to become a language, and it is not just a set of tools. Its code was released in mid-1990s. Israel's Andi Gutmans and Zeev Suraski did a major job in 1997 with the goal of using PHP to run an e-commerce site. Their version, named PHP 3.0, had more of the features we expect and see today.

WHY DO WE LEARN PHP?

There are various programming languages for you to learn, which may lead you to wonder if you should start learning PHP. We understand you need to learn and use the best tools for the job at hand, and for many jobs, PHP is a great tool. It is a wonderful tool to learn, and here are just a few great reasons to dive in and learn. In the beginning years of the Internet, most destinations were static content pages. As the Internet grew, people needed sites with more advanced functionality. For example, visitor books and contact frames. PHP was the ideal instrument and it still is. It is an exceptionally strong and experienced programming language.

VERSIONS OF PHP

- **Version 1.0:** Its development started in 1994 and was developed by Rasmus Lerdorf. He used it as a scripting language and wrote several Common Gateway Interface (CGI) programs where CGI is used for simple interactive applications. It works like a web browser, submitting the information to the server. The server passes that data to an application and then the application responds. It goes back to your web browser as a result, and something might be performed by the database or sending an email. CGI applications can be written in any of the programming languages. Common languages like Perl, PHP, and Python are often called CGI scripts. They tend to be scripting languages and they are often called CGI scripts. It can be written in other programming languages like ASP, Java, C++, but it is important to know that CGI application runs on the server.

First, Lerdorf used it to maintain his personal homepage, and later on, he extended these codes to work with web forms and databases. This implementation was called Personal Home Page or Forms interpreted.

This version of PHP already had several basic functionalities like it has form handling capabilities variables and the ability to work with HTML. The syntax was also similar.

- **Version 2.0:** This version of PHP was released for public usage in 1995. It continued to grow, and a formal developer team was formed to work on the inconsistencies of version 1.0. Once the discrepancies were overcome, updated language was released as version 2.0 in 1997.

- **Version 3.0:** As PHP grew, it attracted the attention of Zeev Suraski and Andi Gutmans then. In 1997, they rewrote the PHP parser and the basic structure for PHP 3.0. The PHP 3.0 was launched in June 1998 when the public testing was completed. Later, Suraski and Gutmans started to rewrite the core PHP and made the Zend engine in 1999. This led to the beginning of Zend Technologies in Israel.

- **Version 4.0:** In the year 2000, PHP version 4.0 was powered by Zend Engine and was released for public usage. Then, by 2008, PHP version 4.0 had reached to 4.4.9 version. Although, it is no more supported for security updates.

- **Versions 5.0 and 6.0:** In 2004, versions 5.0 and 6.0 were released and powered by Zend Engine 2. They have several new features and better support for Object-Oriented Programming (OOP) and PHP Data Objects (PDO) extension, which give programmers a lightweight interface for accessing databases and many other performance improvements. They level up to version 5.6.0.

In December 2018, its official support for PHP security ended, but Debian provided security support until 2020. When the developers used PHP 5.0 for the development of their applications, that PHP 5.0 had insufficient support for Unicode encoding. But in 2005, Andrei

Zmievski took to overcome this problem. He launched a project to embed Unicode support throughout the PHP system and included the ICU, i.e., International Components for Unicode library across the basic PHP system. The text strings in PHP were represented as 16-bit Unicode Transformation Format or commonly known as UTF-16. This was partially completed when it was realized that conversion UTF-16 could cause several performance issues. In March 2010, PHP version 6.0 was released with non-Unicode features like traits and closure binding.

- **Version 7.0:** In the period of 2016 and 2017, PHP went through major changes, and the update was released as PHP 7.0. It is based on phpng, which stands for PHP next Generation. It (PHP Next Generation) was an initiative by developers to overcome the high-performance constraints of the previous versions. The phpng served as the base branch for PHP version 7.0, which provided several optimizations and performance improvements. It included an in-build caching mechanism for better performance.

- **Current Version:** PHP 8.1.x is the latest version. It was released in May 2022.

PHP

What Is PHP?

It's a server-side programming language that's been around for almost 25 years. It is also known as Hypertext Preprocessor. It's a popular open-source general-purpose scripting language that's especially well-suited for web development and can be embedded in HTML. It is an open-source and server-side scripting language, mainly used for developing web applications. The syntax of the PHP language is similar to the C language. It is used to manage dynamic web content, databases, session tracking, and to build entire e-commerce sites. It comes with a number of popular databases, including MySQL, PostgreSQL, Oracle, Sybase, Informix, and Microsoft SQL Server.

What Can We Do with PHP?

People in business need their website to be developed without any well-maintained structure. The PHP application will provide maintenance like maintenance of any machine or website at every period of time needs to be updated.

Following are some of the reasons that simply explain why PHP programming language is the good choice for web development:

- **Boost simplicity:** PHP made coding easy. It is also used to create and run the website in the most efficient manner possible.

- **Works exceptionally:** It trends toward the adaptive content created a CMS customization, a crucial competitive need for the business.

- Increased programming is used to create a large modification and building and lower the cost per hour for those services.

- **Adaptive:** It has made the responsive websites and fluid grid systems even more pertinent for the organizations.

- **Standard library:** It simplifies and speeds the data processing ability of the language.

- Content management system development.

- Apps development for small businesses.

- Small video games development.

- Data transfer.

Main Components

- **MVC-based architecture:** It mainly works on model-view architecture that helps in managing the code and separates the model, view, and controller files, and helps in connecting the database easily, and the changes can be done easily without affecting other files or modules.

- **Web server:** It mainly works on web server software and uses the Apache server (WAMP, XAMMP).

- **Database:** It may use with any database; however, MySQL is the most popular.

- **PHP parser:** It helps in parsing the PHP instructions to HTML code writing and then sends it to a browser to display the content.

- **Encryption:** PHP can encrypt the data or access and set the cookie variable. Using PHP, a developer can restrict the other users from accessing the pages.

- **Filters:** These filters are used to validate the data by using the filter function. It helps in checking the invalid input that has been submitted to avoid the security problem and break of web pages.

- **System functions:** The system functions are the ways to open a file. It helps in creating, reading, and writing the file as well.

- **Handle forms:** Forms can be used to get the data from files, save the data, send the email, and return the data to a user in the form of a result.

- **Frameworks:** It has various frameworks such as Laravel, Aura, Yii, Symfony, and Zend. These will help to get well-ordered and clear code syntax that is easily manageable and make the development easier for the developers.

- **Autosuggest:** The components are ready to use to implement the search form with an autosuggest feature using PHP and database MySQL.

Pros and Cons of PHP

Every programming language has pros and cons. But here, let's discuss the pros and cons of PHP.

Pros:

- The most important pros is open-source and free-to-use technology, which can be downloaded anytime and be ready for website development and considerable savings for the development budget.

- Various online tutorials, manuals, and other reference materials are available over the Internet for PHP, which facilitate the development and may provide help and the source of inspiration in tough situations.

- It is an independent and cross-platform language. Application-based PHP can run on every operating system such as UNIX, Linus, Windows, etc. It can easily download and connect with databases.

- Its speed is higher than in any other languages. It is understandable for beginners and easy to use, and simple. It is about three times faster than Python in some scenarios.

- Moreover, several frameworks, such as Laravel, Code Igniter, and various CMS, such as WordPress and Drupal, help to extend the functionality of PHP and make the development process easier and more effective.

- If you know basic C programming, then you can easily work with PHP.

- It is more stable than several years before by the help of providing different versions.

- PHP version 5.0 or later version has supported OOP Object-oriented.

- It has supported powerful libraries to modularize functions for data representations easily.

- Modules connecting with databases are pre-integrated in PHP, reduce time and efforts for development.

- The release of PHP version 8.0 brings faster speed.

- PHP has great collaboration with HTML with various benefits provided by cloud solutions.

- Flexibility makes the PHP code able to combine with many other programming languages effectively.

Cons:

- PHP is not as secure as other languages, so the project needs to promote security and should not use PHP.

- It is not suitable for web apps that need to handle huge content.

- PHP is a weak type not as tight as Java, which leads to incorrect information and data for users.

- Using PHP Frameworks needs to learn Built-in Function (pre-integrated in PHP) to avoid rewriting the function.

- Using PHP Frameworks functions can cause poor performance.

- It cannot offer equally fast and effective alternative dedicated libraries like Python's TensorFlow, Scikit-learn, Theano, and Keras.

- It has a bad reputation related to its security due to the low-entry barrier for novice programmers.

- It is not suitable for huge content-based web applications.

- It does not allow to change or modification in the core behavior of the web applications.

Built-in Templating Engine

Many templating engine libraries allow you to separate the view layer from the rest of the application. In most cases, you can implement such a library by yourself. You don't even need another library; sometimes, it is enough just to separate your view of the template HTML files into a different directory, prepare some variables in the simple controller, and include the templates.

PHP framework provides some kind of templating engines. Most of the programmers use plain PHP by default, including Symfony 1.x, Zend Framework, and CakePHP, but many other standalone libraries can be plugged into your framework or custom application.

Here is the list of some templating engines:

- **Smarty:** It was one of the most famous templating engines and was developed as a subproject of the PHP, but has lost its popularity in recent years due to poor performance and backward compatibility with PHP version 4.0. Also, it has lacked many modern features such as templating inheritance. Now, it is back with version 3.0. Many other frameworks, such as Django, have inherited some of the basics.

- **PHPTAL:** It is a template engine based on a very different syntax and concept. It implements the Zope Page Templates syntax, where Zope is an application server written in Python. It is based on well-formed XML/XHTML, for example, that comes from the project page. If you have good experience with ZOPE or XML, then this template engine is helpful for you.

- **Twig:** It is the last PHP template engine designed by the authors of Symfony, which is the default view library of this framework PHP version 2.0. Its advantages are rich features, extensibility, good documentation, and speedy compilation of your templates to the native PHP language.

By knowing how to use a library or framework is not enough. A good programmer should also know how to stuff works, the relationship between the components, and possible caveats. This will give you an idea of how more advanced libraries work.

PHP from the Command Line

The command-line interface, or CLI, was introduced in PHP 4.3 in December 2002, as its default Server API or SAPI. Now, it is CGI.

The command-line option-v (version) in PHP will reveal whether your Server API is a CLI binary or other in your current installation,

```
C:\Users\PC>php -version
PHP 7.4.14 (cli) (built: Jan 5 2021 15:12:29)
( ZTS Visual C++ 2017 x64 )
Copyright (c) The PHP Group
Zend Engine v3.4.0, Copyright (c) Zend Technologies
```

You will see the above line when you run php-version in your local system.

PHP command line has so many commands to execute in the command prompt, you can check list in one go like,

```
C:\Users\PC>php -help
Usage: php [options] [-f] <file> [--] [args...]
    php [options] -r <code> [--] [args...]
    php [options] [-B <begin_code>] -R <code> [-E <end_
code>] [--] [args...]
    php [options] [-B <begin_code>] -F <file> [-E <end_
code>] [--] [args...]
    php [options] -S <addr>:<port> [-t docroot] [router]
    php [options] -- [args...]
    php [options] -a
  -a                 It run as interactive shell
  -c <path>|<file> It look for php.ini file in this
directory
  -n                 Only no configuration (ini) files
will be used
  -d foo[=bar]      It define INI entry foo with value
'bar'
  -e                 It generate extended information for
debugger/profiler
  -f <file>          It parse and execute <file>.
  -h                 It is used for help
  -i                 It gives you the PHP related
information
```

```
  -l                   It is syntax check only (lint)
  -m              It  is syntax show compiled in modules
  -r <code>       It   syntax run PHP <code> without
using script tags <?..?>
  -B <begin_code> It runs PHP <begin_code> before
processing input lines
  -R <code>       It runsPHP <code> for every input
line
  -F <file>        It can parse and execute <file> for
every input line
  -E <end_code>    It runsPHP <end_code> after
processing all input lines
  -H              It can hide any passed arguments
from external tools.
  -S <addr>:<port> It runswith built-in web server.
  -t <docroot>     It specify document root <docroot>
for built-in web server.
  -s               It can output HTML syntax highlighted
source.
  -v               It is version number
  -w               It is output source with stripped
comments and whitespace.
  -z <file>        It loads Zend extension <file>.
args          It is arguments passed to script. Use
-- args when first argument
 It starts with - or script is read from stdin
  --ini           It shows configuration file names
  --rf <name>     It shows information about function
<name>.
  --rc <name>       It shows information about class
<name>.
  --re <name>       It shows information about extension
<name>.
  --rz <name>       It shows information about Zend
extension <name>.
  --ri <name>       It shows  configuration for
extension <name>.
```

Using PHP-a starts either the PHP interaction mode or shell. Run the command like,

```
C:\Users\PC>php -a
Interactive shell
PHP >
```

Here we will see how to run PHP scripts from the command line. We start with our simple 'Hello, PHP' program in PHP.

So open your file and make sure it has a .php extension. Write the basic PHP program.

Example:

```
<?PHP
        echo 'Hello, World!';
?>
```

Save it as Firstprogram.php. This file can execute from the terminal by running the command,

```
PHP Firstprogram.php
```

Upgrading PHP in macOS

To check the PHP version that is currently installed in your system by executing the following command line:

```
PHP -v
```

To update the PHP version you can use,

```
brew upgrade PHP
```

Upgrading PHP in Windows

If you are using Windows, it is easy to run your PHP application on pre-packaged localhost environments such as WAMP or MAMP servers. These applications come with PHP preinstalled and configured. You just need to update that to their latest version or install it using the built-in tool to get the latest PHP version.

Both WAMP and MAMP provide you an option within the application to easily switch PHP.

Upgrading PHP in Ubuntu

As mentioned before, you should first check the PHP version that's in your Ubuntu machine.

In Ubuntu, the package can be installed from the Ondrej/PHP repository. First, run the following command by tapping the repository.

```
sudo add-apt-repository PPA:Ondrej/PHP
sudo apt-get update
```

Then, you can run the following commands, which will install PHP 7.4, some PHP extensions and packages, and the PHP CLI.

```
sudo apt-get install php7.4 php7.4-common php7.4-cli
```

Why Is PHP Still So Widely Used?

Although PHP is not considered as the most popular language these days, but here are some key PHP benefits that help explain why it is still so important in web development:

- One of the main reasons why PHP became so commonplace is that it is simple and straightforward to get started with. Even without extensive knowledge or prior experience in web development, most people can create a web page with a single PHP file in a short period of time. Its syntax is simple, and command functions are easy to learn.

- This also helps developers to get started with PHP – it can be installed quickly and at zero cost. There is also open access to a wide range of PHP frameworks such as Laravel and Symfony.

- PHP is platform-independent, meaning it can be used on macOS, Windows, Linux and supports most web browsers. It also supports all the major web servers, making it easy to deploy on different systems and platforms at minimal additional cost.

- Now, PHP has a large and loyal community base to support it. There are a lot of online tutorials, FAQs, and tips and tricks to help new PHP developers and to continue pushing the boundaries of what the language can achieve through regular updates.

- PHP code has been put to the test in all kinds of real-life environments.

- The bugs have been found and fixed, making the language more stable and trusted by developers.

PHP Prerequisites

Before installing PHP, you need to be sure that your server can handle it. The requirements are basic, and a lot of the software is already installed on your computer.

It requires Windows 2008/Vista. Either 32-Bit or 64-bit, PHP does not run on Windows RT/WOA/ARM where new PHP 7.2.0 Windows 2008 and Vista are no longer supported.

It requires the Visual C runtime (CRT). You must download the x86 CRT for PHP x86 builds, and the x64 CRT for PHP x64 builds.

INSTALLATION OF PHP

How to Install PHP on Windows

If you are working over the Windows system, then you do not need to install PHP through the command line.

The best and easy way to install PHP is to enable IIS, i.e., you can enable it by running the command in the Run box or by keyboard shortcuts Windows + R named appwiz. Cpl. The Program and Features Control Panel will open as a result of this. On left side, click the "Turn Windows features on or off" link. Click on the "Turn Windows features on or off" link on the left side. Now click on the Internet Information Services check box. By default, it installs all the stuff needed to host a website, but you need some more developers. After clicking OK, this dialog box will appear on your screen for a while, and then use WebPI to install PHP. After launching WebPI, you can find it under the Products tab. Click Add on the version you want, and then click Install.

You can download PHP for Windows and manually configure it to work with IIS.

If all this looks complicated, you could install web server instead of WampServer or XAMPP, as these come with everything you need to start working with a web server: Apache, a database, and of course PHP.

How to Install PHP on Linux

Before installation, you should be familiar with the terminal and how to operate Unix. These command-line codes work on every Linux distribution that uses the basic syntax in the terminal.

First, make sure your packages are up to date, so run this command in the terminal.

```
sudo apt-get update && sudo apt-get upgrade
```

Now it's ready to install PHP in your local.

```
sudo apt-get install PHP
```

What if you want to install any particular version of PHP such as PHP 7.4?
Type in the following command:

```
sudo apt install php7.4
```

You can change this version number with whatever PHP version you want.

Installing PHP on Ubuntu

For Ubuntu, there are not many specific concerns. It is one of the most well-known distributions, so Linux guides are practically made for that system. One other available option is to download a LAMP stack. LAMP's full form is Linux, Apache, MySQL, and PHP. It is a bundle of all the software you need to get a server up and running.

You can manually download every one of these tools separately, and you could get Taskel, which is a bundle that will install all these at once. By running these two commands in the terminal:

```
sudo apt install tasksel
sudo tasksel install lamp-server
```

How to Install PHP on macOS

PHP comes preinstalled on most the macOS systems, so you usually do not need any manual installation.

And all you have need to do is uncomment a line of code in the Apache configuration file httpd.conf, which you can usually find at location '/private/etc/apache2/httpd.conf'. You need to uncomment these two lines of code by removing the hashtag symbol.

```
# LoadModule php5_module libexec/httpd/libphp5.so
# AddModule mod_php5.c
```

You can always check the PHP version using the "PHP-v" command to make sure PHP was installed correctly.

If you want to download PHP manually, then you should install Homebrew (it is Missing Package Manager for macOS (or Linux)) and use this simple command:

```
brew install PHP
```

Installing a Text Editor

You need a text editor to write some beautiful PHP. Ideally, any text editor would do. Even the default one is a notepad on windows or for macOS X can be used when writing PHP. We can use notepad++ because it has some features used to write clean and efficient code quickly such as syntax highlighting and autocompletion.

These text editors will save your time just downloading it.

Here is the list of some code editors for PHP projects:

- Sublime Text
- Visual Studio Code
- Atom
- Notepad++
- Novi HTML Visual Editor
- Coda
- Brackets
- SlickEdit

Starting Apache to Run PHP Scripts

First, you need to install XAMPP to start the apache web service in order for the browser to be able to run PHP scripts. To do the same, open up the Control Panel of XAMPP by double-clicking on the XAMPP icon. By default, it starts Apache automatically, but you can start it manually by clicking "Start."

Key to remember: Some other applications installed on your computer can cause Apache not to work because they are using the same port Apache is configured to, e.g., Skype.

Place Your Project in the Root Directory of XAMPP

Grab the files that you have created and place them in the root directory of your server in the folder named "htdocs," you are ready to run it in your browser. Always start your Apache and MYSQL in XAMPP Control Panel to execute PHP scripts. The file will use the localhost.

Example:

```
http://localhost:8080/index.php.
```

Printing Hello PHP on the Web Browser with a PHP File

There are some basic setup to print the content on the browser using a PHP file,

- First, open the folder htdocs under the xampp folder. It locates at C:\xampp\htdocs.

- Then create a new folder called PHP-coding there.

- And now, create a new file called index.php under the PHP-coding folder and place the following code in the file:

```
<!DOCTYPE html>
<html lang="en">
<head>
    <meta charset="UTF-8">
    <meta name="viewport"  initial-scale=1.0"
content="width=device-width,>
    <title> PHP</title>
</head>
<body>
        <h1><?php echo 'Hello, PHP!';?></h1>
</body>
</html>
```

The above code in the PHP-coding.php file looks like a normal HTML document except the part <?php and?>.

The code between the opening <?php and closing tag?> is PHP:

```
<?php echo 'Hello, PHP';?>
```

This code prints out the Hello, PHP message inside the <h1> tag using the echo statement.

When PHP executes the PHP-coding.php file, it executes the code and returns the Hello, PHP! message.

Then, launch a web browser and open the URL using,

```
http://localhost:8080/PHP-coding/
```

PHP Hello World on the Command Line

Open the command prompt on Windows or terminal on macOS or Linux.

```
Go to the folder c:\xampp\htdocs\PHP-coding\.
```

Now, type the following command to execute the PHP-coding.php file.

Example:

```
c:\xampp\htdocs\helloworld>php PHP-coding.php
```

Points to Remember:

- Always place the PHP code between <?php and? > to mix PHP code with HTML.

- Use the echo construct to output one or more strings to the screen.

PHP BASICS

- **Tags and Syntax:** We will start our journey with PHP syntax and execute our first file.

  In PHP, syntax word is most important, you need proper syntax for your server to know where it should start parsing PHP, and you have to show the parsing PHP via the open and close PHP tags, as shown here:

```
<?PHP
?>
```

Using these PHP tags lets you add your code anywhere in the document. Then suppose that if you have an HTML website, you can just add these tags, along with some PHP code, and it will process. Using the open and close PHP tags, you must also use the .php extension in your file. Let's get started with a quick example.

Here, we are going to use what we've learned how to display a string to the user:

  i. Open your code editor.

  ii. Create a new file and name it index.php.

  iii. Enter the following, and save your document:

```
<?php?>
```

  iv. Open your working directory in the terminal.

  v. Type the following command: php index.php

vi. Switch back to your document and enter the following:

```
<?PHP
echo "Hello World";
?>
```

vii. Go back to the terminal and type the following:

```
PHP index.php
```

Now we are going to discuss the important topic for writing codes in PHP scripts files. So, the first topic is written below.

- **Comments:** If you'd want to leave a special note for yourself or others in your coding team, then comments help a lot in the trouble of remembering your code working and make for an excellent way to document what your thoughts were at the time. They can also be used to exclude certain pieces of code altogether.

```
// this is a single line comment
# this is another single line comment
/*
```

This is a comment block. Everything here will be ignored and can span multiple lines.

```
*/
```

- **Variables:** If you want to build your website, you will need data and a way to store this data. Data can be a name, a number, a date, or a picture. PHP language offers a way for you to store them in memory by using a variable.

So, the variable is basically used to store any other data.

Each variable in PHP language must be preceded by the dollar ($) sign followed by the variable name without any spaces in between the sign and variable name.

Example:

```
$myInt = 10;
```

Let's see some of code in action with the following code:

```
<!DOCTYPE html>
<html>
```

```
<body>
<?php
$txt = "My PHP script!";
echo $txt;
?>
</body>
</html>
```

If you run this script in the browser, it should output the following:

```
"My PHP script!";
```

Naming Conventions for PHP Variables

1. It is case-sensitive means $Name and $name are two different variables.

2. All variables in PHP start with a $ sign, followed by the name of the variable.

3. It must always start with a letter or underscore.

4. A variable name must start with a letter or the underscore character _.

5. It cannot start with numbers.

6. A variable name in PHP can only contain alphanumeric characters and underscores (A-z, 0-9, and _).

7. It is a loosely typed language, and therefore you don't need to define the data types for variables. Depending on its value, it will automatically convert the variable to the correct data type.

8. A variable name cannot contain spaces.

- **Scope:** The variable scope is defined as the portion of the program within which it is defined and can be accessed.
  There are three scopes of the variable,

  i. **Local variables scope:** It is a scope that is declared within a function or block is called local variables for that particular function/block. These variables cannot access outside the function. Otherwise, it will show an error.

     ```
     <?PHP
         function scope()
     ```

```
    {
        $num = "Local variable scope";   //local
variable
        echo "This is the way to declared: "
. $num;
    }
    scope();
?>
```

ii. **Global variables scope:** These variables can be declared outside the function, and these can be accessed anywhere in the program. To access these within a function, use the GLOBAL keyword before the variable or without any keyword.

```
<?PHP
    $name = "PHP";            //Global Variable
    function scope()
    {
        global $name;
        echo "Variable inside the function:
". $name;
        echo "</br>";
    }
    scope();
    echo "Variable outside the function: ". $name;
?>
```

iii. **Static variable scope or static scope:** Use the static keyword before the variable, and this variable is called a static variable.
It only exists in a local function, but it does not free its memory after the program execution leaves the scope.

```
<?PHP
    function scope()
    {
        static $num1 = 3;        //static
variable
        $num2 = 1;                //Non-static
variable
        //increment in non-static variable
        $num1++;
```

```
            //increment in static variable
            $num2++;
            echo "Static: " .$num1. "</br>";
            echo "Non-static: " .$num2 ."</br>";
        }

//first function call
        scope();

        //second function call
        scope();
    ?>
```

The output will be like this,

```
Static: 4
Non-static: 2
Static: 5
Non-static: 2
```

- **PHP Constants:** It is a name or identifier for a fixed value like variables, except that they cannot be undefined or changed once they are defined. When we define a constant, we use the define() method followed by parameters in the parenthesis that give it a name of the variable and a value of it.

Example:

```
<?PHP
// Here defining constant
define("variable_name", "value");
// Here using constant
echo 'This is how to declare constant  -.
' variable_name;
?>
```

Some rules to remember about constants:

i. They must start with a letter and an underscore, not the $ sign.

ii. They can move globally across the entire script automatically.

- **Echo and Print Statements:** Here we will learn how to use the PHP echo and print statements to display the output in a web browser.

Echo Statement

It is used to output one or more strings (should be in lowercase). Generally, the echo statement can help to display anything on the browser such as string, numbers, variable values, the results of expressions, and so on.

Since it is a language construct, not actually a function. You can use it with or without parentheses, for example, echo or echo (). Also, if you want to pass more than one parameter to echo, the parameters must not be enclosed within parentheses.

With Multiple Paramters	With Single Paramters
```<?php```	```<?php```
```// Displaying string of text```	```// Displaying string of text```
```echo "Hello World!";```	```echo(Hello)```
```?>```	```?>```

- **Display HTML code:** Below is the example that will show you how to display HTML code using the echo statement:

```php
<?php
// Displaying HTML code
echo "<h4>This is a h4 heading tag.</h4>";
echo "<h4 style='color: red;'>This is heading with
color red.</h4>";
?>
```

- **Display variables:**

```php
<?php
// Defining variables
$txt = "Hello PHP";
$number = 123
$alphabets = array("A", "B", "C");
```

```php
// Displaying variables with echo statement:

echo $txt;
echo "<br>";
echo $number;
echo "<br>";
echo $alphabets [0];
?>
```

The output of the code in PHP will look something like this:

```
Hello PHP
123
A
```

- **The PHP print statement:** You can use the print statement to display output to the browser. Same as echo, the print is also a language construct, not a function; you can also use it without parentheses like print or print().

  Both echo and print work the same way except that the print statement can only output one string and always returns 1. That's why the echo statement is considered faster than the print statement.

Displaying Strings with the Print Statement

The example tells you how to display a string of text with the print statement:

```php
<?PHP
// Displaying string of text
print "Hello PHP!";
?>
```

The output of the above PHP code will look something like this:

```
Hello PHP!
```

- **Display HTML code:** The example will show you how to display HTML code using the print statement:

  ```php
  <?php
  // Displaying HTML code
  print "<h4>This is a h4 heading tag</h4>";
  print "<h4 style='color: red;'>This is heading
  with color red.</h4>";
  ?>
  ```

- **Display variables:** The example will show you how to display variable using the print statement:

  ```php
  <?php
  // Defining variables
  $txt = "Hello PHP";
  ```

```
$number = 123;
$alphabets = array("A", "B", "C");

// Displaying variables
print $txt;
print "<br>";
print $number;
print "<br>";
print $alphabets[0];
?>
```

The output of the above PHP code will look something like this:

```
Hello PHP
123
A
```

WHAT IS HTML (HYPERTEXT MARKUP LANGUAGE BASICS)?

It is a computer language that creates most web pages and applications. A hypertext is a simple text that refers to other pieces of text, while a markup language is a series of markings that tells the web servers to style and structure a document.

It is not considered a programming language as it cannot create dynamic functionality. Instead, using HTML, web users can create and structure sections, paragraphs, and various navigation links using elements, tags, and attributes.

This HTML file ends with a .html or .htm extension. A browser reads the HTML file and renders its content so that users can view it.

All HTML pages have a set of HTML elements consisting of a set of tags and attributes. These elements are the building blocks of a web page. A tag tells the browser where an element begins and where its ends, whereas an attribute describes the characteristics of an element.

There are three main parts of an element are:

- **Opening tag:** It is used to tell that where an element starts to take effect. The tag is enclosed with opening and closing angular brackets. For example, use the start tag as <p> to create a paragraph.

- **Content:** It is the output that other users see.

- **Closing tag:** It is the same as the opening tag but with a forward slash before the element name. For example, </p> to end a paragraph.

Most Used HTML Tags and HTML Elements

The most used HTML tags and two main elements are:

- Block-Level Elements

- Inline Elements

Block-Level Elements

A block-level element takes the entire width of a page and always starts a new line in the document. For example, a heating element will be in a separate line from a paragraph element.

Every HTML page uses these three tags:

- **\<html>:** This tag is the root element that defines the whole HTML document.

- **\<head>:** This tag holds meta information such as the page's title and charset.

- **\<body>:** This tag encloses all the content that appears on the page.

Other block-level tags are:

- **Heading tags:** These range from \<h1> to \<h6>, where heading \<h1> is largest, getting smaller as they move up to \<h6>.

- **Paragraph tags:** These are all enclosed by using the \<p> tag.

- **List tags:** These have different variations. Use the \<ol> tag for an ordered list, and use \<ul> for an unordered list. Then, enclose individual list items using the \<li> tag.

Inline Elements

It formats the inner content of block-level elements such as adding links and emphasized strings. These elements are most commonly used to format text without breaking the flow of the content.

For example:

- a \<strong> tag would render an element in bold.

- \<em> tag would show it in italics.

- \<a> tag and a href attribute to indicate the link's destination.

Using PHP and HTML on a Single Page

You can utilize both HTML and PHP on the same page to take benefit of what they both have to offer if you want to add HTML code to a PHP file when HTML and PHP are two independent computer languages.

With these methods, you can easily embed HTML code in your PHP script to format it better and make them more user-friendly.

This method depends on your specific situation.

- **HTML code in PHP script:** The first way is to design the page like a typical HTML web page with HTML tags, then wrap the PHP script code in separate PHP tags. You may even place the PHP code in the center of the file and use the <?PHP and?> tags to close and reopen it.

  This method is useful if you have a lot of HTML code and want to also include some code in PHP.

  Here the example of putting the HTML outside of the tags,

  ```
  <html>
  <title>HTML with PHP</title>
  <body>
  <h1>My Example</h1>

  <?php
  // PHP content
  echo "Hello PHP!";
  ?>

    <b>Here is some more HTML</b>

  <?php
  // PHP content
  echo "Hello PHP!";
  ?
    </body>
    </html>
  ```

- **Another way of using html in PHP file:** Another way is the opposite of the previous one; it is how you can add HTML to a PHP file with PRINT or ECHO, where PHP construct is used to print HTML on the page simply. You can include the HTML inside of the PHP tags by this method.

  This is a method to use for adding HTML to PHP if you only have a line or so to do.

Example:

```
<?php
  echo "<html>";
echo "<title>HTML With PHP</title>";
echo "<b>My Example</b>";
//your php code here
print "<i>Print works too!</i>";
?>
```

CSS (CASCADING STYLE SHEETS)

What Is CSS?

CSS is a language for specifying how your documents are presented to users, how they are styled, laid out, etc.

Usually, a document is a text file structured using a markup language (HTML). It is the most common markup language, but you may also come across other markup languages such as SVG or XML.

CSS Syntax

It is a rule-based language that defines rules specifying groups of styles that applied to specific elements or groups of elements on your web page. For example, "I want the main heading on my page to be shown as large red text."

The following code shows a very simple CSS rule that would achieve the styling as described above:

```
h1 {
    color: yelloe;
    font-size: 3em;
}
```

We have a set of curly { } braces. Inside those curly braces, you can declare one or more declarations, which take the form of property and value pairs. Each pair specifies the single property of the element(s) we are selecting, then a value that we'd like to give the property where before the colon we have the property and after the colon we have the value of the property. Its properties have different allowable values, depending on which property is specified.

In the above example, we have the color property, which can take various color values, i.e., "yellow." We also have the font-size property, which can take various size values, i.e., "3rem."

A CSS style sheet will contain many such rules, written one after the other.

```
h1 {
    color: yellow;
    font-size: 3em;
}

p {
    color: black;
}
```

Using CSS with PHP

PHP is a server-side language, where CSS is cascading style sheets that allow you to create great-looking web pages and both not interact with each other. You can use CSS to interact with your HTML in a good manner. Using CSS with PHP is more simple than you might think. Similar to echoing a text string in PHP, CSS is echoed in the same way. You can use CSS echoed out through PHP just like you would in HTML.

If you want to include an entire style sheet in the HTML <head> tag the following code will work for example,

```
<PHP> echo '<link rel="stylesheet" type="text/css"
href="style.css"></head>'; <PHP>
```

You can include a CSS file via PHP using include (). This will help to insert the file into this position on the page when it is executed just like copy and paste.

```
<PHP> include('style.css'); <PHP>
```

Note: You will need to include your CSS in the <style> tags,

```
<style>
body{
font-size:20px;
}
</style>
```

<>Tags at the beginning and end of the CSS file if using this method.

Data Types

A variables in PHP are represented by a dollar (\$) sign followed by an alphanumeric name beginning in a letter or underscore. These are case-sensitive. They don't need to be declared, and their data types are inferred from the assignment statement.

PHP supports the following data types:

- boolean

- integer

- float

- string

- array

- object

- resource

- NULL

Here is the example of various data type,

```php
<?php
$bool = TRUE;
$name = "String";
$age = 25;
$pi = 3.14159;
echo $bool ;
echo "<br>";
echo $name;
echo "<br>";
echo $age;
echo "<br>";
echo $pi;
echo "<br>";
?>
```

- **Statements:** Some basic PHP statements include:

    i. **echo:** It shows the output of one or more strings.

    ii. **print:** It also shows output but only of one string.

iii. **Assignment statement:** It is used to assign a value to a variable using this operator =.

iv. **include:** It is used to include and evaluate the specified external file.

v. **require:** It is the same as included, except it shows a fatal error on failure instead of a warning.

Examples:

```
include 'file.php' // The code in file.php will
be evaluated here
echo "Hello PHP.";
echo "Text with
multiple lines. Newlines will
output as well or can be done like this.";
echo $bool?  'true' : 'false' //Conditional
Operators
$a = ($b = 5) + 4; // the value a = 9, b = 5
echo $a,$b;
$c = 'A equals '.  $a;
print $c;
```

- **Expressions:** PHP expressions can include:

    i. $a = $b = 5; //The assignment statement

    ii. $b = $a++; //Post-increment a variable

    iii. $b = ++$a; //Pre-increment a variable

    iv. $x = $bool? $a : $b; //Ternery conditional

    v. The last expression evaluates to if ($bool) $x = $a else $x = $b

- **Operators:** These symbols tell the PHP processor to perform specific actions. For example, the plus (+) symbol is an operator that tells PHP to add two variables or values, while the greater-than (>) symbol is an operator that tells PHP to compare two values.

    There are various operators in the PHP language.

    i. PHP Arithmetic Operators

    ii. PHP Assignment Operators

iii. PHP Comparison Operators

iv. PHP Incrementing and Decrementing Operators

v. PHP Logical Operators

vi. PHP String Operators

vii. PHP Array Operators

viii. PHP Spaceship Operators

- **String:** It is a sequence of characters used to store and manipulate text. PHP supports a total of 256 character sets and does not offer native Unicode support.

   There are four ways to specify a string literal in PHP.

   i. **single-quoted:** We can create a string by enclosing the text in a single quote ('String'). It is the easiest way to specify a string in PHP.

      For a literal single quote, escape it with a backslash (\) and to specify a literal backslash (\) use double backslash (\\).

```php
<?php
        $string='Text within single quote';
        echo $string;
?>
```

   You can store multiple line text, special characters, and escape sequences in a single-quoted PHP string.

```php
$str1='Text for
multiple line
text in between single-quoted string';
```

   ii. **double quoted:** We can get the string through enclosing text in between double-quote also. But escape sequences and variables will be interpreted using double-quote PHP strings.

   Example:

```php
<?php
$str="Hello text within double quote";
echo $str;
?>
```

iii. **heredoc syntax:** It (<<<) is the third way to delimit strings. An identifier is provided after this heredoc <<< operator, and immediately a new line is started to write any text.

iv. **new doc syntax:** It is similar to the heredoc, but in the new doc, parsing is not done. It is also identified with three less than symbols (<<<) followed by an identifier. It is a single-quoted string, whereas heredoc is a double-quoted string.

- **PHP escape sequences:** These are used for escaping characters while the string parsing. It is used to give special meaning, like representing line breaks, tabs, alerts, and more.

   These sequences are interpolated into strings enclosed by double quotations or heredoc syntax. The escape sequence will not work when a string is within the single quotes or in docs to get the expected result.

   These are started with the escaping backslash (\). It is followed by the character, which may be an alphanumeric or a special character. If it is an alphanumeric character, it gives special meaning to represent the line breaks \n, carriage return \r, and more.

```
<?PHP
echo "Escape Sequences:\n Backslash \\ is used as
an escaping character.";
?>.
```

- **Widely used escape sequences:** Here we complete a list of some of the commonly used escape sequences. It describes how they are used to escape the special character or to give meaning by combining with some alphanumeric characters.

   i. \': It is to escape 'within a single-quoted string.'

   ii. \": It is to escape "within the double-quoted string."

   iii. \\: It is to escape the backslash.

   iv. \$: It is to escape $.

   v. **\n:** It is to add line breaks between strings.

   vi. **\t:** It is to add tab space.

   vii. **\r:** It is to for carriage return.

- **Arrays:** It is used to store one or more similar types of values in a variable. For example, if you want to store 20 values, then instead of defining 20 variables, it is easy to define an array of 20 lengths.

  There are three various kinds of arrays in PHP:

- **Numeric array:** An array with a numeric index and its values are stored and accessed linearly.

Example:

```
<?PHP

$numbers = array( 1, 2, 3, 4, 5);

foreach( $numbers as $value ) {
   echo "Value is $value <br />";
   }
?>
```

- **Associative array:** An array with strings as an index and stores element values in association with key values rather than in strict linear index order.

```
<?php
/* Method to associate create array. */
        $alphabets = array("A" => 1, "B" => 2,
"C" => 3);

   echo "First alphabets is A and Number is ".
$alphabets ['A'].  "<br />";
   echo "First alphabets is B and Number is ".
$alphabets ['B'].  "<br />";
   echo "First alphabets is C and Number is ".
$alphabets ['C'].  "<br />";
?>
```

- **Multidimensional array:** An array containing one or more arrays and values are accessed using multiple indices.

```
<?php
        $marks = array(
           "Student" => array (
```

```
                    "English" => 15,
                    "Maths" => 30,
                    "Chemistry" => 39
                )
        );

        /* multi-dimensional array values */
        echo "Marks for Student in English is : " ;
        echo $marks['Student']['English'].
"<br />";
?>
```

- **Conditional statement**

  - **if statement**

    Syntax:

    ```
    if: if (expr) statement
    <?php
    $a= 15;
    $b= 14;
    if ($a > $b)
     echo "a is greater than b";
    ?>
    ```

  - **if-else statement**

    Syntax:

    ```
    if-else: if (expr) statement1; else
    statement2;
    <?php
    $a= 11;
    $b= 14;
    if ($a > $b)
    echo "a is greater than b";
    else
    echo "b is greater than a";
    ?>
    ```

- **if-elseif statement (Multiple elseifs can be included in the same if statement)**

  Syntax:

  ```php
  <?php
  $a= 11;
  $b= 14;
  if ($a > $b)
   echo "a is greater than b";
  elseif ($b > $a)
   echo "b is greater than a";
  else
   echo "Both are equal";
  ?>
  ```

- **switch statement**

  Syntax:

  ```php
  <?php
  $a = 3;
  switch ($a) {
    case 1:
      echo "1";
      break;
    case 2:
      echo "2";
    case 3:
      echo "3";
      break;
    case 4:
      echo "4";
      break;
    default:
      echo "0";
  }
  ?>
  ```

- **Looping statements**

    i. **for loop:** Syntax, for (expr1; expr2; expr3) statements;
       Same syntax as Java/C++

    ```php
    <?php
    for ($j = 0; $j < 10; $j++) {
        echo "Number is $j ";
        echo "<br>";
    }
    ?>
    ```

    ii. **while:** Syntax, while (expr) statements execute statements while
       the expression is true.

    ```php
    <?php
    $x = 1;

    while($x <= 5) {
        echo "The number is: $x <br>";
        $x++;
    }
    ?>
    ```

    iii. **do...while:** Syntax, do {statements; } while (expr);
       Similar to while loops, except that the condition is checked
       after the body of the loop, meaning that the body will always be
       executed at least once.

    ```php
    <?PHP
    $x = 1;

    do {
        echo "The number is: $x <br>";
        $x++;
    } while ($x <= 5);
    ?>
    ```

    iv. **Continue:** Syntax, continue [int arg];
       It skips the rest of the loop's code for the current iteration and
       continues execution at the beginning of the next iteration.

    v. **Break:** Syntax, break [int arg];
       It ends the execution of the current loop. The optional arg tells
       it how many levels of loops it should break out of.

vi. **Foreach:** Syntax, foreach (array_expression as [$key =>] $value) statements;

    Loops over the array is given by array_expression. On every iteration, the value of the current element is assigned to $value and the internal array pointer is advanced by one. If specific, the current element's key will be assigned to $key each iteration.

```
<?php
$colors = array("red", "green", "blue",
"yellow");

foreach ($colors as $value) {
   echo "$value <br>";
}
?>
```

- **Functions:** It is defined as a reusable piece or block of code that performs a specific action with the following syntax:

```
function funct($arg_1, $arg_2, ..., $arg_n) {
   echo "This is a function.";
   return $value;
}
```

By default, the function parameters are passed by value so that we can change the value of the argument within the function, and it does not get changed outside of the function.

- **Classes and OOP:** It stands for Object-Oriented Programming basically; it is a programming model that is based on the concept of objects and classes. Unlike procedural programming, where the main focus is on writing procedures or functions that perform operations on the same data, but OOP only focuses on the creations of objects that contain both data and functions together.

    Where a class is a set of variables and methods working with these variables, classes are defined the same as Java except that "->" (arrow notation) is used instead of "when referring to functions and elements of a class."

    There are various terms used in the OOP concepts in PHP are as follows,

    i. Initializing variable

    ii. Encapsulation

    iii. Inheritance

    iv. Abstract classes

    v. Parent

    vi. Constructors

    vii. :: (Scope resolution operator)

    viii. Comparing Objects

- **Opening and creating files in PHP:** The present files can be opened, and new files are created using the PHP function fopen() where the fopen() accepts two arguments and returns a filehandle used for all future read and write interactions with that particular file. The first argument is the name having the path of the file to open. This path is relative to the web server file system root, not your server root. The other argument is an attribute that indicates the mode in which to open the file (create, read-only, write-only, etc.).

Mode	Description
r	It is a read-only account. The pointer is at the beginning of file.
r+	It is read and write access and the pointer is positioned at the start of the file.
W	It is write-only access. The pointer is placed at the beginning of the file, and if it does not already exist, the file is created.
w+	It is read and write access. The pointer is relocated to the beginning of the file, and the file is created if it does not already exist.
A	It is write-only access, and the pointer is positioned at the end of the file, and the file is created if it does not already exist.
a+	It is read and write access, and the pointer is positioned at the end of the file, and the file is created if it does not already exist.
x+	It is created and opens for reading and writing. The pointer is at the beginning of file. If the file already exists, return false.
x	It is created and open for write-only. The pointer is at the beginning of file. If the file already exists, return false.

PHP 5.0 vs. PHP 7.0 comparison

Parameter	PHP 5.0	PHP 7.0
Version	It uses the old version of the engine called Zend II. It performs poorly in terms of speed when compared to PHP 7.0.	It uses a new model of engine known as PHP-NG or Next generation. These engines can considerably enhance performance with optimized memory usage.
Return type	It does not allow programmers to specify the return type of a function or method.	It enables the declaration of the return type of the functions as per the expected return value, making the code robust and accurate.
Handling of fatal errors	It is quite tough to handle fatal errors in PHP version 5.0.	The procedure for dealing with fatal mistakes has been simplified. This script function is used to execute return types. After the parenthesis of an argument, programmers must declare the return type. Major problems may be turned into exceptions with this script, making them easier to deal with.
64-bit compatibility	It does not support 64-bit numbers or huge files since it does not support 64-bit support.	It features 64-bit support, which allows programmers to use a native 64-bit integer and huge files and, as a result, operate a wide range of programs on 64-bit system architectures without defects.
Coalescing Operator	There is no coalescing operator in PHP 5.0. If the value is not accessible, the programmer must write explicit code to return null.	Another notable feature of PHP 7.0 is the coalescing operator, which is symbolized by a double question mark (??). The operator is used to show whether or not something exists.
Spaceship Operator	There is no one in the charge of spaceship.	Comparisons necessitate the usage of a large number of operators. It comes with a new operator known as the spaceship operator, which is denoted by the symbol <=>. When the value is not available, the function might automatically return to null.

(Continued)

Parameter	PHP 5.0	PHP 7.0
The concept of anonymous class	In PHP 5.0, there is no concept of anonymous classes.	To reduce the execution time, an anonymous class is employed.
Namespaces are declared.	An Individual declaration for common namespaces is included.	It provides Group Use Declaration, which allows developers to include classes from the same namespace in their code, making it more easy and concise.
Asynchronous programming support	In previous PHP 5.0 versions, it was difficult to perform several activities simultaneously.	It has effectively resolved this problem as this enables seamless execution of a variety of tasks. One can access the database, network, set timers, and perform several I/O operations simultaneously and without any obstruction.
Examples of advanced features	Improvements to the XML extension, superior soap implementation, and other advanced features in PHP 5.0 are examples.	Return type declaration, CSPRNG functions, and other advanced features of PHP 7.0 are examples.

- **New PHP 7.0 features:** Let's have a look over the new feature of PHP. Here is the list of features:

  - **Scalar type hints:** The scalar types (integers, floating-point numbers, Booleans, and strings) can also be used as type hints. They have been available in PHP for a while now, but they were restricted to classes, arrays, and callable.

  - **Return type declarations:** Type hints to ensure input consistency and return type declarations ensure output consistency, use a colon before the opening curly brace of a function to hint the return type.

  - **Anonymous classes:** These classes are useful for simple one or off objects. The anonymous classes can define a class and instantiate an object inline.

  - **The Closure::call() method:** These are anonymous functions that are declared inline and assigned to a variable. It also can be used as a callback for later execution. In PHP version 5.0, it was good to bind an object to the scope of the closure as if it was a method.

The "call" method in the PHP version 7.0 features was introduced to simplify the process.

- **Generator delegation:** Generators are easy, but sometimes it is hard to explain. Using them is very simple. It is all about the "yield" keyword. By using "yield," a generator is returned yielded value. It implements an iterator which makes it easy to use in a while or for loops.

  The generator delegation was introduced in PHP 7.0. It means a generator from another function can be addressed.

- **Generator return expressions:** As mentioned in the above feature, values can be yielded and an iterator over it by using the yield keyword. But return values are ignored by generators.

  Then the "getReturn" method was added to the Generator class to allow return values in generators.

- **The null coalesce operator:** It is a shorthand for checking if a value is set and not null within inline comparisons. Instead of doing the old "isset" check over and over again, just use "??" to return the value if it is set or an alternative value instead.

- **The spaceship operator:** It makes it easier to compare values. Instead of returning a typical true or false value, the space ship operator returns one of the following values based on the result of the evaluation:

  The result will be,

     i. 0 is when both values are equal.

    ii. −1 is when the left value is less than the right value.

   iii. 1 is when the left value is greater than the right value.

- **Throwables:** A big change in PHP 7.0 is that errors are no longer raised the way they used to be. Errors behave in a similar way as exceptions. They can inherit from the Throwable interface, it means that errors can now be caught in a try-catch block. You can get both exceptions and errors named Throwables and catch errors as Error objects.

There are different kinds of errors we can catch while coding in PHP:

i. ArithmeticError

ii. DivisionByZeroError

iii. AssertionError

iv. ParseError

v. TypeError

- **Level support for the dirname() function:** It is used more often than you think. It is the function relatively refers to directories.

  Its function has a second argument that indicates how many levels you're going up the directory tree. If you don't enter any value, then 1 is the default.

- **The integer division function:** The intdiv returns the integer value of a division, whereas simple divisions can return a float.

- **Uniform variable syntax:** This standard changes the indirect access to array keys, properties, and methods are evaluated. In PHP 7.0, the interpretation enforces a strict left-to-right evaluation.

However, PHP 8.0 has now been released with new and further improved features.

CHAPTER 2

Data Types and Operators

IN THIS CHAPTER

➤ Data types

➤ Expression and variables

➤ Various operators

In the previous chapter, we have learned what PHP is, its basic terms, installation on various platforms, installation in operating Windows, Linux, macOS, use of HTML and CSS in PHP, including the external file in PHP scripts, its data types, and different oops concepts and its data types.

In this chapter, we will cover variables with their scopes, data types, and various operators in PHP languages.

CODING BUILDING BLOCKS

To create programs in PHP that do something helpful, you will have to understand the blocks of reusable code called methods or functions and temporarily store data that cannot be executed in variables. We discuss evaluations, which allow your code to make intelligent mathematical principles and user data education choices.

DOI: 10.1201/9781003308669-2

43

VARIABLES

Since we expect that some of you have not done any programming, we get that variable maybe another idea. A variable stores a value, for example, the text string "Hi PHP to this World!" or the integral value 1. A variable can then be reused all through your code, rather than needing to sort out the integral value again and again for the whole life of the variable, which can be disappointing and tiring.

Give careful consideration to some key elements in the form of variables. The dollar ($) sign should look at all-time fill the prefix space of your variable name. The next character after the dollar sign must be either a letter or an underscore. It cannot under any circumstances be a number; generally, your code won't execute, so watch those grammatical mistakes!

- PHP variables may be made up of alphanumeric characters and underscores; for instance, a-z, A-Z, 0-9, and _.

- Variables in PHP are case-sensitive. This implies that $variable_name and $Variable_Name are different.

- Variables with more than one word can be isolated with underscores to make them simpler to understand; for instance, $test_variable.

- Variables can be assigned values that use the equal (=) sign.

- Always end with a semicolon (;) to finish assigning the variable.

Reading a Variable's Value

To get to the value of a variable that has previously been assigned, just specify the dollar ($) sign followed by the variable name, and utilize it as you would the value of the variable in your code. You don't need to remove your variables when your program finishes. They're temporary since PHP naturally tidies them up when you finish using them.

- **Variable types:** Variables store all types of information. PHP naturally picks a data variable taking into account the value assigned. These information types comprise strings, numbers, and more complex components such as arrays. We'll talk about arrays later. What's vital to know is that unless you have the motivation to care about the type of data. PHP handles all the points of interest, so you don't have to stress over them. When a particular sort of information is needed, for example, the numerical division operation, PHP endeavors to convert the data types naturally. If you have a string with a single "2," it will be changed over to a whole number estimation of 2. This change is dependably exactly what you need PHP to do, making coding consistent for you.

- **Variable scope:** PHP helps keep your code sorted out by verifying that on the off chance that you use code that somebody else composed (and you likely will) the names of the variables in your code don't clash with other beforehand composed variable names. For instance, in case you're utilizing a variable called $name that has an estimation of Bill, and you use another person's code that additionally has a variable called $name, however, utilizes it to stay informed concerning the filename log.txt, your worth could get overwritten. Your code value for $name of PHP will be supplanted by log.txt, and your code will make say Hello log.txt rather than Hello PHP, this would be a major problem.

  To keep this from happening, PHP sorts out code into functions. Functions permit you to gather a piece of code together and then execute that code by the variable name. To keep your variables in your code separate from variables in functions, PHP gives separate storage of variables inside every function. This different storage room implies that the scope, or where a variable's value cab be admitted, is the nearby the local storage of the value.

- **Global variables:** Global variables permit you to cross the limit between discrete capacities to get to a variable's worth. The worldwide proclamation indicates that you need the variable to be the same variable everywhere regarded as global. Global variables ought to be utilized sparingly because adjusting a variable is simple without acknowledging the unintentional results. This sort of error can be extremely hard to find. Also, when we examine functions in detail, you will discover that you can pass in values to functions when you call them and get values returned from them when they are done. You don't need to use global variables. On the chance that you need to use a variable in a particular function without losing the worth every time the function ends. However, you would prefer not to use a global variable but rather a static variable.

- **Static variables:** Static variables give a variable that isn't decimated when a function ends. You can utilize the static variable value again whenever you call the capacity, and it will have the same value as when it was last utilized as a part of the function. The easiest approach is to consider the variable as global yet open to simply that function. The estimation of $age is currently held every time the birthday function is called. The worth will stay around until the program ends.

  Value is spared on the grounds that it's announced as static. In this way, we've talked about two types of variables, yet there's still one more to examine, superglobal.

- **Superglobal variables:** PHP uses uncommon variables called super-globals to give data about the PHP script's surroundings. These variables don't require any announcement as global. They are habitually accessible, and they give imperative data past the script's code itself, for example, values from a user's input.

  In PHP 4.01, the superglobals are termed as arrays. Arrays are unique accumulations of values that we'll talk about in later chapters. The more established superglobal variables such as those beginning with $HTTP_* that were not in clusters still exist, but their use is not recommended, as they are deprecated.

Types of Variables

1. **Constant variable:** It is a name or an identifier for a simple value. Its value cannot change during the execution of the script. By default, it is case-sensitive. To define a constant, you need to use the define() function and retrieve the value of a constant, or simply specify its name and can also use the function constant() to read a constant value if you wish to obtain the constant name dynamically.

2. **Global variables:** It can access anywhere in the program. A global variable must be declared global in the function in which it is to be modified. By keeping the keyword GLOBAL in front of the variable that recognizes as global. This keyword prefix is an existing variable that tells PHP to use the variable with that name.

   Example:

```
<?PHP
    $val = 15;
    function add() {
```

```
    GLOBAL $val;
    $somevar++;
    print "Value is $val ";
  }
  add();
?>
```

3. **Local variables:** It is declared in a function is considered local; it can be referenced solely in that function. Any assignment of variable outside of that function will be considered to be an entirely different variable from the one contained in the function.

```
<?php
  $x = 4;
  function get () {
    $x = 0;
    print "Value of x inside the get function is
$x. <br />";
  }
  get();
  print "Value of x outside get the function is
$x. <br />";
?>
```

4. **Static variables:** This type of variable scoping is known as static. You can declare a variable static simply by placing the keyword STATIC in front of the variable name.

   The STATIC variable will not lose its value when the function exits and will still hold that value should the function be called again.

```
<?php
  function inc() {
    STATIC $count = 0;
    $count++;
    print $count;
    print "<br />";
  }
  inc();
  inc();
  inc();
?>
```

PREDEFINED VARIABLES

PHP provides various predefined variables to all scripts. External variables to built-in variables, last error messages, and so on are represented by the variables. All of this data is stored in predefined variables.

1. **Superglobals:** These are built-in variables always available in all scopes inside the PHP script.

2. **$GLOBALS:** It is used to access global variables from anywhere in the PHP script. It is $GLOBALS[], where the index holds the global variable name, accessed.

3. **$_SERVER:** It is server and execution environment information.

4. **$_GET:** HTTP GET variables and collect data sent in the URL or submitted in an HTML form.

5. **$_POST:** HTTP POST variables are used to gather data from an HTML form and pass the variable to the server.

6. **$_FILES:** It is HTTP File Upload variables which is a two-dimensional associative global array of items which are uploaded by via HTTP POST methods and hold the attributes of file such as [name] – represents the name of the which is uploading, [size] – represents the size of the file, [type] – represents the types of the files like pdf, jpeg, png, etc., [tmp_name] –represents a temporary address where the file is located before processing the upload request, [error] – represents types of errors occurred when the files uploading.

7. **$_REQUEST:** HTTP Request variables and used to collect data after submitting an HTML form. It is not used mostly because $_POST and $_GET perform the same task and are widely used.

8. **$_SESSION:** It is an associative array that contains all session variables. It is used to set and get session variable values.

9. **$_ENV:** It is another superglobal associative array in PHP. It stores environment variables available to the current script.

10. **$_COOKIE:** It is a variable used to retrieve a cookie value and an associative array containing a list of all the cookies values sent by the browser in the current request, keyed by cookie name.

11. **$php_errormsg:** It's a variable that holds the text of the most recent PHP error message. Only the scope in which the issue occurred and if the track errors configuration option is enabled and disabled by default will this variable be available.

12. **$HTTP_RAW_POST_DATA:** It contains the raw POST data.

13. **$http_response_header:** It's an array that works in the same way as the get_headers() method. The HTTP response headers are stored in $http_response header when using the HTTP wrapper. $http_response_header will create in the local scope.

14. **$argc:** The argc stands for argument count, and argv stands for argument values. The number of arguments passed to script.

15. **$argv:** It is an Array holding all the arguments passed to the PHP script.

IS PHP A CASE-SENSITIVE LANGUAGE?

In PHP, variable names are case-sensitive; however, function names are not.

Explanation: If you defined PHP variable in lowercase, then you need to use it in lowercase everywhere in the code. If we define a variable $name = "PHP," then we must need to use $name, but the variable name with uppercase like $NAME will not work.

It will work if you define function names in lowercase but call them in uppercase. For example, if we define function add() {} then calling ADD() will also work.

Here is the difference between the case sensitive and case insensitive:

Case sensitive (both user-defined and PHP defined):

- variables

- constants

- array keys

- class properties

- class constants

Case insensitive (both user-defined and PHP defined)

- functions

- class constructors

- class methods

- keywords and constructs (if, else, null, for each, echo, etc.)

REGULAR EXPRESSION

It is commonly known as "regex" or "RegExp," which are especially formatted as text strings used to find patterns in text. It is one of the most useful tools for effective and efficient text processing and manipulations for your code. For example, it can verify any data, whether it is the format of data, i.e., name, phone number, email, etc., passed by the coder was find or replace a matching string within text content, and correct or not on.

PHP version 5.3 and later supports Perl-style regular expressions (or regex) via its preg_ family of functions.

Function	Its Description
preg_match()	It performs a regular expression match.
preg_match_all()	It performs a global regular expression match.
preg_replace()	A preg replace performs a regular expression search and replace.
preg_grep()	It returns the elements of the input array that matched the pattern.
preg_split()	It splits up a string into substrings using a regular expression.
preg_quote()	It is quoted for regular expression characters found within a string.

Why Does Perl Style Regular Expressions?

Because Perl (stands for Practical Extraction and Report Language) is a general-purpose programming language that is used to develop generic applications, and PHP is a scripting language that can be used to develop web applications. It was the first programming language that provided integrated support for the regular expressions in PHP language, and it is well known for its stronger support of regular expressions and its extra text processing and manipulation capabilities.

Let's have a brief overview of the commonly used PHP built-in pattern-matching functions in the world of regular expressions.

Regular Expression Syntax

Its syntax includes the use of special characters to make sure you do not confuse with the special HTML characters.

These characters are having special meaning within a regular expression, are:., *, ?, +, [,], (,), {, }, ^, $, |, \.

You just need to backslash these characters when you want to use them in your code.

For example, if you would like to match ".", you have to write \.. like

```
$pattern = "/aa[kf]e/";
```

All other characters are automatically assuming their specific literal meanings. The following describes the various options available for pattern formatting.

Character Classes in Regular Expression

The big square brackets [ ] surrounding a pattern of characters are called a character class, for example, [xyz]. It always matches a single character out of a list of particular characters, meaning the expression [xyz] matches only x, y, or z.

Regular Expression	What It Does
[abc]	It matches any one of the characters a, b, or c.
[^abc]	It matches any one character other than a, b, or c.
[a-z]	It matches any one character from lowercase a to lowercase z.
[A-Z]	It matches any one character from uppercase a to uppercase z.
[a-Z]	It matches any one character from lowercase a to uppercase Z.
[0-9]	It matches a single digit between 0 and 9.
[a-z0-9]	It matches a single character between a and z or between 0 and 9.

Built-in Regular Expression Functions in PHP

It is built-in functions in PHP that allows us to work with regular functions, which we will learn in this PHP Regular Expressions tutorial. The above section will get all the Regular useful expressions, but we will only discuss some of the most used regular expressions.

Let's look at the commonly used regular expression functions in PHP.

Built-in Regular Expression Functions	Description	Example
preg_match()	This preg match performs pattern matching in PHP on a string and returns true if a match is found and false if a match is not found.	```<?php $my_url = "This is the preg_match() function"; if (preg_match("/preg_ match/", $my_url)) { echo "The given URL contains preg_match."; } else { echo "The given URL does not contain preg_match."; } ?>```
preg_split()	This preg split function is used to perform a pattern match on a string and then split the results into a numeric array.	```<?php $my_text="This is Regular Expressions"; $my_array = preg_split ("/ /", $my_text); print_r($my_array); ?>```
preg_replace()	This preg replace function is used to perform a pattern match on a string and then replace the match with the specified text.	```<?PHP $text = "PHP is a widely-used open source general-purpose scripting language. PHP is especially suited for web development and can be embedded into HTML"; $text = preg_replace("/PHP/", '<span style="backgr ound:yellow">PHP</span>', $text); echo $text; ?>```

The syntax for a regular expression, such as PHP preg_match(), PHP preg_split(), or PHP preg_replace(), is given below,

```
<?php
function_name('/pattern/',subject);
?>
```

Regular Expression Metacharacters

The metacharacters allow us to perform more complex pattern matches such as testing the validity of an email address. Now have a look at the commonly used metacharacters.

Metacharacter	Description	Example
.	It matches any single character except a new line.	/./ matches anything that has a single character
^	It matches the starting off, or string / excludes characters.	/^PH/ It matches any string that starts with PH
*	It matches any zero (0) or more characters	/com*/ matches computer, communication etc.
$	It matches the pattern at the end of the string $	/com$/ matches youtube. com,google.com etc.
+	It requires preceding character(s) to appear at least once	/yah+oo/ matches yahoo
\	It is used to escape meta characters	/yahoo+\.com/ treats the dot as a literal value
[..]	It is character class	/[abc]/ matches ABC a-z
a-z	It matches lower case letters	/a-z/ matches cool, happy etc.
A-Z	It matches upper case letters	/A-Z/ matches WHAT, HOW etc.
0-9	It matches any number between 0 and 9	/0-4/ matches 0,1,2,3,4

DATA TYPES

What Is a Data Type?

A data type or type in any programming language is an attribute of data that tells the compiler or interpreter how the programmer plans to use the data. This type defines the operations that can be performed on the data, also the meaning of the data, and the way values of that type can be stored.

The values assigned to any PHP variable may be of different data types, including simple string and numeric types, to more complex data types like arrays and objects.

PHP language supports a total of eight primitive data types:

- Integer
- Floating point number or float
- String
- Booleans
- Array
- Object
- Resource
- NULL

All the above data types are divided into various types:

1. **Scalar Types:** A variable is called scalar type if it holds a single value only. There are four scalar data types in PHP:

   - boolean
   - integer
   - float
   - string

   The above data types are used to construct variables. Now let's discuss each one of them in detail.

2. **Compound Types:** A variable is called a compound if it holds more than one value within. There are two compound data types.

   - array
   - object

3. **Special Types:** There are two special data types.

   - resource
   - NULL

Integers

These are the whole numbers without a decimal point (–2, –1, 0, 1, 2). It can be specified in decimal (base 10), hexadecimal (base 16 or prefixed with 0x), or octal (base eight or prefixed with 0) notation, extra preceded by a sign (— or +).

Here the some example of conversion from decimal to integer's value,

```php
<?php
$a = 123; // decimal number
var_dump($a);
echo "<br>";
$b = -123; // a negative number
var_dump($b);
echo "<br>";
$c = 0x1A; // hexadecimal number
var_dump($c);
echo "<br>";
$d = 0123; // octal number
var_dump($d);
?>
```

The output of the following code,

```
int(123)
int(-123)
int(26)
int(83)
```

Strings

These are sequences of characters, where every character is the same as some bytes. The string can hold letters, numbers, and also special characters, and it can become as large as up to 2GB, i.e., 2147483647 bytes maximum. The easiest way to specify a string is to enclose it in single quotes (example, 'Hello world!'). However, you can also use double quotes ("Hello world!").

```php
<?php
$a = 'Hello PHP!';
echo $a;
echo "<br>";
$b = "You are learning PHP langauge!";
echo $b;
echo "<br>";
$c = 'You I\'ll be learning PHP.'
echo $c;
?>
```

There are four ways to specify a string literal in PHP:

1. **single-quoted:** We can also create a string by enclosing the text in a single quote ('String'). It is the easiest way to specify a string in PHP.

   For a literal single quote, escape it with a backslash (\) and to specify a literal backslash (\) use double backslash (\\).

   ```php
   <?php
           $string='Text within single quote';
           echo $string;
   ?>
   ```

   You can store multiple line text, special characters, and escape sequences in a single-quoted PHP string.

   ```php
   $str1='Text for
   multiple line
   text in between single-quoted string';
   ```

2. **double quoted:** We can get the string through enclosing text in between double-quote also. But escape sequences and variables will be interpreted using double-quote PHP strings.

   Example:

   ```php
   <?php
   $str="Hello text within double quote";
   echo $str;
   ?>
   ```

3. **heredoc syntax:** It (<<<) is the third way to delimit strings. An identifier is provided after this heredoc <<< operator, and immediately a new line is started to write any text.

4. **new doc syntax:** It is similar to the heredoc, but parsing in the new doc is not done. It is also identified with three less than symbols <<< followed by an identifier. It is a single-quoted string, whereas heredoc is a double-quoted string.

WHAT IS PHP'S STRING FUNCTION?

The "string" term refers to a series of characters. PHP language supports several data types, including strings. The alphanumeric characters are allowed in string variables. When these conditions are met, strings are generated. It is likely to perform a variable and allow it to string characters. With the echo parameter, they are using PHP Strings directly. String functions in PHP are languages created that help in taking terms.

String Functions

Then according to string functions in PHP programming languages, these functions are used to modify a string or query knowledge about a string. The length of the string function is the most fundamental example of a string function. This function returns the length of a literal string.

Here is the list of string functions used in PHP.

String Function	Description
addslashes()	It returns a string with backslashes in front of characters that need to be escaped.
bin2hex()	It converts a string of ASCII characters to hexadecimal values.
addcslashes()	It returns a string with backslashes in front of specified characters.
chop()	It removes space or other characters from the right end of a string.
chr()	It returns a character from a specified ASCII value.
chunk_split()	It splits a string into a series of smaller chunks.
convert_cyr_string()	It converts a string from a Cyrillic character set to another.
convert_uudecode()	It decodes a uuencoded string.
convert_uuencode()	It encodes a string using uuencode.
count_chars()	It returns information about the characters in a string.
crc32()	It calculates a 32-bit CRC for a string.
crypt()	Returns a hashed string.
echo()	It can output one or several strings.
explode()	It can break down a string into an array.
fprintf()	It can write a formatted string to a specified output stream.
get_html_translation_table()	It returns the translation table used by htmlspecialchars() and htmlentities().
Hebrew()	It can transform Hebrew text to visual text.
hebrevc()	It can convert Hebrew text to visual text and implement HTML line breaks.
hex2bin()	It can translate hexadecimal values to ASCII characters.
html_entity_decode()	It can turns HTML entities to characters.
htmlentities()	It can converts characters to HTML entities.

(Continued)

String Function	Description
htmlspecialchars_decode()	It can transform special HTML entities into characters.
htmlspecialchars()	It switches predefined characters to HTML entities.
implode()	It retrieves a string from the elements of an array, same as join().
lcfirst()	It can change a string's first character to lowercase.
levenshtein()	It can calculate the Levenshtein distance between two strings.
localeconv()	It can return information about numeric and monetary formatting for the locale.
ltrim()	It can remove spaces or other characters from the left side of a string.
md5()	It can calculate the MD5 hash of a string and return it.
md5_file()	It can calculate the MD5 hash of a file.
Metaphone()	It can provide the Metaphone key of a string.
money_format()	It can return a string as a currency string.
nl_langinfo()	Gives specific locale information.
nl2br()	It can insert HTML line breaks for each new line in a string.
number_format()	It can format a number, including grouped thousands.
ord()	It can return the ASCII value of a string's first character.
parse_str()	It can parse a string into variables.
print()	It can output one or several strings.
printf()	It can output a formatted string.
quoted_printable_decode()	It can convert a quoted-printable string to an 8-bit binary.
quoted_printable_encode()	It goes from an 8-bit string to a quoted-printable string.
quotemeta()	It can return a string with a backslash before metacharacters.
rtrim()	It can strip whitespace or other characters from the right side of a string.
setlocale()	It can set locale information.
sha1()	It can calculate a string's SHA-1 hash.
sha1_file()	Does the same for a file.
similar_text()	Determines the similarity between two strings.
soundex()	It can calculate the soundex key of a string.
sprintf()	It can return a formatted string.
sscanf()	It can parse input from a string according to a specified format.
str_getcsv()	It is used to parses a CSV string into an array.
str_ireplace()	It is used to replace some characters in a string (case-insensitive).
str_pad()	It is used to pads a string to a new length.

(Continued)

String Function	Description
str_repeat()	It is used to repeat a string a specified number of times.
str_replace()	It is used to replace some characters in a string. It is case-sensitive.
str_rot13()	It is used to perform the ROT13 encoding on a string.
str_shuffle()	It is used to shuffle all characters in a string randomly.
str_split()	It is used to splits a string into an array.
str_word_count()	It is used to count the number of words in a string.
strcasecmp()	It is used to compare two strings (case-insensitive).
strchr()	It is used to find the first occurrence of a string inside another string and alias of strstr().
stripcslashes()	It unquotes a string quoted with addcslashes().
strcoll()	It is used to compare two strings or the Locale-based string comparison.
strcmp()	It is used to compare two strings, and also it is case-sensitive.
strcspn() part of some specified characters are found	It is used to return the number of characters found in a string before any.
strip_tags()	It is strips HTML and PHP tags from a string.
stripos()	It returns position of the first occurrence of a string inside another string, and it is case-insensitive.
stripslashes()	It unquotes a string quoted with addslashes().
stristr()	It finds the string's first occurrence inside another string, and it is case-insensitive.
strlen()	It returns the length of a string.
strncasecmp()	It is used for the comparison of the first n characters, and it is case-insensitive
strnatcmp()	It is used to compare two strings using a "natural order" algorithm (case-sensitive)
strnatcasecmp()	It is used to compare two strings using a "natural order" algorithm, and it is case-insensitive.
strncmp()	It is a string comparison of the first n characters (case-sensitive).
strrev()	It reverses a string.
strrchr()	It finds last occurrence of a string inside another string.
strpos()	It returns the position of the first occurrence of a string inside another string (case-sensitive).
strpbrk()	It searches a string for any of a group of characters.
strripos()	It finds the string position of the last occurrence inside another string, and it is case-insensitive.
strrpos()	It finds position of the last occurrence of a string inside another string, and it is case-sensitive.
strspn()	It returns the number of characters found in a string that contains only characters from a specified charlist.

(Continued)

strstr()	It finds the string first occurrence inside another string, and it is case-sensitive.
strtok()	It splits a string into smaller strings.
strtolower()	It converts a string to lowercase letters.
strtoupper()	It converts a string to uppercase letters.
strtr()	It translates certain characters in a string.
substr()	It returns a part of a string.
substr_compare()	It compares two strings from a specified start position or binary safe and optionally case-sensitive.
substr_count()	It can count the number of times a substring occurs in a string.
substr_replace()	It replaces a part of a string with another string.
trim()	It removes whitespace or other characters from both sides of a string.
ucfirst()	It converts the first character of a string to uppercase.
ucwords()	It converts the first character of a word in a string to uppercase.
vfprintf()	It is used to write a formatted string to a specified output stream.
wordwrap()	It is used to wrap a string to a given number of characters.
vprintf()	It outputs a formatted string.
vsprintf()	It is used to write a formatted string to a variable.

ESCAPE SEQUENCES

The combination of the escape character \ and a letter is used to tell that the character after the escape character should be treated.

You can get the same effect in double-quoted strings by using the escape character, which, in PHP, is a backslash \.

Here is the list of commonly used Escape sequences in PHP language.

Escape Sequences	Meaning
\"	It prints the next character as a double quote, not a string closer.
\'	It prints the next character as a single quote, not a string closer.
\n	It prints a newline character or linefeed.
\t	It is printed a tab character.
\r	It prints a carriage return but does not use very often.
\$	It prints the next character as a dollar, not as part of a variable.
\\	It is printed the next character as a backslash, not an escape character.
\e	It is used for escape.
\f	It is used for a form feed.

(Continued)

Escape Sequences	Meaning
\v	It is used for the vertical tab.
\[0-7]{1,3}	It is the sequence of characters matching the regular expression is a character in octal notation, which silently overflows to fit in a byte.
\x[0-9A-Fa-f]{1,2}	It is the sequence of characters matching the regular expression is a character in hexadecimal notation.
\u{[0-9A-Fa-f]+}	It is the sequence of characters matching the regular expression is a Unicode code point, which will be output to the string as that code point UTF-8 representation.

FLOATING POINT NUMBERS OR DOUBLES

Floating point numbers are also known as "floats," "doubles," or "real numbers" are decimal or fractional numbers, like display in the example below.

```php
<?php
$a = 0.234;
var_dump($a);
echo "<br>";
$b = 40.2e3;
var_dump($b);
echo "<br>";
$c = 1E-10;
var_dump($c);
?>
```

Here is the output of the following code,

```
float (1.234)
float (10200)
float (4.0E-10)
```

Booleans

These are like a switch that has only two possible values, either 1 (true) or 0 (false).

Example:

```php
<?php
// Assign the value TRUE to a variable
$result = true;
var_dump($result);
?>
```

Here is the output of the following code,

```
True
```

Arrays

It is a variable that holds more than one type of value at a time. It is useful to set a series of related items together such as country or city names.

It is formally defined as an indexed collection of data values. Each index, also known as the key of an array, is unique and references a corresponding value.

```php
<?php
$name = array("Sam", "John", "Ray");
var_dump($name);
echo "<br>";

$colors = array(
    "Red" => "#ff0000",
    "Green" => "#00ff00",
    "Blue" => "#0000ff"
);
var_dump($colors);
?>
```

Here is the output of the following code,

```
array(3) { [0]=> string(3) "Sam" [1]=> string(4)
"John" [2]=> string(3) "Ray" }
array(3) { ["Red"]=> string(7) "#ff0000" ["Green"]=>
string(7) "#00ff00" ["Blue"]=> string(7) "#0000ff" }
```

There are three various kinds of arrays in PHP:

- **Numeric array:** An array with a numeric index and its values are stored and accessed linearly.

  Example:

  ```php
  <?PHP

  $numbers = array( 1, 2, 3, 4, 5);
  ```

```
foreach( $numbers as $value ) {
   echo "Value is $value <br />";
   }
?>
```

- **Associative array:** An array with strings as an index and stores element values in association with key values rather than in strict linear index order.

```
<?php
/* Method to associate create array. */
        $alphabets = array("A" => 1, "B" => 2,
"C" => 3);

   echo "First alphabets is A and Number is
".$alphabets ['A'].  "<br />";
   echo "First alphabets is B and Number is
".$alphabets ['B'].  "<br />";
   echo "First alphabets is C and Number is
".$alphabets ['C'].  "<br />";
?>
```

- **Multidimensional array:** An array containing one or more arrays and values are accessed using multiple indices.

```
<?php
        $marks = array(
           "Student" => array (
               "English" => 15,
              "Maths" => 30,
              "Chemistry" => 39
           )
        );

        /* multi-dimensional array values */
        echo "Marks for Student in English is : " ;
        echo $marks ['Student'] ['English'].
"<br />";
?>
```

Array	Functions
array_change_key_case	It changes all keys in an array to uppercase or lowercase.
array_chunk	It splits an array into chunks.
array_column	It retrieves the values from a single column in an array.
array_combine	It merges the keys from one array and the values from another into a new Array.
array_count_values	It counts all values in an array.
array_diff	It arrays and returns the difference (values only).
array_diff_assoc	It arrays and returns the difference (values and keys).
array_diff_key	It arrays and returns the difference (keys only).
array_diff_uassoc	It arrays (keys and values) through a user callback function.
array_diff_ukey	It arrays (keys only) through a user callback function.
array_fill	It fills an array with values.
array_fill_keys	It fills an array with values, specifying keys.
array_filter	It filters the elements of an array via a callback function.
array_flip	It exchanges all keys in an array with their associated values.
array_intersect	It compares arrays and returns their matches (values only).
array_intersect_assoc	It compares arrays and returns their matches (keys and values).
array_intersect_key	It compares arrays and returns their matches (keys only).
array_intersect_uassoc	It compares arrays via a user-defined callback function (keys and values).
array_intersect_ukey	It compares arrays via a user-defined callback function (keys only).
array_key_exists	It checks if a specified key exists in an array, alternative: key_exists
array_keys	It returns all keys or a subset of keys in an array.
array_map	It applies a callback to the elements of a given array.
array_merge	It merges one or several arrays.
array_merge_recursive	It merges one or more arrays recursively.
array_multisort	It sorts multiple or multi-dimensional arrays.
array_pad	It inserts a specified number of items (with a specified value) into an Array.
array_pop	It deletes an element from the end of an array.
array_product	It calculates the product of all values in an array.
array_push	It pushes one or several elements to the end of the array.
array_rand	It can pick more than one random entry out of an array.
array_reduce	It can reduce the array to a single string using a user-defined function.
array_reduce	It can reduce the array to a single string using a user-defined function.

(Continued)

Array	Functions
array_replace	It can reduce elements in the first array with values from the following array.
array_replace_recursive	It can recursively replace elements from later arrays into the first array.
array_reverse	It returns an array in reverse order.
array_search	It can search the array for a given value and returns the first key if successful.
array_shift	It can shift an element from the beginning of an array.
array_slice	It extracts a slice of an array.
array_splice	It can remove a portion of the array and replace it.
array_sum	It can calculate the sum of the given values in an array.
array_udiff	It can compare arrays and return the difference using a user function.
array_udiff_assoc	It can compare arrays and return the difference using default and a user function (keys and values).
array_udiff_uassoc	It can array and return the difference using two user functions (values and keys).
array_uintersect	It can compare arrays and return the matches via user function (values only).
array_uintersect_uassoc	It can compare arrays and return the matches via two user functions (keys and values).
array_unique	Removes duplicate values from an array.
array_unshift	It can add one or more elements to the beginning of an array.
array_values	It returns all values of an array.
array_walk	It applies a user function to every element in an array.
array_walk_recursive	It recursively applies a user function to every element of an array.
arsort	It sorts an associative array in the descending order according to the value.
asort	It sorts an associative array in the ascending order according to the value.
count	It counts all elements in an array - alias of sizeof.
current	It returns the current element in an array, and an alternative is a position.
each	It can return the current key and value pair from an array.
end	It sets the internal pointer to the last element of an array.
extract	It imports variables from an array into the current symbol table.
in_array	It checks if a value exists in an array.
key	It fetches a key from an array.
krsort	It sorts an associative array by key in reverse order.

(Continued)

Array	Functions
ksort	It sorts an associative array by key.
list	It can assign variables as if they were an array.
natcasesort	It sorts an array using a "natural order" algorithm independent of the case.
natsort	It sorts an array using a "natural order" algorithm.
next	It advances the internal pointer of an array.
prev	It moves the internal array pointer backward.
range	It creates an array from a range of elements.
reset	It sets the internal array pointer to its first element.
resort	It sorts an array in reverse order.
shuffle	It shuffles an array.
sort	It sorts an indexed array in ascending order.
uasort	It sorts an array with a user-defined comparison function.
uksort	It arranges an array by keys using a user-defined comparison function.

Operator Keywords

There are three compound assignment operators. They are:

Operator	Equivalent
&=	and_eq
|=	or_eq
^=	xor_eq

Objects

It is a data type that allows storing data and knows how to process that data. It is a specific instance of a class that serves as the template for objects. These are created based on this template via the new keyword.

Every object has various properties and methods corresponding to its parent class. Every object instance is fully independent, with its own properties and methods, and can be manipulated independently of other objects of the same class.

Example:

```php
<?php
// Class definition
class greets{
    // properties
    public $str = "Hello World!";
```

```
    // methods
    function show_greeting() {
        return $this->str;
    }
}
// Create object from class
$message = new greets;
var_dump($message);
?>
```

NULL

It is a special data type which is used to represent empty variables in PHP languages. A variable of type is a variable without any data. It is the only possible value of type null.

Example:

```
<?php
$a = NULL;
var_dump($a);
echo "<br>";

$b = "Hello PHP!";
$b = NULL;
var_dump($b);
?>
```

Explanation: When a variable is created with an empty value in PHP like $name, it is automatically assigned a value of NULL type. Many developers get confused about it. Usually they considered both $var1 = NULL and $var2 = "" are same, but this is not true. Both are different. The $var1 has a null value where $var2 indicates no value assigned to it.

Resources

It is a special variable, holding a reference to an external resource. The resource variables hold special handlers to opened files and database connections.

Example:

```
<?php
// Open a file for reading
```

```
$handle = fopen("note.txt", "r");
var_dump($handle);
echo "<br>";

// Connect to MySQL database server with default
setting
$link = mysqli_connect("localhost", "root", "");
var_dump($link);
?>
```

Here we have the list of the types of Boolean values equivalents:

Data Types	True Value	False Value
Integer	All non-zero values	0
Floating point	All non-zero values	0.0
Strings	All other strings	Empty strings ()"" and The zero string()"0"
Null	Never	Always
Array	If it contains at least one element	If it does not contain any elements
Object	Always	Never
Resource	Always	Never

Typecasting

PHP language supports type-casting in the same way as C to allow the type of an expression to be changed. By placing the name in parentheses, PHP converts the value to the desired type.

The rules for converting types are commonly easy, but conversions are mostly not so simple. The following examples show how various values of $variable are converted using the (int), (bool), (string), and (float) casting operators.

- Cast to integer:
  (int) $var or (integer) $var

- Cast to Boolean:
  (bool) $var or (boolean) $var

- Cast to float:
  (float) $var, (double) $var or (real) $var

- Cast to string:
  (string) $var

- Cast to array:
  (array) $var

- Cast to object:
  (object) $var

Type conversion with casting operators conversion values:

Casting	Value of $var	(int) $var	(bool) $var	(string) $var	(float) $var
Casting null to int, bool, string, and float	null	0	False	""	0
Casting true to int, bool, string, and float	true	1	True	"1"	1
Casting false to int, bool, string, and float	false	0	False	""	0
Casting 0 to int, bool, string, and float	0	0	False	"0"	0
Casting 7.3 to int, bool, string, and float	7.3	7	True	"7.3"	7.3
Casting "0" to int, bool, string, and float	"0"	0	False	"0"	0
Casting "18" to int, bool, string, and float	"18"	18	True	"18"	18
Casting "1968 to present" to int, bool, string, and float	"1968 to present"	1968	True	"1968 to present"	1968
Casting "hello" to int, bool, string, and float	"hello"	0	True	"hello"	0

We can use the var_dump function to display variable information. This function displays structured information about expressions, including their type and some value.

Automatic Type Conversion

It occurs when two different typed variables are combined in an expression, or a variable is passed as an argument to a function that expects a different type. When a variable of one type is used, PHP automatically converts the variable to a value of the required type.

```
<?PHP
// $var is set as an integer = 25
$var = "10" + 15;
echo $var;
?>
```

IMPLICIT AND EXPLICIT CASTING

PHP language is a loosely typed language that allows declaring a variable and its type simply by using it. It also automatically converts values from one type to another data type whenever required. This is called implicit casting.

Example:

```
<?php
$str = "10 is a string";
// integer
$num1 = (int) $str;
echo $num1; //10
?>
```

EXPRESSIONS

An expression is that can be evaluated to produce a value. The common expressions are literal values and variables. A literal value evaluates itself, where a variable evaluates the value stored in the variable. More complex expressions are formed using simple expressions and operators.

Almost everything in a PHP file is an expression and anything that has a value is an expression. In a typical assignment statement ($x=10), a literal value, a function or operands processed by operators is an expression, anything that shows to the right of assignment operator (=).

- $x=10; //10 is an expression

- $a=$b+$c; //b+$c is an expression

- $c=add($a,$b); //add($a,$b) is an expression

- $val=sqrt(100); //sqrt(100) is an expression

- $var=$x!=$y; //$x!=$y is an expression

Expressions with ++ and –– Operators

These operators are called increment (++) and decrement (––) operators, respectively. They are called unary operators, need just one operand, and can be used in a prefix or postfix manner, although with a different effect on the value of the expression.

Both prefix and postfix ++ operators increment value of operand by 1 and whereas – operator decrements by 1. However, when used in assignment expression, prefix makes increment/decrement first and then followed by assignment. In case of postfix, assignment is done before increment/decrement.

```php
<?php
$x=10;
$y=$x++;
echo "x = $x "
?>
```

The output will be

```
x = 11
```

Another example of unary operators prefix to the variable,

```php
<?php
$x=10;
$y=++$x;
echo "x = $y";
?>
```

Expressions with Ternary Conditional Operator

This operator has three operands. One is a logical expression. If it is TRU, second operand expression is evaluated otherwise third one is evaluated.

Example:

```php
<?php
$marks=50;
```

```
$result= $marks<40?  "fail" : "pass";
echo $result;
?>
```

The result will be displayed as

Pass

OPERATORS

Operators take some values or the operands and do something, for instance, add them together. These operators are written as punctuation symbols – for example, the + and – familiar to us from math. Some operators modify their operands, while others do not.

- **Operator Precedence:** The precedence decides the order of execution of operators in an expression. For example, in 6+6/3, division of 6/3 is done first, and then the addition of 6+2 is done because division operator / has higher precedence over addition operator +. Parentheses should be required to force a specific operator to be called before others. Some of the operators have the same level of precedence. The order of associativity decides the order of operations. The operators of the same precedence level but are non-associative cannot be used next to each other.

  The only use of parentheses, where necessary, can often increase the readability of the code by making grouping.

  The following lists PHP operators with decreasing order of precedence.

Operator	What It Does
clone new	clone and new
**	Exponentiation
++ ——	increment/decrement
~(int) (float) (string) (array) (object) (bool)	Casting
Instanceof	Types
!	Logical
* /	multiplication / division
%	Modulo
+ –.	arithmetic and string
<< >>	bitwise shift

(Continued)

Operator	What It Does
< <= > >=	Comparison
== != === !== <> <=>	Comparison
&	bitwise and/references
^	bitwise XOR
|	bitwise OR
&&	logical and
||	logical or
??	null coalescing
? :	Ternary
= += -= *= **= /=. = %= &= |= ^= <<= >>=? ?=	assignment operators
yield from	yield from
Yield	Yield
print	Print
and	Logical
Xor	Logical
or	Logical

- **Arithmetic Operators:** PHP provides common arithmetic operators that allow performing addition, subtraction, multiplication, division, exponentiation, and modulus operations.

  It requires numeric values. Applying an arithmetic operator to non-integer values will convert them to integer values before performing any arithmetic operation.

Operator	Name	Example	Description
+	Addition	$x + $y	It might the sum of $x and $y
−	Subtraction	$x − $y	It might be the difference of $x and $y
*	Multiplication	$x * $y	It might be the product of $x and $y
/	Division	$x / $y	It might the quotient of $x and $y
**	Exponentiation	$x ** $y	It might return the result of raising $x to the $y'th power
%	Modulo	x % $y	$ It might be the remainder of $x divided by $y

- **Assignment Operators:** These operators store a value in the object specified by the left operand.

There are two types of assignment operations:

- **Simple assignment:** In which the value of the second operand is stored in the object specified by the first operand. For example, = (simple assignment operator).

  All assignment operators in the given table except the = operator are compound assignment operators.

- **Compound assignment:** In which arithmetic, shift, or bitwise operation is performed before storing the result.

Operator	Meaning
=	It stores the value of the second operand in the object specified by the first operand; this is called a simple assignment.
*=	It multiplies the value of the first operand by the value of the second operand; stores the result in the object specified by the first operand.
/=	It divides the value of the first operand by the value of the second operand; stores the result in the object specified by the first operand.
<<=	It shifts the value of the first operand left the number of bits specified by the value of the second operand; stores the result in the object specified by the first operand.
%=	It takes the modulus of the – first operand specified by the value of the second operand; stores the result in the object specified by the first operand.
+=	It can add the value of the second operand to the value of the first operand; stores the result in the object specified by the first operand.
−=	It subtracts the second operand's value from the first operand's value; store the result in the object specified by the first operand.
|=	It obtains the bitwise inclusive OR of the first and second operands; stores the result in the object specified by the first operand.
^=	It obtains the bitwise exclusive OR of the first and second operands; stores the result in the object specified by the first operand.
&=	It obtains the bitwise AND of the first and second operands; stores the result in the object specified by the first operand.
>>=	It shifts the value of the first operand right to the number of bits specified by the value of the second operand; store the result in the object specified by the first operand.

- **Bitwise Operators:** It performs bit-level operations on the operands. The operators are converted to bit-level, and then the calculation is performed on the operands. The operations, such as addition, subtraction, multiplication, etc., can be performed at bit-level for processing.

These operators allow operating on the bitwise.

- **Bitwise AND operator:** This operator AND works on two operands. This operator in PHP takes two numbers as operands and performs AND on every bit of two numbers. The result of AND operator is one only if both bits value is 1.

- **Bitwise OR:** This operator is working on two operands. This operator takes two numbers as operands and does OR on every two numbers. The OR operator's result is one of any of the two bits value is 1.

- **Bitwise XOR:** This operator works on two operands, and it is also known as the Exclusive OR operator. It takes two numbers as operands and does XOR on every two numbers. The result of XOR is 1 if the two bits are different.

- **Bitwise NOT:** This operator works on only one operand. It takes one number and inverts all bits of it.

- **Bitwise Left Shift:** This operator works on two operands. Bitwise Left Shift operator takes two numbers. The left shifts the bits of the first operand and the second operand decides the number of places to shift.

- **Bitwise Right Shift:** This operator works on two operands. The operator takes two numbers, right shifts the bits of the first operand; the second operand decides the number of places to shift.

These operators allow operating on the bitwise representation of their arguments.

Operator	Name	Example	Result
&	& (Bitwise AND)	$x & $y	The bits that are set in both $x and $y are set.
|	| (Bitwise OR)	$x | $y	The bits that are set in either $x or $y are set.
^	^ (Bitwise XOR)	$x ^ $y	The bits set in $x or $y but not both are set.
~	~ (Bitwise NOT)	~$x	The bits set in $x are not set, and vice versa.
<<	<< (Bitwise Left Shift)	$x << $y	Shift the bits of $x $y steps to the left.#
>>	>> (Bitwise Right Shift)	$x >> $y	Shift the bits of $x $y steps to the right.*

- **Comparison Operators:** Use this section as a reference for comparison and logical operators. These operators are used to performing operations on some values. We can describe an operator that takes some values, performs some operations on them, and gives a result.

  Like other programming languages, PHP also supports various operations like arithmetic operations like addition, subtraction, etc., logical operations like AND, OR, etc. Increment/Decrement Operations (––, ++) etc.

  It provides us with many operators to perform such operations on various operands, variables, or values. These operators are just symbols needed to perform operations of various types.

- **Arithmetic Operators:**

Operator	Name	Syntax	Operation
+ (plus)	Addition	$x + $y	It is used to sum the operands.
–	Subtraction	$x – $y	It is used to subtract the operands.
*	Multiplication	$x * $y	It is used to multiple operands.
/	Division	$x / $y	The quotient of the operands.
**	Exponentiation	$x ** $y	$x raised to the power $y.
%	Modulus	$x % $y	It is the remainder of the operands.

  Example:

```php
<?php
  $x = 12; // Variable 1
  $y = 14; // Variable 2

  // Some arithmetic operations on these two
variables
  echo ($x + $y), "\n";
  echo($x - $y), "\n";
  echo($x * $y), "\n";
  echo($x / $y), "\n";
  echo($x % $y), "\n";
?>
```

- **Logical or Relational Operators:** These are used to operate with conditional statements and expressions. These are based on conditions. The output of a conditional statement can either be true or false. Here are the logical operators with their syntax and operations in PHP.

Operator	Name	Syntax	Operation
and	Logical AND	$x + $y	It returns True if both the operands are true else false.
Or	Logical OR	$x or $y	It returns True if either of the operands is true; else false.
xor	Logical XOR	$x xor $y	It returns True if either of the operands is true and false if both are true.
&&	Logical AND	$x && $y	It returns True if both the operands are true else false.
||	Logical OR	$x || $y	It returns True if either of the operands is true else false.
!	Logical NOT	!$x	It returns True if $x is false.

Example:

```php
<?php
$x = 10;
$y = 20;
    if ($x == 10 and $y == 20)
        echo "and Success \n";

    if ($x == 10 or $y == 20)
        echo "or Success \n";

    if ($x == 10 xor $y == 20)
        echo "xor Success \n";

    if ($x == 10 && $y == 20)
        echo "&& Success \n";

    if ($x == 10 || $y == 20)
        echo "|| Success \n";

    if (!$z)
        echo "! Success \n";
?>
```

- **Comparison Operators:** These are used to compare two elements and outputs the result in Boolean. Here are the comparison operators, along with their syntax and operations in PHP.

Operator	Name	Syntax	Operation
==	Equal To	$x == $y	It returns True if both operands are equal.
!=	Not Equal To	$x != $y	It returns True if both operands are not equal.
===	Identical	$x === $y	It returns True if both operands are equal and are of the same type.
!==	Not Identical	$x !== $y	It returns True if both operands are unequal and are of different types.
<	Less Than	$x < $y	It returns True if $x is less than $y.
>	Greater Than	$x > $y	It can return True if $x is greater than $y.
<=	Less Than or Equal To	$x <= $y	It can return True if $x is less than or equal to $y.
>=	Greater Than or Equal To	$x >= $y	It can return True if $x is greater than or equal to $y.

Example:

```php
<?php
  $a = 20;
  $b = 30;
  $c = "20";

  echo $a == $c;
echo $a != $b;
  echo $a <> $b;
  echo $a === $c;
```

Operator	Name	Operation
?:	Ternary Operator	If the condition is true ? then $x : or else $y. It means that if the condition is true, then the left result of the colon is run; otherwise, the result is on the right.

```php
  echo $a !== $c;
  echo $a < $b;
  echo $a > $b;
  echo $a <= $b;
  echo $a >= $b;
```

```
//Output of all of the above is 1 because
1 means True
?>
```

- **Conditional or Ternary Operators:** These operators are used to compare two given values and take either of the results simultaneously, depending on whether the output is TRUE or FALSE. These are also used as a short notation for the if-else statement.

Syntax:

```
$var = (condition)? value1: value2;
<?php
  $var = 20;
  echo ($var > 0)?  'The given number is
positive' : 'The given number is negative';
?>
```

- **Assignment Operators:** These are used to assign various variables, with or without mid-operations. Here are the operators with their syntax and operations that PHP provides for the operations.

Operator	Name	Syntax	Operation
=	Assign value	$x = $y	This operand obtains the value of the operand on the right.
+=	Add then assign value	$x += $y	This operand simply adds same as $x = $x + $y.
-=	Subtract then assign value	$x -= $y	This operand simply subtract same as $x = $x – $y.
*=	Multiply then assign value	$x *= $y	This operand simply product same as $x = $x * $y.
/=	Divide then assign the quotient value	$x /= $y	This operand simply division same as $x = $x / $y
%=	divide then assign the remainder value	$x % = $y	Simple division same as $x = $x % $y

Example:

```
<?php
  // Simple assign operator
  $y = 75;
  echo $y, "\n";
```

```php
// Add then assign operator
$y = 100;
$y += 200;
echo $y, "\n";

// Subtract then assign operator
$y = 70;
$y -= 10;
echo $y, "\n";

// Multiply then assign operator
$y = 30;
$y *= 20;
echo $y, "\n";

// Divide then assign(quotient) operator
$y = 100;
$y /= 5;
echo $y, "\n";

// Divide then assign(remainder) operator
$y = 50;
$y %= 5;
echo $y;
?>
```

• **Spaceship Operators:** The spaceship operator comparison operator is denoted by "<=>." These are used to compare values but return the Boolean results, and it returns integer values. If both the operands are equal, it returns 0. If the right operand is greater, it returns −1. If the left operand is greater, it returns 1.

Operator	Syntax	Operation
$x < $y	$x <=> $y	Identical to −1 (right is greater).
$x <= $y	$x <=> $y	Identical to −1 (right is greater) or identical to 0 (if both are equal).
$x >= $y	$x <=> $y	Identical to 1 (if left is greater) or identical to 0 (if both are equal).
$x == $y	$x <=> $y	Identical to 0 (both are equal).
$x != $y	$x <=> $y	Not identical to 0.

- **Array Operators:** These are used in the case of arrays. PHP provides the array operators' syntax and operations for the array operation.

Operator	Name	Syntax	Operation
+	Union	$x + $y	It performs a union of both, i.e., $x and $y.
==	Equality	$x == $y	It returns True if both have the same key-value pair.
!=	Inequality	$x != $y	It returns True if both are unequal.
===	Identity	$x === $y	It returns True if both have the same key-value pair in the same order and of the same type.
!==	Non-Identity	$x !== $y	It returns True if both are not identical to each other.
<>	Inequality	$x <> $y	It returns True if both are unequal.

- **Increment/Decrement Operators:**

Operator	Name	Syntax	Operation
++	Pre-Increment	++$x	It first increments the value of $x by one, then returns $x.
—	Pre-Decrement	–$x	It first decrements the value of $x by one, then returns $x.
++	Post-Increment	$x++	It first returns $x, then increments the value of it by one.
—	Post-Decrement	$x–	It first returns $x, then decrements the value of it by one.

Example:

```php
<?php
  $x = 3;
  echo ++$x, " First increments then prints
\n";
  echo $x, "\n";

  $x = 3;
  echo $x++, " First prints then increments
\n";
  echo $x, "\n";
```

```
$x = 3;
echo --$x, " First decrements then prints \n";
echo $x, "\n";

$x = 3;
echo $x--, " First prints then decrements \n";
echo $x;
?>
```

- **String Operators:** The concatenation operator ('.') is used to join two or more strings together with this operator. We can use the concatenating assignment operator ('.=') to append the argument from right to left.

Operator	Name	Syntax	Operation
	Concatenation	$x.$y	Concatenated $x and $y.
.=	Concatenation and assignment	$x.=$y	First concatenates then assigns, same as $x = $x.$y.

Example:

```
<?php
$x = "We";
$y = "Learn";
$z = "PHP";
$x .= $y . $z;
echo $x;
?>
```

- **Error Control Operators:** The @ symbol is defined as Error Control Operator. When it is prefixed to any expression, any error encountered by the PHP parser while executing it will be suppressed, and the expression will be ignored.

Operator	Name	Example	Explanation
@	At	@file ('non_existent_file')	Intentional file error

```
<?php
$fp = @fopen("file.txt","r");
echo "Hello World";
?>
```

- **Execution Operators:** PHP supports one execution operator, i.e., backticks ("). These are not single quotes, but they look like they! It attempts to execute the contents of the backticks as a shell command, and the output will be returned. The use of the backticks operator is identical to shell_exec().

Example:

```php
<?php
$output = 'ls -al';
echo "<pre>$output</pre>";
?>
```

- **Incrementing/Decrementing Operators:** PHP supports pre and post-increment and decrement operators. These increment/ decrement operators operate on variables and not on any value.

  Here is the list of increment/decrement operators.

Operator	Name	Description
++$x	Pre-increment	Increments $x by one, then returns $x
$x++	Post-increment	Returns $x, then increments $x by one
--$x	Pre-decrement	Decrements $x by one, then returns $x
$x--	Post-decrement	Returns $x, then decrements $x by one

```php
<?php
echo "<h3>Post Increment</h3>";
$a = 5;
echo "Result will be 5: ". $a++. "<br />\n";
echo "Result will 6: ". $a. "<br />\n";

echo "<h3>Pre Increment</h3>";
$a = 5;
echo "Result will 6: ". ++$a. "<br />\n";
echo "Result will 6: ". $a. "<br />\n";

echo "<h3>Post Decrement</h3>";
$a = 5;
```

```
echo "Result will 5: ".  $a--.  "<br />\n";
echo "Result will 4: ".  $a.  "<br />\n";

echo "<h3>Pre Decrement</h3>";
$a = 5;
echo "Result will 4: ".  --$a.  "<br />\n";
echo "Result will 4: ".  $a.  "<br />\n";
?>
```

- **Logical Operators:** These PHP operators are symbols that help perform the logical operations with ease flow. These PHP operators are symbols that help perform logical operations with ease. The logical operators consist of operators, like addition (+), greater than (>), etc., which instruct the compiler to perform the necessary operation. It can check various operations and then determine which of the conditions are true. The values of particular operators use are known as operands. These operators are not similar to functions. PHP has logical operators that help in combining conditional statements.

  PHP languages support the standard logical operators, or, not, and xor. Logical operators can convert their operands to boolean values and then compare them.

  Here is the list of logical operators:

Operator	Name	Example	Result
&&	And	$x && $y	It is true if both $x and $y are true.
||	Or	$x || $y	It is true if either $x or $y is true.
Xor	Xor	$x xor $y	It is true if either $x or $y is true, but not both.
!	Not	!$x	It is true if $x is not true.
and	And	$x and $y	It is true if both $x and $y are true.
or	Or	$x or $y	It is true if either $x or $y is true.

- **String Operators:** There are two operators for string data types. The '.' (Dot) operator is used for the concatenation operator in PHP. Two string operands are joined together, meaning the characters of the right-hand string are appended to the left-hand string and return a new string. PHP language also has a .= operator, which can be called a concatenation assignment operator string on the left is updated by appending characters of the right-hand side operand.

Example:

```php
<?php
$x="Hello";
$y=" ";
$z="PHP";
$n="\n";
$str=$x . $y . $z . $n;
echo $str;
?>
```

- **Array Operators:**

Symbol	Name	Example	Result
+	Union	$x + $y	It is a Union of $x and $y. The + operator appends remaining keys from the right-sided array to the left-handed, but duplicated keys are not overwritten.
==	Equality	$x == $y	Returns TRUE if $x and $y have the same key/value pairs.
===	Identity	$x === $y	Returns TRUE if $x and $y have the same key/value pairs in the same order and of the same types.
!=	Inequality	$x != $y	It can return TRUE if $x is not equal to $y.
<>	Inequality	$x <> $y	It can return TRUE if $x is not equal to $y.
!==	Non-Identity	$x !== $y	Returns TRUE if $x is not identical to $y.

- **Union of arrays (+):** By adding the right-hand array to the left-hand array, the Union operator unites two arrays together. If key exists in both arrays, the left-hand array's elements will be used instead of the right-hand array's matching elements.

- **Comparison of arrays equality (==) and identity (===) operator:** The two arrays are known as equal if they have the same key-value pairs. The equality operator returns true when two arrays have the same key-value pairs. In contrast, the identity operator returns false as the key-value of the comparing arrays are the same but not in the same order.

- **Type Operators:** The type operator object named instanceof is used to determine whether an object, its parent, and its derived class are the same type or not.

    This operator determines the certain class the object belongs to. It is used in (OOPS) object-oriented programming.

    Syntax example, if ($variable instanceof Class)

CHAPTER SUMMARY

This chapter covers the variable's scopes, data types, and various operators, like logical operators, bit wise operator, ternary operators, and so on, in PHP languages. Operand symbols like increment and decrement are used for various operations. The string operator and array operator are also described.

CHAPTER 3

Control Statements

IN THIS CHAPTER

➤ Introduction to control statements

➤ Control statement

➤ Looping statements

The previous chapter covered the variable"s scopes, expression, variables with their scopes, data types, and various operators like increment and decrement in PHP languages logical operators, bit wise operator, ternary operators, and so on.

In this chapter, we will discuss control structures and loops in PHP scripts. We will show you how to use all the control structures supported by the PHP such as if, else, for, foreach, while, switch, and more.

INTRODUCTION TO CONTROL STATEMENTS

In straightforward, a control structure allows controlling the flow of code execution in your coding application. Generally, a program is executed, line by line, sequentially, and a control structure allows altering that flow, usually depending on certain conditions.

These control structures are core features of the PHP language or any other that allows your script to respond differently to several inputs or situations and could let your script give several responses based on user input, file contents, or some other data. Statements usually end with a semicolon in PHP, and they can be grouped into a statement group by encapsulating a group of statements with curly braces.

DOI: 10.1201/9781003308669-3

Or

These are called conditional statements that can execute a block of statements if the condition is true. The statement inside the block will not execute until or unless the condition is satisfied.

The number of statement types is described in this chapter.

PHP supports several different control structures,

- if

- else

- else-if/elsc if

- Alternative syntax for control structures

- while

- do-while

- for

- foreach

- break

- continue

- switch

- match

- declare

- return

- require

- include

- require_once

- include_once

- goto

All these are pre-available in PHP languages. These are called keywords. We cannot use them as a variable anywhere in the code. Suppose we declare some function and function name is the function, then it will give you an error because the function is already a keyword in PHP language.

LIST OF KEYWORDS AVAILABLE IN PHP

What Is a Keyword?

In PHP, certain words are reserved for special use, and we cannot use these words when naming our custom variables, constants, arrays, functions, interfaces, and classes.

These keywords have special meaning and are only used in special contexts. While nothing strictly stops us from prefixing a keyword with a dollar ($) sign, it is conventionally considered bad practice, making code difficult and slow to read.

All these words have a special kind of meaning in language. Some represent things that look like functions, some look like constants, and so on – but they're not, really: they are language constructs. The following words cannot be constants, class names, functions, or method names. They are, however, allowed as property, constant, and method names of classes, interfaces, and traits, except that class, may not be used as the constant name.

PHP Keywords				
__halt_compiler()	abstract	and	array()	as
break	callable	case	catch	class
clone	const	continue	declare	default
die()	do	echo	else	elseif
empty()	enddeclare	endfor	endforeach	endif
endswitch	endwhile	eval()	exit()	extends
final	finally	fn (as of PHP 7.4)	for	foreach
function	global	goto	if	implements
include	include_once	instanceof	insteadof	interface
isset()	list()	match (as of PHP 8.0)	namespace	new
or	print	private	protected	public
readonly (as of PHP 8.1.0) *	require	require_once	return	static
switch	throw	trait	try	unset()
use	var	while	xor	yield
yield from				

Operands Lvalue and Rvalue

The two kinds of expressions in PHP are Lvalues and Rvalues. The operand on the left-hand side of the assignment is the Lvalue and the operand on the right-hand side is the Rvalue.

Lvalue

An Lvalue can have a value assigned so it allowed to appear on either the left side or right side of an assignment.

Output: Lvalue, the left operand

```php
<?php
// lvalue (var1) may be on the left
$var1 = 10
// or on the right side of the =
$var2 = $var1
?>
```

Rvalue

An Rvalue is an expression that cannot assign a value, so it may only appear on the right side of a position.

Output: Rvalue is the left operand

```php
<?php
// rvalue (20) may only be on the right
var1 = 20
// and cannot be on the left
20 = 20
?>
```

The key points to remember:

1. A variable name in PHP is always prefixed with the $ symbol.

2. A variable name cannot start with a numerical value.

3. A variable name may start with uppercase or lowercase alphabetical letters and underscores.

4. A variable name may not contain special characters.

5. Some variable names are case-sensitive.

6. By using reserved keywords for names is considered bad practice.

7. Be consistent in the casing that you use. This series will use camel-Case for variables, attributes, functions, and methods and PascalCase for classes.

8. The reserved keywords have special meaning and should only be used in special contexts.

9. An Lvalue is an operand on the left or right of the =.

10. An Rvalue is an operand on the right of the =.

LIST OF CONTROL STATEMENTS

The if Statement

The if statement is the most used, common, and important feature of many languages, PHP included. It allows for the conditional execution of code in fragments. PHP has features an if structure that is similar to that of the C language.

The if statement executes if the expression inside the parenthesis is evaluated as true or the code is skipped to the next statement block. It can be a single statement followed by a semicolon, and it is a compound statement enclosed by curly braces, and an else statement appears immediately after the statement and have a statement of itself. It is executed only when the last expression is false, or else it is not executed.

Here is the basic syntax of the if statement,

```
if (expr)
    statement
```

Let have a simple example of if statement,

The following example display "a is bigger than b" when $a is bigger than $b:

```
<?php
$a=15;
$b=12;
if ($a > $b)
  echo "a is bigger than b";
?>
```

The else Statement

The last section discussed the if statement, which allows executing a code if the expression evaluates true. On the other side, if the expression evaluates to false, it does not do anything, and more often than not, you also want to execute a different code if the expression evaluates to false.

You always use the else statement block with an if statement block. You can check it as shown in the following code.

Syntax:

```
if (expression)
{
    // code is executed here if the expression
evaluates to TRUE
}
else
{
    // code is executed here if the expression
evaluates to FALSE
}
```

Let's have the example to understand how it works.

```php
<?php
$age = 12;
if ($age < 18)
{
  echo "Your age is less than 18!";
}
else
{
  echo "Age is greater than or equal to 18!";
}
?>
```

else-if Statement

The else-if statement provides an extension to the if-else construct block. If you have more than two options to choose from, you can use the else-if statement.

Let's look at the basic structure of the else-if statement, as shown in the following code.

```
if (expression1)
{
    // code is executed here if the expression1
evaluates to TRUE
}
```

```
else if (expression2)
{
  // code is executed here if the expression2
evaluates to TRUE
}
else if (expression3)
{
  // code is executed here if the expression3
evaluates to TRUE
}
else
{
  // code is executed here if the expression1,
expression2, and expression3 evaluate
}
```

Let's have the example to understand how it works.

```php
<?php
$a=20;
$b=15;
if ($a > $b) {
    echo "a is bigger than b";
} elseif ($a == $b) {
    echo "a is equal to b";
} else {
    echo "a is smaller than b";
}
?>
```

switch Statement

The switch statement is similar to the else-if statement, which we have discussed in the last section. The only difference is the expression that is being checked.

In the case of the else-if statement, you have various conditions at once, and appropriate action will be executed based on a condition. On the other side, if you want to compare a variable with different values, you can use the switch statement.

Here we have an example which is the best way to understand the switch statement.

```php
<?php
$favorite_color = 'Purple';
```

```php
switch ($favorite_site) {
  case 'Red':
    echo "My favorite color is Red!";
    break;
  case 'Green':
    echo "My favorite color is Green!";
    break;
  case 'Yellow':
    echo "My favorite color is Yellow!";
    break;
  case 'Orange':
    echo "My favorite color is Orange!";
    break;
  case 'Purple':
    echo "My favorite color is Purple!";
    break;
  default:
    echo "I like everything at Black";
}
?>
```

Explanation: As you can get the point in the above code example, we want to check the value of the $favorite_color variable, and based on the value of the $favorite_color variable, and we want to print a message.

You have to define the case block for each value you want to check with the $favourite_color variable. If the value is matched with a case, the code associated with that case block will be executed. After that, you need to use the break statement to end code execution. If you don't use the break statement, script execution will continue up to the switch statement's last block.

Finally, if you want to execute a code if the variable's value doesn't match any case, you can define it under the default block. Of course, it's not mandatory – it's just a way to provide a default case.

Other example of switch statement,

```php
<?php
  $day = date(" l ");
  switch($day)
  {
  case "monday":
      print($day);
      break;
```

```
case "tuesday"
    print($day);
    break;
case "wednesday":
    print($day);
    break;
case "thursday":
    print($day);
    break;
case "friday":
    print($day);
    break;
case "saturday":
    print($day);
    break;
default:
  print($day);
}?>
```

The ? Operator

Expressions with the Ternary Conditional Operator

This operator has three operands. One is a logical expression. The second operand expression is evaluated; otherwise, the third one is evaluated. It is represented as a PHP ternary operator and used as a conditional operator. It is mainly evaluated as false or true. If false, the expression next to the ternary operator is executed, or the expression between the ternary operator and colon is executed.

Syntax:

```
condition expresion?  true : false;
```

Example:

```
<?php
$marks=50;
$result= $marks<40?  "fail" : "pass";
echo $result;
?>
```

The result will be displayed as

```
Pass
```

Alternative Syntax for Control Structures (if, else-if)

PHP language offers an alternative syntax for some of its control structures namely if, else, if-else, while, for, foreach, and switch. In each case, the common form of the alternate syntax is to change the opening brace to a colon (:) and the closing brace to endif;, end-while;, end-for;, endforeach;, or endswitch;, respectively.

```php
<?php if ($a == 20) :?>
A is equal to 20
<?php endif;?>
```

In the example, the block "A is equal to 20" is nested within an if statement written in the alternative syntax. The HTML block display only if $a equals to 20.

The alternative syntax of else and elseif as well. The following is the structure of if with elseif and else in the alternative format:

```php
<?PHP
if ($a == 20):
    echo "a equals 20";
    echo "...";
elseif ($a == 6):
    echo "a equals 6";
    echo "!!!";
else:
    echo "a is neither 5 nor 6";
endif;
?>
```

while Loop

The while loop is used when you repeatedly execute a piece of code until the while condition evaluates to false.

You can define it as shown in the following code.

Syntax:

```php
while (expression)
{
    // code to execute until the expression
    evaluates to TRUE
}
```

Let's have a look at single example to understand how the while loop works in PHP.

```php
<?php
//Declare the variable "a" and assign it value
$i = 1;
while ($i <= 15) {
    echo $i++;  /* the printed value would be
                    $i before the increment
                    which is known post-increment) */
}
$i = 1;
while ($i <= 5):
    echo $i;
    $i++;
endwhile;
?>
```

Write the Fibonacci series program in PHP.

```php
<?php
$max = 0;
echo $i = 0;
echo ",";
echo $j = 1;
echo ",";
$result=0;

while ($max < 15 )
{
    $result = $i + $j;

    $i = $j;
    $j = $result;

    $max = $max + 1;
    echo $result;
    echo ",";
}
?>
```

Here is the output of the following,

```
0, 1, 1, 2, 3, 5, 8, 13, 21, 34, 55 and so on.
```

If you are known about the Fibonacci series, you can recognize what the above program does. It outputs the Fibonacci series for the first ten numbers. This while loop is generally used when you do not know the number of iterations that will take place in a loop.

do-while Loop

The do-while loop is so similar to the while loop, with the only difference being that the while condition is checked at the end of the first iteration loop. Thus, we can use that the loop code is executed at least once, irrespective of the result of the whole expression.

Let's have a look at the syntax of the do-while loop.

```
do
{
   // code to execute here
}
while (expression or condition);
```

Here the example of the do-while loop,

```php
<?php
$x = 1;
do {
   echo "The number is: $x <br>";
   $x++;
} while ($x <= 5);
?>
```

for Loop

Generally, this loop is used to execute a code for a specific number of times. On another side, if you already know the exact number of times you want to execute, a particular code block, then the for loop is a good choice.

Have a look at the syntax of the for a loop.

```
for (condition1; condition2; condition3)
{
   // code to execute here
}
```

The condition2 expression is used to initialize variables, and it is always executed. The condition2 expression is also executed at the beginning of a loop, and if it evaluates to true, the loop code is executed. After execution of the loop code, condition3 is executed. Generally, the expr_3 is used to alter the value of a variable used in the condition2 expression.

Here the following example to see how it works,

```php
<?php
for ($var=1; $var<=10; ++$var)
{
   echo sprintf("The result of the square ofof %d is
%d.</br>", $var, $var*$var);
}
?>
```

The output of the following code,

```
The result of the square of 1 is 1.
The result of the square of 2 is 4.
The result of the square of 3 is 9.
The result of the square of 4 is 16.
The result of the square of 5 is 25.
The result of the square of 6 is 36.
The result of the square of 7 is 49.
The result of the square of 8 is 64.
The result of the square of  9 is 81.
The result of the square of 10 is 100.
```

The above code shows the output of the square of the first ten numbers from 0 to 10. It initializes $var to 1, repeats as long as $var is less than or equal to 10, and adds 1 to $var at each iteration.

Breaking Out of the Loop

There are times when you want to break out of a loop before it runs out. This can achieve easily with the break keyword and will get you out of the current for, foreach, do-while, or switch structure.

You can use the Break to get out of various nested loops by giving a numeric argument. For example, using Break two will break you out of 2 nested loops. Therefore, you cannot pass a variable as the numeric argument if you use a PHP version greater than or equal to 5.4.

The break keyword is used to stop the loop, and the program control resumes at the next statement of the loop. To terminate the control from any other loop, we need to use the break keyword. The break keywords are used to end the current execution, foreach, do-while, or switch structure. The statement break can be used to jump out of a loop.

```
<?PHP
for ($x = 0; $x < 10; $x++) {
   if ($x == 4) {
      break;
   }
   echo "The number is: $x <br>";
}
?>
```

Syntax:

```
break number_of_loop_to_terminate;
```

By default, the break keyword followed by a numeric argument which is 1. By passing variables and 0 as a numeric argument is not allowed.

Here are the examples of the break:

- break 2; // It terminates second outer loop.

- break 0; // The 0 is not a valid argument to pass.

```
<?php
for ($x = 0; $x < 10; $x++) {
   if ($x == 4) {
      break;
   }
   echo "The number is: $x <br>";
}
?>
```

foreach

The foreach provides a good way to iterate over arrays. The control statement foreach works only on arrays and objects and will create an issue or error when you try to use it on a variable with a different data type or any other uninitialized variable.

There are two syntax of for each:

```
foreach (iterable_condition as $value)
    statement
foreach (iterable_condition as $key => $value)
    statement
```

The first traverse the iterable given by iterable_condition. The current element's value is assigned to $value on each iteration.

The second form will assign the current element key to the $key variable on each iteration.

Continue

The continued statement breaks a single iteration in the loop. If a specified condition occurs, the code of that condition will not execute and continues with the next iteration in the loop.

The following example skips the value of 5:

```
<?php
for ($x = 0; $x < 10; $x++) {
  if ($x ==5) {
    continue;
  }
  echo "The number is: $x <br>";
}
?>
```

Break and Continue in while Loops

You can further use Break and continue in while loops.

Here the example of Break,

```
<?PHP
$x = 0;

while($x < 10) {
  if ($x == 4) {
    break;
  }
  echo "The number is: $x <br>";
  $x++;
}
?>
```

Here the example of Continue,

```php
<?php
$x = 0;

while($x < 10) {
  if ($x == 4) {
    $x++;
    continue;
  }
  echo "The number is: $x <br>";
  $x++;
}
?>
```

match

The match expressions are evaluated based on an identity-check of a value. Same as a switch statement, a match expression has an expression that is compared against multiple alternatives. Unlike switch, it will evaluate to a value much like ternary expressions. And the comparison is an identity check (===) rather than a weak equality check (==).

For example, match expression in PHP 7:

```php
<?php
  echo match (1.0) {
    '1.0' => "Hello World!",
    1.0 => "Looks Good!",
  };
?>
```

For example, match expression in PHP 8:

```php
<?php
  echo match (2) {
    1 => 'Company',
    2 => 'Department',
    3 => 'Employee',
  };
?>
```

Key points for match expression:

- The match expression does not use the switch-case statements 'case and break' structure. It supports joint conditions and returns a value rather than entering a new code block.

- We can store match output in a variable because it is an expression.

- The match expression does not need a break statement like a switch. It supports only single-line expression.

declare

The declare keyword sets an execution block of code. If a block does not follow the declaration statement, then the directive applies to the rest of the code in the file.

Syntax:

```
declare (directive)
    statement
```

Example:

```php
<?php
declare(strict_types=1);
function sum(int $a, int $b) {
   return $a + $b;
}

// It throws a fatal error because '5' is a string
instead of a number
sum("5", 1);
?>
```

There are three types of directives that can be declared:

- **Ticks:** It sends a tick event each time a specified number of instructions execute. A tick function can register, which will run each time a tick event fires.

- **Encoding:** It is used to indicate what character encoding the file is using. It cannot use on a block, and it has to apply to the whole file.

- **strict_types:** When the strict_types directive is set, values of the wrong type passed into function arguments with type hints will throw a fatal error instead of casting to the correct type.

return Statement

The keyword return ends a function and uses the result of an expression as the function's return value.

If the return statement is outside of a function, it stops the code in the file from running. If the file included any of them include, include_once, require, or require_once, the result of the expression is used as the return value of the include statements.

```
<?PHP
function add($x) {
   return $x + 1;
}
echo "5 + 1 is " . add(5);
?>
```

require Statement

The keyword required is used to embed any PHP code from another file. If the file is not getting, then a fatal error is thrown, and the program stops.

Suppose we have a file named coding.php, for using the code of the same file in another file, then you need to declare the file using include or require keyword, for example:

The file name is coding.php:

```
<?PHP require 'coding.php';?>
```

Note: When you are using the required keyword, always remember that it is a statement, not a function. It's not necessary to write like below:

Function	Statement
<?PHP require ('somefile.php'); ?>	<?php require 'somefile.php'; ?>

include Statement

The keyword include is used to embed PHP code from another file. If the file is not found, some warning is shown, and the program continues to run.

File name is coding.php:

```php
<?php include 'coding.php';?>
```

Example:

fruits.php	display.php
| ```php
<?php
$color = 'green';
$fruit = 'apple';
?>
``` | ```php
<?php
echo "A $color $fruit";
include 'fruits.php';
echo "A $color $fruit";
?>
``` |

require_once Statement

The keyword require_once is used to embed the PHP code from another file. If the file is not getting, then a fatal error is thrown, and the program stops. If the file was previously included, this statement would not include it again. The use require_once keyword to add another page to a page:

Syntax:

```php
<?PHP require_once 'header.php';?>
<?PHP require_once 'footer.php';?>
```

include_once Statement

The keyword include_once is used to embed PHP code from another file. If the file is not getting, a warning is shown, and the program continues to run. If the file was previously included, this statement would not include it again.

The behavior similar to the include statement, with the only difference, is that if the code from a file has already been included, it will not be included again, and include_once returns true. As per name suggests, the file will be included just once.

It is used in those cases where the same file might be included and evaluated more than once during a particular execution of a script. In this case, it may help avoid problems such as function redefinitions, variable value reassignments, etc.

The use include_once keyword to add another to a page:

```php
<?php include_once 'footer.php';?>
```

goto Operator

The goto operator can use to jump to another section in the program. The main point is specified by a case-sensitive label followed by a colon, and the instruction is given as goto followed by the desired target label. This is not a full unrestricted goto. The pointed label must be within the same file and context, meaning that you cannot jump out of any of the functions or methods, nor can you jump into one statement. You also cannot jump statements into any sort of loop or switch structure. You can jump out of these, and common use is to use a goto in place of a multilevel break.

Example:

```php
<?php
goto a;
echo 'Hello';
a:
echo 'PHP';
?>
```

WHAT IS THE BOOLEAN EXPRESSION IN PHP?

A Boolean expression is a way to express the results in a Boolean value that is either true or false.

A simple Booleans expression is written as,

```
Operand_1 Comparison Operator Operand_2
```

where, Operand_1 and Operand_2 can be values, variables, or math expressions.

Comparison Operator can be equal (=), Not equal (!=), Greater than (>), Less than (<), Greater than or equal to (>=), Less than or equal to (<=).

Boolean Constant

A Boolean constant can have TRUE and FALSE, where TRUE is 1 and FALSE is 0.

CHAPTER SUMMARY

This chapter discusses the control structures and loops in PHP. It also discusses how to use the control structures supported by the PHP such as if, else, for, foreach, while, switch, and more.

PHP Functions

In the previous chapter we have covered the topic related the control structures and loops in PHP. Also covered how to use all the control structures supported by the PHP such as if, else, for, foreach, while, switch, and more. Other keywords, like break and continue, have also been discussed.

In this chapter, we will cover functions, including how to define them, and various arguments passed through.

FUNCTIONS

The functions in PHP are similar to other programming languages. A function is just a piece of code that takes one more input in the form of a parameter, does some processing, and returns a value. You might have seen many functions like fopen(), fread(), etc. They are built-in functions, but PHP gives you the option to create your own functions.

DOI: 10.1201/9781003308669-4

Syntax:

```
//define a function
function function_name($arg1, $arg2, ... $argn)
{
    statement1;
    statement2;
    ..
    ..
    return $val;
}
//call function
$result = function_name($arg1, $arg2, ... $argn);
```

DECLARING A FUNCTION

When you declare a function, you can start with the function statement. Next comes a name for your function, and inside the parentheses is a list of arguments separated by commas. You can also choose to have no arguments. The following code shows you the form of a function declaration.

```
function function_name(arguments)
{
Code of block
}
```

In other programming languages, including different versions of PHP, you must declare a function above any call to it but not confirmed in PHP 4. You may write a function declaration after calls are made to it. When you call a function, you write its name followed by parentheses, even if there are no arguments to pass.

Example:

```
function function_name();
```

The functions allow you to put together a block of code that you will repeat several times in your script file. The primary purpose is to avoid identical typing code in two or more places, or it could be to make your code easier to understand.

Here is the simplest example of function in PHP,

```php
<?php
function printText(){
        print("This is simple example of function");
}

printText();
?>
```

The output of the following code will be,

```
This is a simple example of the function
```

Below is the example of the function with parameter,

```php
<?php
function printText($input){
        print("This is function ".$input);
}
printText("with parameter");
?>
```

The output of the following code will be,

```
This is the function with parameter
```

function return Statement

The user-defined function in following example processes the provided arguments and returns a value to calling environment,

```php
<?php
function addition($arg1, $arg2){
    return $arg1+$arg2;
}
$val=addition(10,20);
echo "Result ". $val. "\n";
echo "<br/>";
$val=addition("10","20");
echo "Result : $val";
?>
```

Output

This will produce the following result,

```
Result 30
Result: 30
```

function with Default Argument Value

While defining a function, a default value of the argument may be assigned. If the value is not set to such an argument while calling the function, this default will be used to process inside the function. In the following example, a function is defined with an argument having a default value.

```php
<?php
function language ($user="PHP") {
    echo "Hello $user\n";
    echo "<br/>";
}
//overrides default
language ("User");
//uses default
language ();
?>
```

Output

This will produce the following result,

```
Hello User
Hello PHP
```

The function within Another function

It can be defined inside another function's body block. However, the inner function cannot be called before the outer function has been invoked.

Example:

```php
<?php
function hello () {
    echo "Hello\n";
    function welcome () {
        echo "Welcome to TutorialsPoint\n";
    }
}
```

```
//welcome();
hello();
welcome();
?>
```

Remove the comment to call welcome() before hello(). Following error message halts the program,

```
Fatal error: Uncaught Error: It calls to undefined
function welcome()
Output
Comment the line and run again
Hello
Welcome to TutorialsPoint
```

The return Statement

A function will be finished, ready to return control to its user at some point.

For example, when a function's execution reaches the end of the particular function block of code. Execution picks up directly after the point where the function was called. Another way to stop the function's execution is to use the return (keyword) statement. You may have various return statements in your function, but you have to consider how this reduces the readability of your code. More return statements can be a barrier to understanding the flow of execution. Ideal functions should have one way in and one way out. There will be some cases where multiple return statements are acceptable in practice.

If you follow return with your expression, the value of the expression will be passed back.

Example: A Simple Function using return statement,

```
<?php
    /* Way of defining a PHP Function */
    function printMessage() {
        $message = "This is the function with
return statement in PHP";
        return $message;
    }

/* Calling a PHP Function */
        print(printMessage());
    ?>
```

Example: A simple function using return statement passing some arguments,

```php
<?php
        function plus($num) {
           return $num += 5;
        }

        function minus($num) {
            return $num -= 6;
        }
        $number = 10;
        $plus = plus( $number );
           echo $plus;
           echo "<br/>";
        $minus =minus( $number );
           echo $minus;
    ?>
```

Scope and the Global Statement

We learned previously that variables inside a function only exist inside a namespace variable separate from the global namespace variables. Variables inside a function have private properties and may never be fetched or manipulated anywhere outside the function.

However, there are two ways a function can access variables in the global scope,

- **The global statement:** It can bring a variable into a function's namespace. After that, the variable may be used as if it were outside the function. Any changes to the variable will persist after the function's execution ceases.

- **The GLOBALS array:** In the same way, it is possible to refer to global variables through the array GLOBALS. Variable names index the array, so if you create a variable named userName, you can manipulate it inside a function by writing $GLOBALS["userName"].

The global statement is the idea of static variables. If a variable is declared to be static, it returns its value between function calls.

Working with print_r()

The print_r() function is a PHP built-in function and is used to print or display information stored in a variable.

Syntax:

```
print_r( $var, $is_store )
```

Explanation:

Parameters: This print_r() function accepts two parameters as shown above syntax and described below:

- **$var:** This parameter specifies the variable to be printed and is a mandatory parameter.

- **$is_store:** This is an optional parameter. This parameter is of the boolean type whose default value is FALSE and is used to store the output of the print_r() function in a variable rather than printing it. If this parameter sets to TRUE, then the print_r() function will return the output it is supposed to print.

Arguments: When declaring a function, you should declare arguments inside the parentheses, and a comma should separate each. A dollar ($) sign must prefix the arguments and become variables inside the function. When the function is called, it expects values to be passed in it to fill the arguments in the order they have declared.

By default, an argument then passed value into the local variable. If the variable is preceded by the & (AND) operator, the variable instead becomes an alias (reference variable) for the passed variable. The changes made to referenced variables change the original.

It is also possible to make an argument optional. Many built-in functions provide this functionality.

For date() function in PHP function, you can pass one or two arguments to date.

Syntax:

```
date(format, timestamp)
```

- The first argument is the format of the return value.

- The second argument is the timestamp, a date expressed in seconds since January 5, 1987. When the second argument is omitted, the current time is used.

How to Pass PHP Variables by Reference

By default, PHP variables are passed by value as the functional arguments. When a variable is passed by value, the variable's scope is defined at the function level bound within the scope of function. Changing either of the variables does not affect either of the variables.

Example:

```php
<?php
// Function used for assigning new value to
$string variable and printing it
function print_string( $string ) {
    $string = "This is simple string"."<br/>";

    // Print $string variable
    print($string);
}

// Driver code
$string = "This is global function "."\n";
print_string($string);
print($string);
?>
```

You may set an argument to be unset by default by making it equal to NULL, a special constant. Other than named arguments, you can also access arguments by their position using three functions, func_get_arg, func_get_args, and func_ num_args.

Explanation of the func_get_arg, func_get_args, and func_ num_args.

- Using func_get_arg, you can either fetch one argument at a time.

- Using func_get_args, you can fetch them all as an array.

- Using func_num_args., you can find out how many arguments were passed.

Pass by Reference

When variables are passed by reference using & (ampersand) symbol need to add before variable argument.

Example:

```
function ( &$xvar )
```

The scope of both global and function variables becomes global as the same reference defines both variables. Therefore, whenever the global variable is changed, the variable inside function also gets changed and vice-versa.

Example:

```php
<?php
// Function used for assigning a new value to
$string variable and printing it
function print_string( &$string ) {
    $string = "Function string <br/>";
    // Printing $string variable
    print( $string );
}

$string = "Global function\n";
print_string( $string );
print( $string );
?>
```

The output will be the same because the string variable works as a reference in the function.

The output will be following,

```
Function string
Function string
```

VARIABLE-LENGTH ARGUMENT FUNCTION

PHP language supports variable-length argument function. It means you can pass n number of arguments in the function. To perform so, you need to use three ellipses such as … (dots) before the argument name.

The three-dot concept is implemented in PHP 5.6.

Let's see an example of the PHP variable-length argument function.

```php
<?php
function addition(...$numbers) {
    $sum = 0;
    foreach ($numbers as $n) {
        $sum += $n;
    }
    return $sum;
}
echo addition(1, 2, 3, 4);
?>
```

Built-in Functions in PHP

These are those functions that are already ready-made for PHP language. These functions are used for a specific purpose. The each built-in function has various functionalities. These built-in functions are used based on their functionality. There are many built-in functions available in PHP.

Examples of some built-in funtions are given below.

- **Echo() function:** This function is a built-in function used to display the statements, or you can say it is used to print the output.

  It is used for more than one string. Its function can take a comma-delimited list of arguments to output. It does not return any value.

  Syntax: Use the double or single quote with an Echo function.

  ```php
  echo "statements";
          or

  echo 'statements';
  ```

  Example:

  ```php
  <?php
  echo "Learn PHP built functions";
  ?>
  ```

  Here, we used the echo function only to display the statement. The functionalities of this built-in function are ready-made in the PHP library.

- **Print() function:** This print() function is also used to display the statement, or you can say it is used to print the output.

  It is a function that is used to only one string. We cannot use multiple strings like the echo() function. The print function is also a built-in function in PHP. The print returns a value. We can use the print() function with parentheses or without parentheses. It is slower than an echo. It always prints return 1.

  Example:
  ```php
  <?php
  $name="Hello PHP";
  print $name;
  //or
  print ($name);
  ?>
  ```

- **Printf() function:** The printf() function is also a built_in function. It is very easy, and you already know about the Printf () function. printf() is a part of the language C printf() function, Most people who start working with PHP find it confusing, but it is so simple to use if you have learned c language.

  Example:
  ```php
  <?php
  $str="This is a simple example of printf";
  $res1=strlen($str);
  $res2=str_word_count($str);
  printf("Your string lenght is  %d. You string
  words count: %d",$res1,$res2);
  ?>
  ```

  Your functions make calls to other functions, and they also make calls to themselves. The process of calling itself is called recursion. This definition usually leads to elegant algorithms. The problem is broken down into a small task that is repeated many times.

Recursion

Your functions make calls to other functions, and they also make calls to themselves. The process of calling itself is called recursion. This definition usually leads to elegant algorithms. The problem is broken down into a small task that is repeated many times.

Example: Write a code for displaying n numbers using the recursive function in PHP.

```php
<?php
function NaturalNumbers($number) {
if($number<=10){
echo "$number <br/>";
NaturalNumbers($number+1);
}
}

NaturalNumbers(1);
?>
```

Dynamic Function Calls

You might find yourself in the problem of not knowing which function should be called when you are writing a script, and you want to decide based on data you have during execution. One way to set this is a variable with the name of a function and then use the variable as if it were a function.

If you follow a variable with parentheses, the value of the variable will be treated as the name of a function.

Example:

```php
<?
function write($text)
{
print($text);
}
function writeBold($text)
{
print("<B>$text</B>");
}
$myFunction = "write";
$myFunction("Hello!");
print("<BR>\n");
$myFunction = "writeBold";
$myFunction("Goodbye!");
print("<BR>\n");
?>
```

Callable

The keyword callable is used to force a function argument to be a reference to a function.

A callable can do one of the following:

- An anonymous function

- A string containing the name of a function

- An array describing a static class method

- An array describing an object method

Example:

```php
<?php
function printMessage(callable $format, $str) {
  echo $format($str);
  echo "<br>";
}
function exclaim($str) { return $str. "!"; }
printMessage("exclaim", "Hello PHP");
?>
```

TYPES OF FUNCTIONS

In PHP, It is a function object or reference with type callable. A callback or callable variable can act as a function, object method, and a static class method. There are multiple ways to implement a callback. Some of them are discussed below:

- **Standard Callback:** The functions can be called by using the call_user_func() function in PHP, where arguments are the string name of the function to be called.

  Example:

  ```php
  <?php

  // PHP program to illustrate working
  // of a standard callback
  ```

```php
// Function to print a string
function function_name() {
    echo "Standard Callback \n";
}

// Standard callback
call_user_func('function_name');
?>
```

The output of the following code will be,

```
Standard Callback
```

- **Static class method callback:** In PHP, the static class methods can call by using call_user_func(), where the argument is an array containing the string name of the class and the method inside it to be called.

Example:

```php
<?php

// PHP program to illustrate the working
// of a Static class method callback

// Sample class
class A{

    // Function used to print a string
    static function function_name() {
        echo "Parent A Class \n";
        echo "<br/>";
    }
}

class B extends A{

    // Function to print a string
    static function function_name() {
        echo "Child B Class";
        echo "<br/>";
    }
}
```

```php
// Static class method callback
call_user_func(array('B', 'function_name'));

call_user_func('B::function_name');

// Relative Static class method callback
call_user_func(array('B', 'parent::
function_name'));
?>
```

The output of the following code will be,

- Child B Class

- Child B Class

- Parent A-Class

- **Object method callback:** Object methods can be called by using call_user_func(), where the argument is an array containing the object variable and the string name of the method to be called. Object methods can also be called if they are made invokable using __invoke() function definition. In this case, the argument for the call_user_func() function is the object variable itself.

```php
<?php

// PHP program to illustrate working
// of a object method callback

// Sample class
class B{

    // Function to print a string
    static function someFunction() {
        echo "Callback\n";
    }

    // Function used to print a string
    public function __invoke() {
        echo "invoke callback\n";
    }
}
```

```php
// Class object
$obj = new B();

// Object method call
call_user_func(array($obj, 'someFunction'));

// Callable __invoke method object
call_user_func($obj);

?>
```

- **Closure callback:** These functions can be made callable by making standard calls or mapping the closure function to an array of valid arguments given to the closure function using array_map() function where arguments are the closure function and an array of its valid arguments.

Example:

```php
<?php

// PHP program to illustrate working
// of a closure callback

// Closure to print a string
$print_function = function($string) {
    echo $string."\n";
};

// Array of strings
$string_array = array("Closure callback",
"A", "B");

// Callable closure
array_map($print_function, $string_array);

?>
```

Language Constructs

The key difference between functions & language constructs is that the PHP parser cannot break down the most basic language units. In contrast, functions have to be broken down before parsing, often into language constructs. In other words, in the same way, that PHP code has to be broken down into lower-level opcode by the PHP parser for the machine to understand it, functions must be broken down to language constructs by the PHP parser before they are parsed. There are interesting consequences of this:

- Language constructs tend to be faster than their function counterparts.

- Language constructs, in some cases, may be able to bypass error handling mechanisms.

- While functions can be disabled in PHP via the configuration file, language constructs cannot.

- Language constructs cannot be used as callback functions.

Function Handling Functions

- **call_user_func_array:** Calls a callback with an array of parameters

- **call_user_func:** Calls the Callback given by the first parameter

- **create_function:** Creates an anonymous (lambda-style) function

- **forward_static_call_array:** Calls a static method and passes the arguments as an array

- **forward_static_call:** Calls a static method

- **func_get_arg:** Returns an item from the argument list

- **func_get_args:** Returns an array comprising a function's argument list

- **func_num_args:** Returns the number of arguments passed to the function

- **function_exists:** Returns true if the given function has been defined

- **get_defined_functions:** Returns an array of all defined functions

- **register_shutdown_function:** Registers a function for execution on shutdown

- **register_tick_function:** Registers a function for execution on each tick

- **unregister_tick_function:** De-registers a function for execution on each tick

- User Contributed Notes

- **boolval:** It gets the boolean value of a variable

- **debug_zval_dump:** It dumps a string representation of an internal zval structure to output

- **doubleval:** It alias of floatval

- **empty:** It determines whether a variable is empty

- **floatval:** It gets float value of a variable

- **get_debug_type:** It gets the type name of a variable in a way that is suitable for debugging

- **get_defined_vars:** It returns an array of all defined variables

- **get_resource_id:** It returns an integer identifier for the given resource

- **get_resource_type:** It returns the resource type

- **gettype:** It gets the type of a variable

- **intval:** It gets the integer value of a variable

- **is_array:** It finds whether a variable is an array

- **is_bool:** It finds out whether a variable is a boolean

- **is_callable:** It verifies that a value can be called a function from the current scope

- **is_countable:** It verifies that the contents of a variable are a countable value

- **is_double:** It alias of is_float

- **is_float:** It finds whether the type of a variable is float

- **is_int:** It finds whether the type of a variable is an integer

- **is_integer:** It alias of is_int

- **is_iterable:** It verifies that the contents of a variable are an iterable value

- **is_long:** It alias of is_int

- **is_null:** It finds whether a variable is null

- **is_numeric:** It finds whether a variable is a number or a numeric string

- **is_object:** It finds whether a variable is an object

- **is_real:** It alias of is_float

- **is_resource:** It finds whether a variable is a resource

- **is_scalar:** It finds whether a variable is a scalar

- **is_string:** It finds whether the type of a variable is the string

- **isset:** It determines if a variable is declared and is different from than null

- **print_r:** It prints human-readable information about a variable

- **serialize:** It generates a storable representation of a value

- **settype:** It sets the type of a variable

- **strval:** It gets string value of a variable

- **unserialize:** It creates a PHP value from a stored representation

- **unset:** It unsets a given variable

- **var_dump:** It dumps information about a variable

- **var_export:** It outputs or returns a parsable string representation of a variable

Flag Parameters

A flag value that indicates as a signal for a function or process. The flag's value is used to determine the next program step. It often used as a binary flags, which contain a boolean value either true or false. When all flags are not binary, it can be used to store a range of values.

You can think of a flag as a small red flag that lying flat when it is false but pops up when it is true. A raised flag says to a program, "Stop - do something separate." A common example of a flag in computer programming is a variable in a while loop. The PHP loop below will iterate until the $flag is set to true.

```
$flag = false;
$i = 1;
while (!$flag)  // stop when $flag is true
{
      echo "$i, ";
      $i++;   // increment $i
    if ($i > 100) $flag = true;
}
```

INTRODUCTION TO PHP USER DEFINED FUNCTIONS

The user-defined functions are functions that you use to organize your code. When defining a function, you can call it the same way as the built-in action and parser functions. It helps you encapsulate and reuse functionality in your policy.

A user-defined function declaration starts with the keyword named function as shown below,

Example:

```
function fun_Name($arg_1, $arg_2, ... $arg_n)
{
// This code to be executed inside a function
//return $value
}
```

fun_Name: This defines the name of the function. The name of a function should begin with a letter or an (_) or (__) underscore. There is no case-sensitivity in function names but any number of arguments can use to define a function. When calling, however, you should provide the same number of parameters.

The syntax to call a PHP user-defined function,

```
$ret=funName($arg1, $arg2, ... $argn);
```

Namespace PHP Functions

With the release of PHP version 5.3, namespaces became popular in PHP and made so much possible, including better autoloading. Most of the time, you will use to see them at the top of every single class file. They can also be used for namespace functions, however.

A standard PHP namespace declaration would look similar to the following at the top of a class file.

```
namespace PHP-code\Html;
class Tag {
    // ...
}
```

You can also declare multiple namespaces in the same file this way, although we won't recommend this in practice much in the same PHP file.

```
namespace PHP-code\Html {
    function get() {
        return '';
    }
}
namespace PHP-code\Utils {
    function get() {
        return '';
    }
}
```

A pure function gives the same input, always returns the same output, and is side-effect free.

```
// This is a pure function
function addition($a, $b) {
    return $a + $b;
}
```

Some side effects are changing the file system, interacting with databases, printing to the screen.

```
// This is an impure function
function addition($a, $b) {
    echo "Adding...";
    return $a + $b;
}
```

PHP KEYWORDS AND IDENTIFIERS TUTORIAL

What Is an Identifier?

An identifier in PHP is how we identify variables, constants, arrays, functions, interfaces, and classes.

It's a name, like Sam would be the name of a person, or BMW would be the brand name of a car.

Rules for Naming Identifiers

PHP language has certain rules that we keep in mind when naming our variables, constants, arrays, functions, interfaces, and classes.

If there are any specific rules and/or conventions other than the below, we will explain each in their respective chapters.

1. Each variable must start with a $symbol. If we don't include the $symbol, the interpreter will assume a constant. This rule does not apply to constants, functions, interfaces, or classes.

```php
<?php
// Variable
$message = "Hello PHP";
// Not a variable
message = "Hello PHP";
?>
```

2. A variable name cannot start with a numeric digit, but may contain a number inside of it.

   Example: Names may not start with a number

```php
<?php
// Not allowed
$21_ABC_Street;
// Allowed
$variable_number_5;
?>
```

A variable name may start with uppercase or lowercase alphabetical letters A - Z or a - z, and underscores _.

Example: Alphabetical letters and underscores are allowed,

```php
<?php

// Allowed
$Name;
$name;
$_name;
?>
```

A variable name may not contain special characters such as $, @, %, etc.

Example: Special characters are not allowed,

```php
<?php
// Not allowed
$^_^;    //underscore
$n@me; /special symbol within variable
$name&surname;
?>
```

A variable name may not contain special characters such as $, @, %, etc.

Example: Special characters are not allowed,

```php
<?php
// Not allowed
$^_^;
$n@me;
$name&surname;
?>
```

Most variables' names are case sensitive, which means a name with lowercase letters is not the same as a name with uppercase letters.

Example: Names are case sensitive,

```php
<?php
// Not the same
$learning;
$LearNing;
$LEARNING;
?>
```

A variable name should not contain a PHP-specific keyword. Keywords are words that PHP reserves for special uses.

Example:

```php
<?php
// Bad practice
$if;
$echo;
$while;
?>
```

Identifier Casing Conventions

Most programming languages have strict data casing conventions such as variables.

For example, in the Python programming variable and function names, use snake_case with underscores separating each word, while classes use camelCase where words are capitalized.

But in PHP, the conventions are less strict, especially in older code that functions are often named with snake_case, but in newer code, camelCase or PascalCase is used.

We also have to consider some popular PHP frameworks and applications. The Zend and Symfony frameworks, for example, do not like underscores but CodeIgniter promotes using snake_case. WordPress also encourages the use of number_case, instead of camelCase.

Let's take a look at the various casings.

- **Snake case:** In the snake case, all letter of the name is lowercase. If any name has multiple words, the words are separated by (_) underscores.

  Example: Snake casing

  ```php
  <?php
  // Snake casing
  $name;
  $first_name;
  ?>
  ```

- **Camel case:** In the camel case, the first character of a name is lowercase. If any name has multiple words, each new word is directly connected to the previous word, but the first letter is uppercase.

Example: Camel casing

```php
<?php
// Camel casing
$name;
$firstName;
?>
```

- **Pascal case:** In the pascal case, the first letter of a word is uppercase. If the name has multiple words, each new word is directly connected to the previous word but the first letter is also uppercase.

Example: Camel casing

```php
<?php

// Pascal casing
$Name;
$FirstName;

?>
```

TYPE HINTS

Using Type hinting, we can specify the expected data type such as arrays, objects, interface, etc., for an argument in a function declaration. This can be most advantageous because it results in better code and improved error messages.

How to Use Array-Type Hinting

When we force a function to get only arguments of the type array, we can put the array keyword in front of the argument name, like the following syntax below:

```php
function functionName (array $argumentName)
{
  //code
}
```

Example:

```php
<?php
function Addition(array $marks)
{
  foreach($marks as $item)
  {
    echo $marksAddition = $item[0];
    echo " : ";
    echo $numberOfMiles = $item[1] + $item[2];
    echo "<br />";
    }
}
$marks = array(
  array('English', 50, 44),
  array('Maths', 50, 41)
);
Addition($marks);
?>
```

How to Use Object-Type Hinting

The Type hinting can be used to force a function to get an argument of type Object. For this purpose, we put the name of the class prefix to the argument name in the function.

In the following example, the class constructor can only get objects that were created from the Driver class. We ensure this by putting the word Driver in front of the argument name in the constructor.

```php
<?PHP
class Car {
  protected $driver;

  // The constructor can only get Driver objects as
arguments.
  public function __construct(Driver $driver)
  {
    $this -> driver = $driver;
  }
}
class Driver {}
$driver1 = new Driver();
$car1    = new Car($driver1);
?>
```

Does PHP Support Any Type Hinting for Some Basic Data Types?

The version PHP5 does not allow type hinting for basic data types like integers, floats, strings, and Booleans. PHP7 does support scalar type hinting.

PHP5 does not support type hinting to primarily data types like integers, strings, or Booleans. So, when we have to validate that an argument belongs to a basic data type, we can use one of the PHP "is_" family functions.

- **is_bool:** It is used to determine whether a variable is a boolean (true or false).

- **is_int:** It is used to determine whether a variable is an integer.

- **is_float:** It is used to determine whether a variable is a float (3.14, 1.2e3, or 3E-10).

- **is_null:** It is used to find out whether a variable is null.

- **is_string:** It is used to determine whether a variable is a string.

THE SPLAT OPERATOR IN PHP

The PHP splat operator (…) has been available in PHP since version 5.6.

The splat operator can unpack parameters to functions or combine variables into an array. If you have seen this operator anywhere in JavaScript, it is usually called the spread operator and works similarly. Let's have some examples of how it works in the PHP language.

Take the any function, this takes two parameters and adds them together, and returns the output.

```php
function add_numbers($number_1, $number_2) {
  return $number_1 + $number_2;
}
```

Now, take the following array of numbers,

```php
$numbers_array = [1, 2];
```

We can call the function in various ways to add these numbers together using the above function. The splat/spread operator allows us to send the array to the function and unpacked into separate variables.

We can call the function using the splat operator like this.

```php
echo add_numbers(...$numbersArray);
```

Here the detailed examples of the splat operator in PHP function.

```php
<?php
function addNumbers(...$numbers) {
  $sum = 0;
  foreach ($numbers as $number) {
    $sum += $number;
  }
  return $sum;
}
//This is called in the following way.
echo addNumbers(1, 2, 3, 4, 5);
?>
```

SIGNATURE

When you run this code, the output will be "15" as each parameter is sent to the function as an array, and the numbers are added together. We can add more parameters to this function as we want. They will be turned into a single array inside the function.

The parameter signature is the definition of parameters in a method's definition (signature). What is meant with the quoted text is to use the same number and type (which is not applicable in PHP) of the parameter when overriding a parent class method.

A signature of a function or method is also referred to as ahead. It contains the name and the parameters. The actual code of the function is called body.

```php
function foo($arg1, $arg2) // signature
{
    // body
}
```

When the return is omitted, the value null will be returned.

Note:

Example of using return:

```php
<?php
function square($num)
{
    return $num * $num;
```

```
}
echo square(3);    // outputs '9'.
?>
```

A function cannot return multiple values at once, but similar results can be obtained by returning an array.

Example of returning an array to get multiple values:

```
<?PHP
function arrary_numbers()
{
    return [0, 1, 2];
}
//way of array de-structuring, which collects each
member of the array individually
[$zero, $one, $two] = arrary_numbers();

// the only equivalent alternative is using list()
construct
list($zero, $one, $two) = arrary_numbers();
```

Here the example of returning a reference from a function:

```
<?php
function &returns_reference()
{
    return $someref;
}
$newref =& returns_reference();
?>
```

"PARAMETER" VS. "ARGUMENT"

A parameter is the variable part of the method signature or method declaration. An argument is an expression used when calling the method.

Here is the following code:

```
void Function_name_1(int i, float f)
{
    // where code will be here
}
void Function_name_2()
{
```

```
    int number_value = 1;
    Function_name_1(number_value, 2.0);
}
```

Here i and f are the parameters, and number_value and 2.0 are the arguments.

Variable Functions

Suppose the name of a variable has parentheses () in front of it. In that case, the parser tries to find a function whose name corresponds to the value of the variable and executes it, and such a function is called a variable function.

This feature helps implement callbacks, function tables, etc.

These functions cannot built language constructs such as include, require echo, etc.

In the following example, the value of a variable matches the function of the name. Parentheses thus call the function in front of a variable.

Here the example of the variable functions in

```
PHP
<?PHP
function PHP(){
    echo "Hello PHP";
}
$var="PHP";
$var();
?>
```

Here is another example of a variable function with arguments,

```
<?php
function addition($x, $y){
    echo $x+$y;
}
$var="addition";
$var(5,5);
?>
```

The output is given below:

30

Anonymous Functions (Lambda)

These functions are also known as closures, and they allow the creation of functions with no specified name. They are most useful as the value of callback parameters, but they also have many other uses.

Anonymous functions are implemented using the Closure class.

As you learn PHP, you must know what a regular function is and define one. We can also create a regular PHP function like this,

```
function regularFunction(){
//function definition here...
}
```

An anonymous functions resemble the regular function as they can contain the same type of code; they accept arguments, return values, and all...

The key difference is the anonymous functions have no name. Here is an example of the definition of an anonymous function,

```
function($argument_1,$argument_2){
//It is an anonymous function definition that goes
here
};
```

If you have noticed that there are two key differences between a regular function and an anonymous function.

There is no function name between the function keyword & the opening parenthesis() it tells we have created an anonymous function.

There should place semicolon after the function definition because anonymous functions definitions are expressions, whereas standard function definition is code constructs.

This function cannot refer anywhere, but you can do a lot of things with it like:

- You can assign these functions to any variable and can call it with the variable name. You can store a different anonymous function in a single array.

- You can pass the function to another function as a parameter. It is known as Callback.

- It returns from within an outer function to access the external function's variables. This is known as closure.

Assigning the Anonymous Function to Variables

While creating an anonymous function, it can be assigned to a variable just like any other value. Here is an example,

```
$addition = function_name($arg_1,$arg_2){
return 'add = '.$arg_1+$arg_2;
};
```

Once you done that, you can call the function with a variable name like,

```
echo $addition(20,50);
```

the output is given below

```
sum = 70
```

Using an Anonymous Function as the Callback

Commonly used by the anonymous function is to create a simple inline callback function. It is a function that you can pass to another function as a parameter. Once you access callback function, the receiving function can use it whenever required. Many built-in functions accept a callback or create your own function.

Here see some of the built-in functions and understand their functionality.

So we have the array_map() function, using this function to run a callback function on each function element. This function accepts a callback function and an array as an argument. It iterates through each element of an array and applies the callback function to every element. Then your callback function needs to return a value that will replace the array value, and array_map returns the modified array.

Here is example,

```
// this is without callback function
$num_array = array(0,1,2,3,4);
foreach ($num_array as $key => $value) {
$new_array[]=$value   + $value;
}
print_r($new_array);
//without the callback function
```

```
$num_array = array(0,1,2,3,4);
foreach ($num_array as $key => $value) {
$new_array[]=$value+$value;
}
print_r($new_array);
this will output-
Array
(
[0] => 2
[1] => 4
[2] => 6
[3] => 8
[4] => 10
)
```

when we use a regular function as a callback function in array_map()

Using regular callback function

```
function addition($num){
return $num*$num;
}
$new_array=array_map('addition', $num_array);
print_r($new_array);
```

Using anonymous function as callback

```
$new_array = array_map(function($num) {
return $num + $num;
}, $num_array);
print_r($new_array);
print_r($num_array);
this will output-

Array
(
[0] => 2
[1] => 4
[2] => 6
[3] => 8
[4] => 10
)
```

```
Array
(
[0] => 2
[1] => 4
[2] => 6
[3] => 8
[4] => 10
)
```

Why Do We Use Functions in a PHP Script?

1. **Better code organization:** PHP functions allow us to write group blocks of related code that perform a specific task together.

2. **Reusability:** Once we define, a function can be called by many scripts in our PHP files. This saves us lots of time reinventing the wheel when we want to perform some routine tasks such as connecting to the database.

3. **Easy maintenance:** It updates to the system only need to be made in one place.

Here we are going to discuss some inbuilt functions in PHP.

Strings functions

str_getcsv()	It is used to parse a CSV string into an array.
str_ireplace()	It is used to replace some characters in a string (case-insensitive).
str_pad()	It is used to pad a string to a new length.
str_repeat()	It is used to repeat a string a specified number of times.
str_replace()	It is used to replace some characters in a string. It is case-sensitive.
str_rot13()	It is used to perform the ROT13 encoding on a string.
str_shuffle()	It is used to shuffle all characters in a string randomly.
str_split()	It is used to split a string into an array.
str_word_count()	It is used to count the number of words in a string.
strcasecmp()	It is used to compare two strings (case-insensitive).
strchr()	It is used to find the first occurrence of a string inside another string and alias of strstr().
stripcslashes()	It unquotes a string quoted with addcslashes().
strcoll()	It is used to compare two strings or the Locale-based string comparison.
strcmp()	It is used to compare two strings, and also it is case-sensitive.

(Continued)

strcspn()	It is used to return the number of characters found in a string before any part of some specified characters are found.
strip_tags()	It strips HTML and PHP tags from a string.
stripos()	It returns the position of the first occurrence of a string inside another string, and it is case-insensitive.
stripslashes()	It unquotes a string quoted with addslashes().
stristr()	It is used to find the very first occurrence of a string inside another string, and it is case-insensitive.
strlen()	It is used to return the length of a string.
strncasecmp()	It is used for the comparison of the first n characters, and it is case-insensitive.
strnatcmp()	It is used to compare two strings using a "natural order" algorithm (case-sensitive).
strnatcasecmp()	It is used to compare two strings using a "natural order" algorithm, which is case-insensitive.
strncmp()	It is a string comparison of the first n characters (case-sensitive).
strrev()	It reverses a string.
strrchr()	It finds the last occurrence of a string inside another string.
strpos()	It returns the position of the first occurrence of a string inside another string (case-sensitive).
strpbrk()	It searches a string for any of a set of characters.
strripos()	It is used to find the position of the last occurrence of a string inside another string, and it is case-insensitive.
strrpos()	It finds the position of the last occurrence of a string inside another string, and it is case-sensitive.
strspn()	It returns the number of characters found in a string that contains only characters from a specified charlist.
strstr()	It finds the very first occurrence of a string inside another string (case-sensitive).
strtok()	It splits a string into smaller strings.
strtolower()	It converts a string to lowercase letters.
strtoupper()	It converts a string to uppercase letters.
strtr()	It translates certain characters in a string.
substr()	It returns a part of a string.
substr_compare()	It compares two strings from a specified start position or binary safe and optionally case-sensitive.
substr_count()	It is used to count the number of times a particular substring occurs in a string.
substr_replace()	It replaces a part of a string with another string.

Numeric functions

Function	Description
abs()	It returns the absolute (positive) value of a number.
acos()	It returns the arc cosine of a number.
acosh()	It is used to return the inverse hyperbolic cosine of a given number.
asin()	It returns the arc sine of a given number.
asinh()	It returns the inverse hyperbolic sine of a number.
atan()	It returns the arctangent of a number in radians.
atan2()	It returns the arctangent of two variables, x and y.
atanh()	It returns the inverse value of the hyperbolic tangent of a given number.
base_convert()	It converts a number from one number base to another.
bindec()	It converts a binary number to a decimal number.
cos()	It returns the cosine of a number.
cosh()	It returns the hyperbolic cosine of a number.
decbin()	It converts a given decimal number to a binary number.
dechex()	It converts a given decimal number to a hexadecimal number.
decoct()	It converts a given decimal number to an octal number.
deg2rad()	It converts a given degree value to a radian value.
expm1()	It returns exp(x) – 1.
exp()	It calculates the exponent of e.
floor()	It rounds a given number down to the nearest integer.
fmod()	It returns the remainder of x/y.
getrandmax()	It returns the largest possible value returned by rand().
hexdec()	It converts a hexadecimal number to a decimal number.
hypot()	It calculates the hypotenuse of a right-angle triangle.
int div()	It performs integer division.
is_finite()	It checks whether a value is finite or not.
is_infinite()	It checks whether a value is infinite or not.
is_nan()	It checks whether a value is 'not-a-number.'
lcg_value()	It returns a pseudo-random number in a range between 0 and 1.
log()	It is used to return the natural logarithm of a number.
log10()	It is used to return the base-10 logarithm of a number.
log1p()	It returns log(1+number).
max()	It returns the highest value in an array or the highest value of several specified values.
min()	It returns the lowest value in an array or the lowest value of several specified values.
mt_getrandmax()	It returns the most significant possible value returned by mt_rand().
mt_rand()	It generates a random integer using the Mersenne Twister algorithm.

(Continued)

Function	Description
mt_srand()	It seeds the Mersenne Twister random number generator.
octdec()	It converts an octal number to a decimal number.
pi()	It returns the value of PI.
pow()	It returns x raised to the power of y.
rad2deg()	It converts a radian value to a degree value.
rand()	It generates a random integer.
round()	It rounds a floating-point number.
sin()	It returns the sine of a number.
sinh()	It returns the hyperbolic sine of a number.
sqrt()	It returns the square root of a number.
srand()	It seeds the random number generator.
tan()	It returns the tangent of a number.
tanh()	It returns the hyperbolic tangent of a number.

Date functions

Function	Description
date_add()	It adds days, months, years, hours, minutes, and seconds to a date.
date_create_from_format()	It returns a new DateTime object formatted according to a specified format.
date_create()	It returns a new DateTime object.
date_date_set()	It sets a new date.
date_default_timezone_get()	It returns the default timezone used by all date/time functions.
date_default_timezone_set()	It sets the default timezone used by all date/time functions.
date_diff()	It returns the difference between two dates.
date_format()	It returns a date formatted according to a specified format.
date_get_last_errors()	It returns the warnings/errors found in a date string.
date_interval_create_from_date_string()	It sets up a DateInterval from the relative parts of the string.
date_interval_format()	It formats the interval.
date_isodate_set()	It sets the ISO date.
date_modify()	It modifies the timestamp.
date_offset_get()	It returns the timezone offset.
date_parse_from_format()	According to a specified format, it returns an associative array with detailed info about a specified date.
date_parse()	It returns an associative array with detailed info about a specified date.

(Continued)

date_sub()	It subtracts days, months, years, hours, minutes, and seconds from a date.
date_sun_info()	It returns an array containing info about sunset/sunrise and twilight begin/end for a specified day and location.
date_sunrise()	It returns the sunrise time for a specified day and location.
date_sunset()	It returns the sunset time for a specified day and location.
date_time_set()	It sets the time.
date_timestamp_get()	It returns the Unix timestamp.
date_timestamp_set()	It rets the date and time based on a Unix timestamp.
date_timezone_get()	It returns the time zone of the given DateTime.
objectdate_timezone_set()	It sets the time zone for the DateTime object.
date()	It formats a local date and time.
getdate()	It returns date/time information of a timestamp or the current local date/time.
gettimeofday()	It returns the current time.
gmdate()	It formats a GMT/UTC date and time.
gmmktime()	It returns the Unix timestamp for a GMT date.
gmstrftime()	It formats a GMT/UTC date and time according to locale settings.
date()	It formats a local time/date as integer.
localtime()	It returns the local time.
microtime()	It returns the current Unix timestamp with microseconds.
mktime()	It returns the Unix timestamp for a date.
strftime()	It formats a local time and/or date according to locale settings.
strptime()	It parses a time/date generated with strftime().
strtotime()	It parses an English textual DateTime into a Unix timestamp.
time()	It returns the current time as a Unix timestamp.
timezone_abbreviations_list()	It returns an associative array containing dst, offset, and the timezone name.
timezone_identifiers_list()	It returns an indexed array with all timezone identifiers.
timezone_location_get()	It returns location information for a specified timezone.

(Continued)

timezone_name_from_ abbr()	It returns the timezone name from abbreviation.
timezone_name_get()	It returns the name of the timezone.
timezone_offset_get()	It returns the timezone offset from GMT.
timezone_open()	It creates new DateTimeZone object.
timezone_transitions_get()	It returns all transitions for the timezone.
timezone_version_get()	It returns the version of the timezonedb.

HTML Code inside the Function in PHP

A function can contain only PHP code. Hence, it is possible to define a function that contains HTML code. The following welcome() function displays the welcome message wrapped in a span tag:

Example:

```php
<?php function welcome($language) {?>
        <span> Hello <?= $language?> </span>
<?php }?>
```

CHAPTER SUMMARY

Here in this chapter, we have discussed the functions in PHP languages, their benefits, some built-in functions of arrays, string, number date commonly used in PHP.

Object-Oriented Programming (OOP)

In the previous chapter, we have discussed the functions in PHP languages, built-in functions of arrays, string, number date commonly used in PHP. In this chapter, we will talk about the OOP concept used in PHP.

INTRODUCTION TO OOP

PHP language is a server-side scripting language used not only for web application development but also used as a general-purpose programming language. PHP OOP is a programming language principle added to PHP version 5 that helps build complex, reusable web applications.

DOI: 10.1201/9781003308669-5

Basically, PHP is not as strong in its OOP feature as other languages. OOP in PHP language has a lot going for it, and it is possible to have a good career without learning and using OOP concepts, but you should be familiar with them. Using both OOP and procedural programming allows you to better choose the right approach for each individual project.

In this chapter, we will be explaining some important topics of the OOP in PHP with some examples. Also, I will explain the syntax of OOP in PHP 5 and later the key underlying OOP theories as well. Here, we will use somewhat simple examples with some practical, real-world code that will be used.

The PHP OOP concepts are:

- **Class:** The class is a defined data type, which includes local functions as well as local data. You also think about class as a template for making many instances of the object's same kind (or class).

- **Objects:** A class defines a single instance of the data structure. You can define a class once and then make multiple objects that belong to it. Objects are also known as instances.

- **Constructor:** It refers to a particular type of function which will be called automatically called whenever there is an object formation from a class.

- **Destructor:** It refers to a special type of function that will automatically be called whenever any of the objects is deleted or goes out of scope.

- **Inheritance:** When a class inherits the existing features and function of a parent class, then it is called Inheritance. For example, the child class will inherit all or a few member functions and variables of a parent class.

- **Interface:** It defines method names and arguments but not the contents of the methods. It is similar to a class except that it cannot contain code. It is declared using the "interface" keyword.

- **Data Abstraction:** It is the essential feature of the OOP programming language. It shows only useful information to the user, and other remains were hidden from the end-user. It is the representation of data in which the implementation details are hidden (abstracted). This type of polymorphism in which all of the operators have separate implementations is depending on the types of arguments. Similarly, the functions can also be overloaded with different implementations.

- **Magic Methods:** These methods are special methods that are aspired to perform certain tasks. These methods are prefixed with a double underscore (__). All these function names are reserved, and they cannot be used for any intention other than associated magical functionality. The magical method in a class must be declared as public. These methods act as interceptors that are automatically called when certain conditions are met.

- **Polymorphism:** It is an object-oriented concept in which the same function can be used for different operations. For example, the function name will remain the same, but it takes various arguments and can do different tasks.

- **Overloading:** It has the ability to create multiple functions of the same name with different implementations.

- **Abstract Class:** It is a class that contains at least one abstract method. It is a method that is declared but not implemented in the code. It is defined with the abstract keyword.

OOP THEORY

Every beginner should need to know and understand that OOP is that it is currently not just only about new syntax but also a new way of thinking about a problem. The most common mistake done by the beginners in OOP programmers makes to inappropriately apply OOP theory. All programming comes down to taking some actions with data. A user enters the data in an HTML form, and then the PHP code validates it, emails it, stores it in a database, and so forth. In OOP, the focus is on the data. With what types of things will the application work? You need to identify both the actions and the data required in both approaches. A class is a well-generalized definition of a thing and thing of classes as blueprints. An object is a basic implementation of that thing.

The two most important terms for OOP are class and object. For example, the think of objects as the house built using the blueprint as a guide, and in OOP, you design your classes and then implement them as objects in your programs when needed. For example, the think of objects as the house built using the blueprint as a guide, and in OOP, you design your classes and then implement them as objects in your programs when needed.

OOP can break applications into specific subparts. Web sites do various things like interact with handle forms, databases, send emails, generate HTML, etc. Each of these things can be defined as a module. There are following the principle of the OOPs like abstraction: it means that classes should be defined broadly. Instead of designing a class for interacting only with a MySQL database, you should also make one that interacts with a nonspecific database. You should define a more particular class for MySQL using Inheritance and overriding. This class should look and act like the general database class, but some of its functionality would be customized accordingly.

Another OOP principle is an encapsulation that separates out and hides how something is accomplished. A properly designed class can do everything you need it to do without your ever knowing how it's being done.

Those are the concepts behind OOP. You will see how they work out in the many OOP examples in this chapter. But before getting into the code, we will talk about the OOP's dark side.

DEFINING A CLASS

OOP programming begins with classes. A class is an abstract definition of a thing: what information must be stored, and what functionality must be possible with that the information passed? A User class can be able to store information such as the user name, user ID, user email address, and so on more information of that user. The more functionality of a user could be login, logout, change password, and more.

Syntactically, a class definition is the word class, with the name of the class. The class name cannot be a fixed word and is frequently written in uppercase as a name convention. After the class name, the class definition is placed within {} (curly braces):

```
class ClassName {
}
```

Classes can include variables and methods, which are referred to as attributes or other properties and methods, respectively. A class's attributes and methods are called its members.

Functions are easy to add to classes:

```
class ClassName {
function functionName() {
```

```
// Function code.
}
}
```

The methods defined within a class are like functions outside of a class. They can take one than one argument, have default and return values, and so on.

An attributes within classes are separate from variables outside of classes.

First, all the attributes must be prefixed with a keyword indicating the visibility of the variables. The keyword options are public, private, and protected. These values would not mean anything to you until you understand Inheritance, so until then, just use public:

```
class ClassName {
public $var1, $var2;
function functionName() {
// Function code.
}
}
```

As shown here, class attributes are listed any method definitions. The second difference between attributes and simple variables is that if an attribute is defined with a set value, that value must be a literal value and not an expression:

```
class Student1 {
public $var1 = 123;
public $var2 = 'string';
public $var3 = array(1, 2, 3);
}
class Student2{
// these won't work!
public $today = get_date();
public $square = $num * $num;
}
```

The class name can be any label, but it cannot be a reserved word.

A class name starts with a letter or underscores, followed by a number of letters, numbers, or underscores. As the regular expression, it would be expressed with: ^ [a-zA-Z_\x70-\xff][a-zA-Z0-9_\x70-\xff]*$.

A class can contain its own constants, variables called properties, and functions defined inside the class as "methods."

Example: Simple Class definition

```php
<?php
class SimpleClass
{
    // property declaration
    public $var = 'a default public value';
    // method declaration
    public function displayVarMethod() {
        echo $this->var;
    }
}
?>
```

NEW KEYWORD

In PHP, the keyword new must be used to create an instance of a class. An object is always created unless the object has a constructor defined that throws an exception on error. Classes should be defined before instantiation.

If a string contains the name of a class is used with new, a new instance of that class creates.

Example of creating an instance,

```php
<?php
$instance = new ClassName();
// This can also be done with a variable:
$class_name = 'ClassName';
$instance = new $className(); // new SimpleClass()
?>
```

WHAT ARE CONSTANTS?

A constant is a name or identifier for a single value. That value cannot be changed during the execution of the script except for magic constants, which are not actually constants. Constants are case-sensitive. By convention, constant identifiers are always uppercase.

```php
<?php
// Some valid constant names
```

```php
define("PHP",        "something");
define("FOO2",       "something else");
define("PHP_LANGAUGE", "something more");

// Invalid constant names
define("5PHP",       "something");
// This is valid, but should not be avoided:
// PHP may one day provide a magical constant
// that will help to break your script
define("__PHP__", "something");
?>
```

Some key differences between constants and variables:

- Constants do not have any other sign or dollar ($) sign before them, but variables have.

- Constants can be accessed and defined anywhere in your file without regard to variable scoping rules such as public, private, and protected.

- Constants cannot be redefined or undefined once they have been set anywhere in the code.

- Constants can only evaluate to scalar values or an arrays.

Defining Constants

```php
<?php
define("CONSTANT", "Hello PHP.");
echo CONSTANT; // outputs "Hello PHP."
echo Constant;  // It will emit an error that is :
Undefined constant variable "Constant"
// It prior to PHP 8.0.0, outputs "Constant" and
issues a warning. (because we declared constant as
Uppercase not in lowercase)
?>
```

Defining Constants using the const keyword:

```php
<?php
// Simple value
const CONSTANT = 'Hello PHP';
```

```php
echo CONSTANT; //It will return you the constant
value, but your constant will be in uppercase.

// Scalar expression
const EXTRA_CONST = CONSTANT.'; Goodbye World';
echo EXTRA_CONST;

const ANIMALS_NAME = array('dog', 'cat', 'bird');
echo ANIMALS_NAME[1]; // outputs "cat" by index
referring

// Constant arrays
define('ANIMALS_LIST', array(
    'dog',
    'cat',
    'bird'
));
echo ANIMALS[1]; // outputs "cat" by index referring
?>
```

How to define a class in PHP, here is an example of the simple class creations which having switch cases:

```php
<?PHP HelloWorld.php
/* This will define the Languages class.
* The class says "Hello, world!" in different
languages.
 */
class Languages {
// This method prints a greeting in different
languages.
 // It takes one argument which language to use.
// The default language is English.
function sayHello($language = 'English') {

 // Put the greeting within P tags:
echo '<p>';

// Print a message specific to a language:
switch ($language) {
case 'Dutch':
 echo 'Hallo, wereld!';
```

```
 break;
 case 'French':
echo 'Bonjour, monde!';
 break;
 case 'German':
 echo 'Hello, Welt!';
 break;
 case 'Italian':
 echo 'Ciao, mondo!';
break;
case 'Spanish':
 echo '¡Hola, Mundo!';
break;
 case 'English':
default:
echo 'Hello, world!';
break;
 } // End of switch.
// Close the HTML paragraph, echo '</p>';
 } // End of sayHello() method.
 } // End of Languages class.
```

CREATING AN OBJECT

If you want to create an object, using OOP is a two-step process. The first is to define a class. You just need to write the HelloWorld class. The second step is to use that class by creating an object or a class instance.

Creating an object is very easy in PHP once you have defined your class. It requires the new keyword example,

```
$object = new ClassName();
```

Now the variable $obj exists and is of type ClassName (instead of data type string or array). The $object is a ClassName instance. This syntax is used to invoke the class's methods:

```
$obj->method_Name();
(This symbol -> can be called the object operator.)
```

If a method takes any arguments, you provide those within parentheses, as in any function call:

```
object->methodName('name',12,  true);
```

To access an object's properties, use

```
$object->propertyName;
```

Note that you cannot use the property variable dollar sign, which is a common cause of parse errors:

```
$object->$propertyName; // Error!
$object-> propertyName; // Correct!
```

Once you have finished with an object, you can delete it as you would any variable using unset(),

```
unset($object);
```

Example, to create an object,

```
<!doctype html>
<html lang="en">
 <head>
<meta charset="utf-8">
<title>Hello, World!</title>
<link rel="stylesheet" href="style.css">
 </head>
<body>
<?php
 /* This page uses the Hello class.
  * This page just says, "Hello, world!".
 */

 // Include the class definition:
require('Hello.php');

 // Create the object:
 $obj = new Hello();

// Call the sayHello() method:
$obj->sayHello();

 // Say hello in different languages:
 $obj->sayHello('Italian');
```

```
$obj->sayHello('Dutch');
$obj->sayHello('French');

// Delete the object:
unset($obj);
?>
</body>
</html>
```

Explanations: Create a new PHP document in your text editor or IDE, to be named hello.php, beginning with the standard HTML:

```
<!doctype html>
<html lang="en">
<head>
<meta charset="utf-8">
<title> Hello, PHP!</title>
<link rel="stylesheet" href="style.css">
</head>
<body>
<?php hello_object.php
```

1. The class definition file contains no HTML, as it is not meant to be used on its own. This PHP page can include all of the code necessary to make a useful HTML page.

2. Include the class definition, require('HelloWorld.php');
   The PHP script must have access to the class definition in order to create an instance of that class. That file must be provided here as a separate file. If the file could not be included, the script will terminate with a fatal error if need() is used.

3. Create the object:

```
$obj = new Hello();
```

There's nothing more to it than the above line of code! You may name the object variable whatever you like.

4. Invoke the sayHello() method using syntax below.

```
$obj->sayHello();
```

This line of code will call the sayHello() method, which is part of the $obj object. The regards will be in the default language of English.

5. Say hello in a few more languages:

```
$obj->sayHello('Italian');
$obj->sayHello('Dutch');
$obj->sayHello('French');
```

An object method can be defined and invoked multiple times, like any other function where different arguments are provided to vary the result.

6. Delete the object and complete the page:

```
unset($obj);
?>
</body>
</html>
```

It will be deleted soon as the script ends.

7. Save the file as hello.php and place it in your Web directory, along with Hello.php.

You do not have to place both documents in the same directory, but if stored separately, you will need to change the required () line accordingly.

8. Test hello.php by viewing it in your Web browser. Note that you should run hello.php, not Hello.php, in your Web browser.

THE $this ATTRIBUTE

The class HelloWorld actually does something, which is very nice, but it's a fairly minimal example. The class includes a method named sayHello(), but it does not contain any attributes such as variables.

As you see in the section "Defining a Class," attributes:

- A variables.

- It must be declared as public, private, or protected.

- If it is initialized, it must be provided a static value, not the result of an expression.

There are some rules for defining a class attribute, but using those attributes requires more information.

As we already explained that through the object, you could access attributes via the object notation operator that is ->.

Example:

```
$object->propertyName;
```

The problem is that you must use an alternative syntax to access the class's attributes within the class itself methods. You cannot do just this:

```
class ClassName {
public $variable;
function methodName() {
// This won't work:
print $variable;
        }
}
```

The methodName() method cannot access $variable in that manner, and the only solution is a special variable called $this. The term $this refers to the currently active instance, which is the object in that class. You may use the example to refer to the instance of a class and its attributes within a method or function.

```
$this->attributeName syntax.
```

Example of Rectangle using class, object instance, and this keyword,

```
class Rect{

// Declare the attributes:
public $width = 0;
 public $height = 0;

 // Method to set the dimensions:
 function setRectSize($w = 0, $h = 0) {
$this->width = $w;
$this->height = $h;
 }
```

```php
// Method to calculate and return the area.
function area() {
 return ($this->width * $this->height);
}

// Method to calculate and return the perimeter.
 function perimeter() {
return ( ($this->width + $this->height) * 2 );
}

// Method to determine if the rectange
// is also a square.
 function isSquare() {
 if ($this->width == $this->height) {
 return true; // Square
} else {
return false; // Not a square
}
}
 } // End of Rect class
//Create the instance of the Rect class,
 // Define the necessary variables:
$width =2;
$height = 7;




// Print a little introduction:
echo "<h2>With a width of $width and a height of
$height...</h2>";
// Create a new object:
$ rectObject = new Rectangle();
// Assign the rectangle dimensions:
 $rectObject->setSize($width, $height);
// Print the area:
 echo '<p>The area of the rectangle is '. $r->area().
'</p>';
// Print the perimeter:
echo '<p>The perimeter of the rectangle is '.
$r->perimeter(). '</p>';
unset($rectObject);
```

Explanations:

1. To create a new PHP document in your text editor or IDE, to be named rect.php

```
<?php
```

2. Begin defining the class:

```
class Rect {
Declare the attributes:
public $height = 0;
public $width = 0;
```

Rect class has two attributes: one for the width and another for its height. Both are initialized to 0.

3. Create a method for setting the rectangle dimensions:

```
function setRectSize($w = 0, $h = 0) {
$this->width = $w;
$this->height = $h;
}
```

The setRectSize() method takes two arguments corresponding to the width and height. Both have default values of 0.

4. Within the method, the class attributes are given values using the numbers that provided when this method is called $w and $h that is the weight and height of the rectangle, respectively. With this $this->width and $this->height refers to this class $width and $height attributes.

5. It is used to create a method that calculates and returns the rectangle's area:

```
function area() {
return ($this->width *  $this->height);
}
```

This method does not need to take any arguments because it can access the class's attributes via $this.

6. Create a method that calculates perimater of the rectangle and returns the perimeter:

```
function perimeter() {
```

```
return ( ($this->width  +  $this->height) * 2 );
}
```

This method is like area().

7. Create a method who find that rectangle is also a square:

```
function isSquare() {
if ($this->width ==   $this->height) {
return true;
} else {
return false;
}
}
```

8. This method compares the rectangle dimensions. If they are similar, the Boolean true is returned, which will indicate that the rectangle is a square.

9. Complete the class:

```
// End of Rectangle class.
```

10. Then save the file as Rectangle.php.

11. Create the Rectangle instance.

12. Define the necessary variables and print:

```
$width = 2;
$height = 7;
echo "<h2>"With a width of $width and a height of $height...</h2>";
```

13. Create the object and assign the rectangle dimensions:

```
$rectObject = new Rect();
$rectObject = setRectSize($width, $height);
```

The first-line code creates an object of type Rect. In the second-line code, the values are assigned to the variables in this code, the $width and $height to the object attributes. The values are assigned to $w and $h in the setRectSize() method when it's called, which are then assigned to $this->width and $this->height within that method.

14. Print the rectangle area,

```
echo '<p>The area of the rectangle  is.
' $rectObject >getArea().  '</p>';
```

To print the rectangle area, you only need to have the object tell you what that value is by calling its area() method.

15. Print the rectangle's perimeter:

```
echo '<p>The perimeter of the rectangle is '.
$ rectObject ->perimeter().  '</p>';
```

16. Delete the object and complete the page:

```
unset($r);
?>
</body>
</html>
```

17. Save the file as rect.php and place it in your directory

CREATING CONSTRUCTORS

A constructor is a special method that differs from standard ones in three ways:

- It cannot have a return statement.

- When object of that class is created, it is automatically and instantly called.

- Its name is always _ _construct().

The syntax of defining a constructor is given below,

```
class ClassName {
public $variable ;
function _ _construct() {
// Function code.
}
}
```

A constructor connects to a database, sets cookies, or initializes the values. Basically, you can use constructors to do whatever should always be done and done first when an object of this class is made.

```
<?PHP
class Student
{
        private $number;
        public function__construct($number)
        {
                $this-$number= $number
        }
}
$object = new Student(1);
?>
```

CREATING DESTRUCTORS

A constructor is used to call automatically when an object is created, whereas the destructor is called when the object is destroyed.

Syntax:

```
$obj = new ClassName();
unset($obj); // Calls destructor, too.
```

It may occur when a script ends at that point PHP releases the memory used by variables.

The destructor is created like so:

```
class ClassName {
// Attributes and methods.
function _ _destruct() {
// Function code.
}
}
```

Example:

```
<?php
class Student
{
```

```
    private $number;
    public function __construct($number)
    {
     echo "In constructor, ";
      $this-$number = "Class object! ";
    }
    public function __destruct($number)
    {
            echo "destroying ".  $this->number
.   "\n";
    }
}
$object = new Student();
?>
```

PHP VARIABLE SCOPE

When you start working with functions and objects in PHP, a variable scope can cause some confusion. Fortunately, PHP variable scope rules are relatively easy to understand. You will learn all you need to know about variable scope in PHP. You'll look at:

The concept of variable scope

- What it is, and what it means

- Differences between global and local scope

- How do we can access global variables from within a function

- PHP superglobals and how they work

- How to use static variables to preserve the state

What Is Variable Scope?

The scope of any variable in PHP is the context where the variable was created and in which it can be accessed easily. PHP has two variable scopes:

- **Global:** The global variable can be accessed from anywhere in the script.

- **Local:** The local variable is only accessible from within the function (or method) that created it.

A local scope makes your code easier to manage and global. They can be read and changed from anywhere in your script. By restricting a variable to a local scope, you limit the amount of code that can access that variable.

```php
<?php
$globalName = "PHP";
function sayHello() {
  $localName = "Java";
  echo "Hello, $localName!<br>";
}

sayHello();
echo "The value of $globalName is: '$globalName'<br>";
echo "The value of $localName is: '$localName'<br>";
?>
```

In this above code, we create two variables:

- $globalName is a global variable since it is not created inside any function.

- $localName is a local variable, created and used inside the function sayHello().

Superglobals Explained

PHP provides a set of predefined global arrays containing various useful informations. These arrays are known as superglobals because they're accessible from anywhere in your script, including inside functions, and you don't need to declare them as global using the global keyword.

Here is a complete list of the superglobals available in PHP:

- **$GLOBALS:** It contains a list of all global variables in the script (excluding superglobals).

- **$_GET:** It just holds a list of all form fields sent by the browser using the GET request.

- **$_POST:** It holds a list of all form fields sent by the browser using the POST request.

- **$_COOKIE:** It holds a list of all cookies sent by the browser.

- **$_REQUEST:** It contains all the keys and values in the $_GET, $_POST, and $_COOKIE arrays combined.

- **$_FILES:** It holds a list of any files uploaded by the browser.

- **$_SESSION:** It allows you to store and retrieve persistent session variables for the current browser.

- **$_SERVER:** It holds server environment info such as the filename of the running script and the IP address of the browser.

- **$_ENV:** It contains a list of environment variables passed to PHP. These can include variables provided by the shell and CGI variables.

For example, we can use the $_GET superglobal to retrieve a value included in the query.

```php
<?php
$yourName = $_GET['yourName'];
echo "Hello, $yourName!";
?>
```

The $GLOBALS superglobal lets you access global variables within functions.

```php
<?php
$globalName = "PHP";
function sayHello() {
   echo "Hello, " .$GLOBALS['globalName'] ."!<br>";
}
sayHello();  // Displays "Hello, PHP!"
?>
```

Static Variables

The Static methods are callable without an instance of the object created. The variable $this is not available inside methods declared as static.

The variables can be accessed without the creation of an object, using the scope resolution operator(::). But the static method cannot access the non-static variables because that requires the creation of the object. So, to access variables of a static class, we should declare them as static using the keyword static.

Example of Static variable example,

```php
<?php
class Class_name {

    // Static variable and static function
    // using static keyword
    public static $var = "text";

    public static function func() {
        echo self::$var;
    }
}

Class_name::func();
?>
```

Example of Static method,

```php
<?php
class ClassName{
    public static function staticMethod() {
        // Rest of the code
    }
}

Foo::StaticMethod();
$classname = 'ClassName';
$classname::StaticMethod();
?>
```

Example of defining variables in class and instances in PHP,

```php
<?php
class Student {
  // Properties
  public $name;
  public $age;

  // Methods
  function set_name($name) {
    $this->name = $name;
  }
```

```
    function get_name() {
        return $this->name;
    }
}
$student_1 = new Student ();
$student_2 = new Student ();
$john->set_name('John');
$sam->set_name('Sam');

echo$john->get_name();
echo "<br>";
echo $sam->get_name();
?>
```

Explanation:

1. You should create a new PHP document in your text editor or IDE, to be named phpClass.php

2. Begin defining the class:

```
class Student{
// Rest of the code
}
```

Using the syntax outlined earlier, start with the keyword class, followed by the name of the class, and by the opening curly brace, which could go on the next line. For the class name, I use the "uppercase camel" capitalization: initial letters are capitalized, as are the first letters of new words.

```
public $name;
public $age
```

3. In-class Students, we have access specified defined that is public, the name and age of the student are defined as public.

4. We set two methods for setting the name of the student with getting the name of the student. In both methods, we have used this keyword.

5. This ($this) is a reserved keyword in PHP, which refers to the current calling object. It is the object to which the method belongs. This keyword is only used inside the internal methods of the class.

```
function set_name($name) {
    $this->name = $name;
```

```
}
function get_name() {
    return $this->name;
}
```

6. Then set the instance of the Student. We have created two instances named student_1, student_2. This is the way to get and set the value to the class

```
.$student_1 = new Student ();
```

7. In next two methods we set the value to the class method set_name that same value will be printed which we passed.

```
$john->set_name('John');
$sam->set_name('Sam');
```

8. Further methods print the values which we have set before.

```
echo$john->get_name();
echo "<br>";
echo $sam->get_name();
```

INTERFACE

It defines a contract which a class must fulfill. If a class is a blueprint for objects, an interface is a blueprint for classes. The interface is written in the same way as the declaration with the interface keyword class.

Interfaces in PHP are limited to:

- Publicly visible methods.

- Publicly visible constants.

Interfaces rule:

- Every method defined as an interface must be public.

- Every method must be implemented within a class.

- The class in the interface must use the same method signatures defined in the interface.

- It can be extended like classes using the extends operator.

- The interface can be extended with another interface using extends keyword.

- You cannot create objects to interface, but the class implementing the interface can have objects.

- You cannot define a variable in an interface.

- If you extend interface, all the methods of the interface must be implemented in the child class.

Example for the interface class,

```php
<?php
interface A {
    public function property($x);
    public function description();
}
class Student implements A {
  public function property($x) {
        $this->x = $x;
    }
    public function description() {
        echo 'Describing' . $this->x . tree;
  }
}
$Student = new Students();
$Student-> property(mango);
$Student-> description();
?>
```

PHP Abstract Class

Mainly, an abstract class defines an interface for other classes to extend, and it is a class that cannot be instantiated.

```
To define an abstract class, you can add the abstract
keyword prefix to the className as follows:
<?PHP
abstract class className
{
    // ...
}
```

An abstract method, like an abstract class, does not have an implementation. You may also use the abstract keyword before the method to declare an abstract method, like in this,

```
abstract function methodName(arguments);
```

Although it is not needed, an abstract class will have at least one abstract method. A class must be abstract if it has one or more abstract methods.

If a class extends abstract class, it must either implement all of the abstract methods or declare itself abstract.

The key point for abstract class,

- It isn't possible to instantiate it. It serves as an extension interface for other classes.

- There is no implementation for an abstract method. A class must be abstract if it has one or more abstract methods.

- A class that extends abstract class must implement all of the abstract class's abstract methods.

```
<?php
// Abstract class
abstract class Base {
        function __construct() {
                echo "this is abstract class
constructor ";
        }

        // This is abstract function
        abstract function printdata();
}
class Derived extends base {
        function __construct() {
                echo "\n Derived class constructor";
        }
        function printdata() {
                echo "\n Derived class printdata
function";
        }
}
$b1 = new Derived;
$b1->printdata();
?>
```

Abstract class vs. interface

Abstract Class	Interface
It can have constants, members, method stubs, methods.	It can only have constants and methods stubs.
The methods and members can have public or protected visibility.	The methods of the interface should only be public, not any other visibility.
The concept of multiple Inheritances is not supported by an abstract class.	An interface can extend, or a class can implement multiple other interfaces.
Child class must implement all the abstract methods of parent class when the extended keyword is used.	There is no need to implement methods from the parent interface when the interface is extending another interface.

INHERITANCE

When the child class accesses the parent class's properties and methods, we call the concept has an Inheritance. The child class can inherit the parent features and give its own method implementation, and this is called overridden method. When a similar method of the parent class is inherited, we call it an inherited method. Now discuss types of Inheritance supported in OOP concept in PHP Inheritance examples.

A PHP use extends keyword to establish a relationship between two classes.

Syntax:

```
class B extends A
```

where A is the base class (also called parent) and B is called a subclass or child class.

Example:

```
<?PHP
class A{
    //properties, constants, and methods of class A
}
class B extends A{
    //public and protected methods inherited
}
?>
```

The keyword extends to define a derived or child class in PHP.

- **Derived class or Subclass:** It specifies the derived class's name. The child class is called a subclass, which inherits the features or characteristics from its parent class. One or more derived classes can inherit from the same base class to perform the Inheritance.

  A few visibility modes are supported in PHP: Public, Private, and Protected.

- **Base class or Parent Class:** It specifies the name of the base from where the child class is inheriting its properties. A base class is also called a parent class. There can be more than one base class in a program. For example, there will be one base class for one child class in a single-level Inheritance, but in a multi-level Inheritance, one child class can inherit from over one base class in more than one level.

Classifications of Inheritance:

- Single Inheritance
- Multi-level Inheritance
- Multiple Inheritance
- Multipath Inheritance
- Hierarchical Inheritance
- Hybrid Inheritance

Mainly the Inheritance has various types, but the PHP only supports the beginning of three.

- **Single Level Inheritance:** In this Level Inheritance, the parent class methods will be extended by the child class. All the methods can be inherited.

```php
<?PHP
    class Parent
    {
        public function display()
        {
```

```php
                echo "Parent Inheritance ";
        }
    }
    class Child extends Parent
    {
        public function view()
        {
                echo "Child Inheritance ";
        }
    }
    $obj= new Child ();
    $obj->display();
    $obj->view();
?>
```

- **Multilevel Inheritance:** In Multilevel Inheritance, the parent class method will be inherited by child class and again subclass will inherit the child class method.

```php
<?php
class A {
        public function GrandParent() {
        return  "age is 80\n";
        }
}
class B extends A {
        public function Parent() {
        return "age is 50\n";
        }
}
class C extends B {
        public function Child() {
        return  "age is 20\n";
            }
         public function Age() {
         echo "Class A ".$this-> GrandParent();
         echo "Class B ".$this-> Parent();
         echo "Class C ".$this-> Child();
         }
}
$obj = new C();
$obj-> Age();
?>
```

- **Multiple Inheritance:** It is the property of the OOP languages in which child class or subclass can inherit the properties of the numerous parent classes or superclasses.

  PHP does not support multiple Inheritance, but we can implement it by using Interfaces in PHP or by using Traits in PHP instead of classes.

```
class child_class_name extends parent_class_name {
    use trait_name;
    . . .
    . . .
    child_class functions
}
```

Example of Multiple Inheritance,

```php
<?php

// Class grandParentClass
class grandParentClass {
  public function gparent() {
  echo "<br>";
      echo "GrandParent";
  }
}

// Trait parentClass
trait parentClass {
  public function p() {
    echo "<br>";
      echo " Parent";
  }
}

class childClass extends grandParentClass {
    use parentClass;
    public function c() {
      echo "<br>";
        echo "Child";
  }
}

$test = new childClass();
$test->gparent();
$test->p();
$test->c();
?>
```

The traits can be inserted into a single class by using them in the use statement, separated by commas.

Syntax:

```
class child_class_name {
    use trait_name;
    ...
    ...
    child_class functions
}
```

Example of using traits in PHP,

```php
<?php

interface C {
    public function bfunction();
}

interface B {
    public function cfunction();
}

class A implements B, C {
    // Function of the interface B
    function bfunction() {
        echo "\nI am in interface B";
        echo "<br/>";
    }

    // Function of the interface C
    function cfunction() {
        echo "\nI am in interface C";
            echo "<br/>";
    }
}

$geeks = new A();
$geeks->bfunction();
$geeks->cfunction();
?>
```

ACCESS SPECIFIERS IN PHP

There are three various Access Specifiers available in PHP: Public, Private, and Protected.

- **Public:** It is class members with this access modifier who will be publicly accessible from anywhere, even from outside the scope of the class.

    Example of Public keyword,

```php
<?php
class parentClass
{
public $name ="PHP";
function show_name()
{
echo $this->name."<br/>";
}
}
class Child extends parentClass
{
function show_inherit_name()
{
echo $this->name;
}
}
$obj = new Child;
echo $obj->name."<br/>";
$obj-> show_name();
$obj-> show_inherit_name();
?>
```

- **Private:** It is class members with this keyword that will be accessed within the class itself. It protects members from outside class access with the reference of the class instance.

    Example of private keyword,

```php
<?php
class parentClass
{
private $name = "PHP";
private function show()
{
echo "This is a private method of parent class";
```

```
}
}
class child extends parentClass
{
function show1()
{
echo $this->name;
}
}
$obj = new child;
$obj -> show();
$obj -> show1();
?>
```

It won't return anything.

- **Protected:** It is the same as private, except by allowing subclasses to access protected superclass members.

```
<?php
class parentClass
{
protected $x = 50;
protected $y = 10;
    function addition()
{
echo $sum = $this->x+$this->y."<br/>";
}
    }
class child extends parentClass
{
function sub()
{
echo $sub = $this->x-$this->y."<br/>";
}
}
$obj = new child;
$obj -> addition();
$obj -> subtraction();
?>
```

The traits can be inserted into a single class by using them in the use statement, separated by commas.

Syntax:

```
class child_class_name {
    use trait_name;
    . . .
    . . .
    child_class functions
}
```

DATA ABSTRACTION

It is an important feature of the OOP programming language. It shows only useful information to the user; others remain hidden from the end-user. It is the representation of data in which the implementation details are hidden (abstracted).

PHP language has abstract classes and methods. Classes defined as abstract cannot be instantiated, and class that contains at least one abstract method also be abstract. When we inherit data from an abstract class, all methods are marked abstract in the parent class declaration should be defined by the child class.

A class is defined with an abstract keyword, and then it becomes an abstract class. A class that contains at least one abstract method is also considered abstract.

ABSTRACT METHODS AND CLASSES

It is a class that is declared abstract. It may or may not include abstract methods. Abstract classes cannot be instantiated, but they can be subclassed.

If any class includes abstract methods, then the class itself declared abstract, as in:

```
public abstract class A {
    // declare fields
    // declare non abstract methods
    abstract void draw();
}
```

ABSTRACT CLASSES COMPARED TO INTERFACES

Abstract classes are similar to interfaces. You cannot instantiate them, but they contain a mix of methods declared with or without an implementation.

However, with abstract classes, you can declare fields that are not static and define public, private, and protected concrete methods.

With interfaces, all fields are public, static, and final automatically. The methods that you declare or define are public.

Also, you can extend only a class. It is abstract, whereas you can implement any number of interfaces.

ABSTRACT CLASSES IMPLEMENTING INTERFACES

A class that implements an interface can implement all of the interface methods. To define a class that does not implement all of the interface methods, that class is declared to be abstract.

Example:

```
abstract class A implements B{
   // implements all but one method of Y
}
class AA extends A{
   // implements the remaining method in Y
}
```

In this case, class A is abstract because it does not fully implement B, but class AA does, in fact, implement B.

CLASS MEMBERS

Abstract classes have static fields and static methods. You can also use these static members with a class reference, for example, AbstractClass. staticMethod()).

Abstract Method

The abstract method only declares it is signature, i.e., its visibility, arguments, and returns type with type hints and don't have any functionality. A class that inherits such an abstract class must override (provide definition) all abstract methods. The corresponding method in child class must carry the same signature as in parent class. The PHP parser throws an exception if the child class doesn't fulfill this condition. A class that extends an abstract class can now be instantiated. Hence, it is called a concrete class.

In the following example, the parent class has two abstract methods, only one of which is redefined in the child class. This results in an error as follows,

```php
<?php
abstract class test_class{
    abstract function a();
    abstract function b();
}
class myclass extends test_class{
    function a(){
        echo "Overrides parent a method";
    }
}
$a=new myclass();
?>
```

Output

Following is the error message,

- **PHP Fatal error:** Class myclass contains one abstract method and must therefore be declared abstract or implement the remaining methods (testclass::hello) in/home/YND5Fr/prog. php on line 14.

  To overcome this error you can remove an extra abstract method,

  ```php
  <?php
  abstract class test_class{
      abstract function a();

  }
  class myclass extends test_class{
      function a(){
          echo "Overrides parent a method";
      }
  }
  $a=new myclass();
  $a->a();
  ?>
  ```

  Output,
  Overrides parent a method

The Abstract Method with Arguments

When an abstract method is defined with arguments, it must be overridden with the same number of arguments in the child class.

In the following example, an abstract method in parent class has two arguments. Child class also defines the same function with two arguments.

Example:

```php
<?php
abstract class test_class{
    abstract function a($name, $age);

}
class myclass extends test_class{
    function a($name,$age){
            echo " Name is $name and my age is
$age";
    }
}
$a=new myclass();
$a->a("ABC",20);
?>
```

Output:

```
Name is ABC, and my age is 20
```

PHP Magic Methods

The magic methods are special methods in a PHP class. These methods override the current actions when the object performs any actions.

The names of these magic methods start with a double underscore (__). And PHP reserves that methods whose start with a double underscore (__) for methods.

You have learned previously that the constructor and destructor use the __construct() and __destruct() methods. Both constructor and destructor are also magic methods.

The __construct() method is invoked when an object is created, and the __destruct() is called when the object is deleted.

Besides the __contruct() and __destruct() methods, PHP also has the following magic methods:

Magic Method	Description
__isset()	It is triggered by calling isset() or empty() on a non-existing or inaccessible property.
__call()	It is triggered when invoking an inaccessible instance method.
__callStatic()	It is triggered when invoking an inaccessible static method.
__get()	It is invoked when reading the value from a non-existing or inaccessible property.
__set()	It is invoked when writing a value to a non-existing or inaccessible property.
__unset()	It is invoked when unset() is used on a non-existing or inaccessible property.
__sleep()	The __sleep() commits the pending data.
__wakeup()	It is invoked when the unserialize() runs to reconstruct any object's resource.
__serialize()	The serialize() calls __serialize(), if available, and construct and return an associative array of key/value pairs that represent the serialized form of the object.
__unserialize()	The unserialize() calls __unserialize(), if available, and restore the properties of the object from the array returned by the __unserialize() method.
__toString()	It is invoked when an object of a class is treated as a string.
__invoke()	It is invoked when an object is called as a function.
__set_state()	It is called for a class exported by var_export().
__clone()	It is called once the cloning is complete.
__debugInfo()	It is called var_dump() when dumping an object to get the properties that should be shown.

Commonly used methods are __set() and __get().

- **The __set() method:** When write to a non-existing or inaccessible property, then PHP calls the __set() method automatically. Here, shows the syntax of the __set() method:

```
public __set ( $name, $value ){
// Here your code
}
```

The __set() method accepts the name and value. Next following example illustrates how to use the __set() method.

```
<?php
class PHP {
```

```php
    public function __set($name, $value)
    {
        $this->$name = $value;
        echo $this->$name;  //just for display
output   the other method__get helps us to get all
the value
    }
}

$obj = new PHP();

// __set() called
$obj -> name = 'You are learning PHP set method';
?>
```

- **The __get method:** The __get() method is the opposite of it. This method is invoked when you try to read data from inaccessible or non-existent object properties. The main purpose of this method is to provide values to such properties.

  Next following example illustrates how to use the __get method.

```php
<?php
class PHP {

    public function __set($name, $value)
    {
        $this->$name = $value;
    }
    public function __get($name)
    {
        If (isset($this->data[$name])) {
            return $this->data[$name];
        }
    }
}
$obj = new PHP();

// __set() called
$obj -> name = 'You are learning PHP set method';
echo $obj->name;
?>
```

- **The __construct() method:** It automatically invokes when an object is instantiated. This method aims to assign some default values to object properties. This method is also called a constructor.

  Next following example illustrates how to use __construct() method.

```php
<?php
class Student {
    private $name;
    private $email;

    public function __construct($name, $email)
    {
        $this->name = $name;
        $this->email = $email;
    }
}

$objStudent = new Student('Student_1', 'student1@
gmail.com');
?>
```

  In the example, when you instantiate a new object with a new student ('Student_1', 'student1@gmail.com'), it calls the __to construct() method in the first place. In the __construct() method, we assign values passed in the arguments to the object properties.

- **The __destruct() method:** This method is called a destructor, and it is called when the object is destroyed. It is called when the script is stopped or exited.

  Next following example illustrates how to use __destruct() method.

```php
<?php
class Student {
    private $name;
    private $email;

    public function __construct($name, $email)
    {
        $this->name = $name;
        $this->email = $email;
    }
```

```php
    public function __destruct()
    {
        echo 'It will be called when the script is
shut down...';
        // save object state/other cleanups
    }
}

$objStudent = new Student('Student_1', 'student1@
gmail.com');
?>
```

- **The __toString() method:** This magic method allows you to define what you would like to display when an object of the class is treated as a string. If you echo or print your object, and you have not defined the __toString() method, it will give an error.

  Next following example illustrates how to use the __toString() method.

```php
<?php
class Student {
    private $name;
    private $email;

    public function __construct($name, $email)
    {
        $this->name = $name;
        $this->email = $email;
    }

    public function __toString()
    {
        return 'Student name: '.$this->name
        .'<br>'
        .'Student email: '.$this->email;
    }
}

$objStudent = new Student('Student_1', 'student1@
gmail.com');
echo $objStudent;
?>
```

- **The __isset() and __unset() methods:** This method is called when you call the __isset() method on inaccessible or non-existent object properties.

  Next following example illustrates how to use __isset() and __unset() method.

```php
<?php
class Student {
    private $data = array();

    public function __isset($name)
    {
        return isset($this->data[$name]);
    }
}

$objStudent = new Student();
echo isset($objStudent->age );
?>
```

  In the example, the age property is not defined in the class, and thus it will call the __isset() method.

  The __unset() function, on the other hand, is invoked when the unset() method is used on inaccessible or non-existent object attributes.

- **The __sleep() and __wakeup() methods:** The __sleep() magic function is not like the others we've looked at so far. It's invoked when you use the object's serialize() method. You only want to store specified attributes during serialization and clear up the object in the case of an extremely big object. The __sleep() function must return an array containing the names of all serialized attributes of the object.

  Next following example illustrates how to use __sleep() and __wakeup() methods.

```php
<?php
class Student {
    private $name;
    private $email;
    private $db_connection_link;

    public function __construct($name, $email,
$phone)
```

```
{
    $this->name = $name;
    $this->email = $email;


}

public function __sleep()
{
    return array('name', 'email');
}

public function __wakeup()
{
    $this->db_connection_link = your_db_
connection_function();
}
}
?>
```

In the example, when you serialize() the Student object, it will call the __sleep() method, and it will preserve the values of the name, email variables.

When the unserialize() function is used on an object, the __ wakeup() magic method is used to re-establish all connections and start-up duties.

- **The __invoke() method:** This special method is called when you try to call an object as a function. Let's see how it works, and then see the purpose of this magic method.

```
<?php
class Student {
    private $name;
    private $email;

    public function __construct($name, $email)
    {
        $this->name = $name;
        $this->email = $email;
    }

    public function __invoke()
```

```
    {
        echo 'Object is called as a function!';
    }
}

$objStudent = new Student('Student_1', 'student1
@gmail.com');
$objStudent();
?>
```

As you see in the example, the $objStudent object is treated as a function, and as we defined the __invoke() method, it'll be called instead of giving you an error. The main purpose of the __invokes () method is that if you want to treat your objects as callable, you can implement this method.

- **The __clone() method:** If you want to make a copy of an existing object, you can use the keyword clone to do that. After cloning, if you modify the properties of the cloned object, you can define the __clone() magic method in your class.

```
<?php
Class Student {
}

class Student {
    private $name;
    private $email;
    private $object_student_school;

    public function __construct()
    {
        $this->object_student_school = new
Student_School();
    }

    public function __clone()
    {
        $this->object_student_school = clone
$this->object_student_school;
    }
}
```

```
$objStudentOne = new Student();
$objStudentclone = clone $objStudentOne;
?>
```

The above approach makes a shallow copy of the object during cloning, and the internal objects of the cloned object will not be cloned.

In the above example, if you have not defined the __clone() method, the cloned object, $objStudentclone, points to the same Student class object referenced by $objStudentOne object. We ensure that the Student class object is cloned along with the main object by using the __clone() method.

The functions __construct(), __destruct(), __call(), __callStatic(), __get(), __set(), __isset(), __unset(), __sleep(), __wakeup(), __toString(), __invoke(), __set_state(), __clone(), and __debugInfo() are magical method in the PHP classes. No function with these names are allowed in any of your classes.

All magic methods MUST declare as public.

The PHP programming language follows an OOP paradigm and other base structures. One of the most useful features is polymorphism. In basic terms, polymorphism is derived from Greek words: poly means many, and morphism means forms. It is a concept that allows creating classes with various functionalities in a single interface.

It is of two types:

- Overloading

- Overriding

Whereas polymorphism in PHP does not support overloading or compile-time polymorphism. The most benefit of polymorphism in PHP is that you don't have to worry about the technicalities of defining which code is written in which class, as all will be used in the same way.

A polymorphic can hold values of different types. An array can be declared as maintaining values of the parent class but, in fact, maintains values from each of the different subclasses of the parent class.

In the overloading, the method name is polymorphic. There is a single abstract function that takes various types of arguments. The actual code executed depends on the arguments given.

Overriding occurs when a subclass inherits a method from a superclass and either hides access to this method or refines it.

IMPLEMENTATION OF POLYMORPHISM IN PHP

Polymorphism in PHP may achieve through the use of abstract classes or concept interfaces. We'll look at several instances to see how we might put it into practice in different ways.

POLYMORPHISM IN PHP TO IMPLEMENT IN INTERFACES

The interface is a blueprint for all the classes. They're similar to classes, with one major distinction. Within interfaces, you may declare and specify method names and parameters. Any class implemented as the interface will implement all its methods.

The syntax of an interface is:

```
interface exampleInterface{
public function methodName();
}
```

The following example uses an interface,

```php
<?php
    interface Calculation {
        public function calcTask();
    }

    class Rectangle implements Calculation {
        private $width;
        private $height;
        public function __construct($width, $height){
            $this -> width = $width;
            $this -> height = $height;
        }
        public function calcTask(){
            return $this -> width * $this -> height;
        }
    }
    $myrect = new Rectangle(3,4);
    echo $myrect->calcTask();
?>
```

Explanation: Interface with the name of "Calculation" commits all the classes that implement it to define an abstract method with the name of calcTask(). The rectangle class implements the calculation interface but defines the method calcTask() with a body different from the Rectangle CalTask() method. Its guideline says that all the methods that calculate the task would have the equivalent name. As a result of we get the area of the rectangle. This keyword is to get the values of the instance on its own.

POLYMORPHISM IMPLEMENTATION IN ABSTRACT CLASSES

The abstract class is the parent class that has methods defined but not the code. They are defined using abstract keywords. You can use them to inherit other classes. Each abstract class can have one or more abstract methods. The different child classes use the methods in the same way. Let's have a better understanding with a polymorphism abstract class example in PHP.

The following example uses an abstract class and method,

```php
<?php
abstract class AbstractClass
{
    // Force Extending class to define this method
    abstract protected function getValue();

    // Common method
    public function printOut() {
        print $this->getValue() . "\n";
    }
}

class ConcreteClass1 extends AbstractClass
{
    protected function getValue() {
        return "ConcreteClass1";
    }
}
$class1 = new ConcreteClass1;
$class1->printOut();
?>
```

OVERLOADING IN PHP

The overloading is the ability to create various functions of the same name with different implementations also used to create properties and methods. Magic methods process these entities. Function overloading contains the same function name, and that function performs different tasks according to the number of arguments.

Property and Rules of overloading in PHP:

- Overloading methods must define as Public.

- After creating the object for a class, we can access a group of entities that are properties or methods.

- That such entity is said to be overloaded properties or methods, and the process is called overloading.

- Working with these overloaded properties or functions, magic methods are used.

Most of the methods will be triggered in object context except __callStatic() method, which is used in a static context.

Types of Overloading

There are two types of overloading,

- Property Overloading

- Method Overloading

Property Overloading: The overloading is used to create dynamic properties in the object context. There is a need to add a separate line of code for creating these properties. A property is associated with a class instance. If it is not declared within the scope of the class, then it is considered an overloaded property.

Following operations are performed with overloaded properties in PHP. Before performing the operations, we should define appropriate magic methods, which are,

- **__set():** It is used to trigger while initializing overloaded properties.

- **__get():** It is used to trigger while using overloaded properties with PHP print statements.

- **__isset():** It is invoked when we check overloaded properties with isset() function.

- **__unset():** It will be invoked on using PHP unset() for overloaded properties.

Method Overloading: This type of overloading is used to create dynamic methods that are not declared within the class scope. Overloading triggers magic methods dedicated to a suitable purpose. Unlike property overloading, PHP method overloading allows function calls on both objects as well as static context.

The related magic functions are,

- **__call():** It is used to trigger while invoking overloaded methods in the object context.

- **__callStatic():** It is used to trigger while invoking overloaded methods in static context.

Static Methods and Properties

Previously, you have learned how to define a class that has methods and properties. To use these methods and properties of the class, you create an object and access these methods and properties via the object instance.

These methods and properties are hooked to an instance of the class, which are called instance methods and properties.

It allows you to access the methods and properties in the context of a class rather than an object; such methods and properties are class methods and properties.

Class methods and class properties are called static methods and properties.

A static method is hooked to a class, not an individual instance of the class, and you cannot access $this variable (keyword) inside the method. You can access a variable called self. The self means the current class.

The following shows how to call a static method from the inside of the class:

```php
self::staticMethod(arguments);
Code language: PHP (php)
```

To invoke static method from the outside of the class, you can use the following syntax:

```php
className::staticMethod(arguments)
```

Example:

```
MyClass::staticMethod()
```

PHP Static properties
    To define a static property, you can use the static keyword:

```
public static $staticProperty;
```

Example:

```
class MyClass
{
    public static $staticProperty;

    public static function staticMethod()
    {
    }
}
```

For accessing a public static property outside of the class, you can use the class name with the:: operator:

```
MyClass::$staticProperty;
```

In the static methods to access static properties from within the class, you use the self instead of $this as follows:

```
self::staticProperty
```

self vs. $this Keyword
The following table shows the differences between the self and $this:

$this	Self
It represents an instance of the class or object	It represents a class only
It always begins with a dollar ($) sign	It is never begin with a dollar($) sign
It is followed by the object operator (->)	It is followed by the :: operator
The property name after the object operator (->) does not have the dollar ($) sign, e.g., $this->property	The static property name after the :: operator always has the dollar ($) sign

WHAT IS SELF KEYWORD?

Self is a pointer to the class. It refers to the class which is using static variables. If we use a static method inside the class, we can use the self-keyword to call. To call self-keyword, a static variable must use this operator::.

Self-keyword is used for the current class, and basically, it is used to access static members, methods, and constants, whereas parent:: keyword is used for the parent class.

::self vs. ::parent

::self	::parent
self:: It is referred to the class itself, not indicate to any object.	Using self:: It can access the static properties and static methods of the current class.
parent:: It is referred to the parent class.	Using parent:: It can access the static properties and static methods of the parent class.

METHOD OVERLOADING IN PHP

It is used to create dynamic methods that are not made within that class scope/scopes. The PHP concept method overloading also helps trigger the magic methods dictated for the appropriate purpose. Separated from the property overloading concept, the PHP method allows function calls/calls on both the object and the static context.

Syntax:

```
Public _call (string $name1, array $arguments1 )
: mixed
Public static _callStatic (string $name1, array
$arguments1 ) : mixed
```

How Does Method Overloading Work?

It works with the declaration inside the class by creating dynamic methods and also works by triggering some magic methods for an appropriate purpose, and it also calls functions calls on both the static context and the object. This concept is too fine with the other programming languages like C, Java, etc. It is also called a static polymorphic concept.

There are some of the magic functions, they are:

- _call(): This function triggers invoking the overloaded method/methods in the object context.

- **_callStatic()**: This function triggers invoking the overloaded concepts/methods in the static context.

What Is Autoloading?

It is the process of automatically loading PHP classes without explicitly loading them with the require(), require_once(), include(), or include_once() functions.

What Is an Autoloader?

It is a function that takes a name of the class as an argument and then includes the file that contains the same class.

Example:

```
function autoloader ( $class ) {
  $path = $DOCUMENT_ROOT . '/classes/';
  require $path . $class . '.php';
}
```

NAMESPACES

In PHP, the use of namespaces allows classes/functions/constants of the same name to be used in various contexts without conflict, thereby encapsulating these items. A namespace is a grouping of classes/functions etc., depending on their relevance. Just as a file with the same name can exist in two different folders, a class of a certain name can be defined in two namespaces.

The use of it to solves two problems.

- To avoiding name collisions between classes/functions/constants defined by someone with third-party classes/functions/constants.

- By providing the ability to alias (or shorten) Extra_Long_Names, thereby improving the readability of source code.

Namespaces provide a way to group related classes, interfaces, functions, and constants. Namespace names are case-insensitive.

Example:

```
<?PHP
namespace my_space;
```

```php
function hello() {
    echo "Hello PHP\n";
}
?>
```

ENCAPSULATION IN PHP

It is described as the wrapping up of data under a single unit (called class), this protected mechanism that binds the code together and manipulates it, and protects the data members and methods present inside the class. Another way to introduce encapsulation is a protective shield that prevents the data from being accessed by the code outside this shield.

Encapsulation is used to make the code more secure and robust. Using encapsulation, we can hide the real implementation of data from the user, and that does not allow others to manipulate data members except by calling the desired operation.

Let's have an example of an encapsulation in PHP,

```php
<?php
class person
{
public $name;
public $age;
function __construct($name, $age)
{
$this->name=$name;
$this->age=$age;
}
public function display()
{
return "My name is ".$this->name."and my age is
".$this->age;
}
}
$person=new person("ABC",28);
echo $person->display();
?>
```

The above code generates the output as follow,

```
My name is ABC, and my age is 28
```

CHAPTER SUMMARY

In this chapter, we have covered the fundamental OOP concepts, definition and creation of classes and objects, declaring a constant, the use of $this keyword, variable scope in class, the concepts of inheritance, encapsulation, polymorphism, etc.

CHAPTER 6

Using HTTP in PHP

IN THIS CHAPTER

➤ HTTP and its structure

➤ General Header and Client Request Headers

➤ HTTP

In the previous chapter, we have covered the fundamental of the OOP's concepts, definition and creation of the class and object, declare constant, use of $this keyword, variable scope in class, the concept of inheritance, etc.

Before learning HTTP, you must know about the basic terms such as Web, Web server and Web browser URL, HTTP protocol, and more things.

WHAT DOES WEB MEAN?

The Web is the common term for the World Wide Web (WWW), a subsection of the Internet that can consist of the pages accessed by any web browser. Many people think that the Web is the same as the Internet and use these terms vice versa. However, the word Internet truthfully refers to the global network of servers that make sharing information possible over the Web. So, although the Web does make up a large portion of the Internet, they are not the same.

WHAT IS HTTP AND WHAT IS THE STRUCTURE OF HTTP REQUEST AND RESPONSE?

If you are a user or an owner of any website, the one word you may come across when browsing is HTTP. It is essential to get the basics of HTTP to

DOI: 10.1201/9781003308669-6

understand how the Internet works, the details sent and received between your browser and the webserver. Here is a beginner's guide to HTTP attempting to explain the basics.

We need to know the three significant terms as prerequisites:

- **Client:** The user that sends the request via a Web Browser.

- **Server:** The one who sends a response back to the user.

- **Protocol:** It is a set of rules that allow you to communicate between a client (front-end) and a server (back-end). We use a protocol in English to share between two people.

- In the same, the Internet uses some protocols to transfer information between a client and server. The commonly used protocol is the HyperText Transfer Protocol (HTTP) for websites. It allows you to transfer files in the text between client and server.

WHAT IS HTTP?

HTTP stands for HyperText Transfer Protocol. This is a basis for data communication on the Internet. The data communication starts with a request sent from a client and ends with the response received from a web server.

A website URL starting with "HTTP://" is entered in a web browser from a computer (client). The browser can be Chrome, Firefox, Edge, Safari, Opera, or anything else.

Then the web browser sends a request to the webserver that hosts the website.

The web server then returns a response as an HTML page or any other document format to the browser. The browser displays the response from the server to the user.

The web browser is called a User-Agent, and another example of a user agent is the crawlers of search engines like Googlebot.

All the web pages are formatted in Hypertext Markup Language (HTML). This language allows other users to click on the page on the Web via links. The web browser primarily uses the HTTP protocol to transmit data and share information. Browsers like Internet Explorer (IE), Google Chrome, or Mozilla Firefox are used to access Web documents or Web pages connected through links.

The Web is how information is shared over the Internet, including email, instant messaging, and File Transfer Protocol (FTP).

Web server as hardware is connected to the Internet and allows data to be exchanged with different connected devices. In contrast, a web server as software controls how a user access files. The web server process is a model of the client/server model. All computers that host websites must hold web server software.

Web servers are used in web hosting or data hosting for websites and web-based applications or web applications.

How Do Web Servers Work?

The web server software is got through the domain names of websites and it ensures the delivery of the user content to the requesting user. The software side also comprises several components, with at least an HTTP server. The HTTP server can understand the HTTP and URLs. A web server as hardware is a computer that stores web-server software and other files related to a website like HTML documents, images, and other files.

Some Examples of Web Server Use

Web servers often come as part of an enormous package of the Internet and Intranet-related programs used to send and receive emails. Also, perform downloading requests for FTP files and build and publish web pages.

Many primary web servers also support server-side scripting, which is used to operate scripts on a web server. Various primary web servers also support server-side scripting, which is used to manage scripts on a server that can customize the response to the user at the front end. Server-side scripting runs on the server, and that typically has a broad feature set, including database access. The server-side process also uses Active Server Pages (ASP), Hypertext Preprocessor (PHP), and various scripting languages. This process will also allow the other HTML documents to be created dynamically to customize the client's response. Server-side scripting runs on a machine that typically has a broad feature set, including database access.

WHAT ARE STATIC WEB PAGES?

Some simple web pages are written in languages like HTML, CSS, JavaScript, etc., and data is stored in a web server. In the topic of static web pages, as shortly as a server accepts a request for a page, it instantly sends a reply to the client with zero additional processing. The server encounters page on the hard disk, adds the HTTP headers to it, then immediately replies with an HTTP response, and it is way, you can view these web pages via a web browser.

One strange thing about static web pages is that all the pages remain the same unless and until a user does some manual changes on the hard disk. The content in these pages has no changes based on the requests. It is the reason behind the name static web pages. One does not require knowledge of database design and web programming to make and manage a static website. All the codes remain fixed for the static web pages. Therefore, the information does not change, and these pages look like printed ones.

WHAT ARE DYNAMIC WEB PAGES?

These are complicated web pages where the information and content displayed change with a different client. The dynamic web pages are used in languages like Asynchronous JavaScript and XML (AJAX), ASP, CGI, ASP. NET, etc. They take much more time in loading than any static web pages, thus used in cases where the content changes very often, for example, education information, stock, weather, news, sports, and other extra updates.

When a server gets some request for a page, it doesn't not that request to send any HTML page in response. In a dynamic, the information data of pages vary according to different visitors. If you suppose that a person needs to change the information on a web page every second, it becomes physically impractical. No one can alter the HTML pages this often. Thus, they need a dynamic web page and not a static web page. There are several tools that help in creating such pages, like the ASP, ASP.NET, Java Server Pages (JSP), AJAX, Common Gateway Interface (CGI), etc.

A dynamic website accesses content from a Content Management System (CMS). It means the website changes made in the database content such sites use server-side scripting, client-side scripting, or both for generating content.

Here the difference between Static Web Pages and Dynamic Web Pages:

Parameter	Static Web Pages	Dynamic Web Pages
Basics introduction	The content on static web pages remains the same unless someone physically changes it on its hard disk or manual alterations.	The dynamic type of web page is behavioral. The content of pages is capable of varying for various users. It keeps on changing with time and other parameters.
Definition	A static web page is a basic HTML written page that directly responds from a browser to the server. All the data and info remain static, and it stays the same unless someone manually makes any changes.	A dynamic web page is written in complex programming languages such as AJAX, ASP.NET, etc. Here, the data gets rendered to some capacity and interpretation to produce varied content for different users visiting the page.

(Continued)

Parameter	Static Web Pages	Dynamic Web Pages
Complexity	Static types of web pages are extremely simple. The data in static pages remain static and need no interpretation before processing and rendering. Therefore, it comes with no extra complexity.	Dynamic types of web pages are more complicated than static pages. Even they go through the process of understanding, making the data dynamic in character. Such pages become way more complex than any static web page.
Frequency change of information	Its content and information rarely change on a static web page.	The content and information frequently change on a dynamic web page.
Loading time of pages	These web pages take a short time to load compared to the dynamic ones, and this is because they contain very static data and info on the pages.	Dynamic web pages take a long time to load as compared to the static web page because of the more complex, dynamic data present in these web pages.
Use of database in pages	The static web pages normally do not use any databases, and they do not require data redecoration very often.	The dynamic web pages mostly use databases because they involve frequent data and redecoration.
Languages used	Languages, like CSS, JavaScript, HTML, and many more, come into play when writing static web pages. It uses only simple languages.	Languages, like ASP.NET, ASP, AJAX, CGI, and many more, come into play when writing dynamic web pages, and it requires some extremely complex languages for a stable operation.
Use of application program	Static pages do not contain any application programs.	Dynamic page has contained application programs for various services.
Cost of development	The designing of dynamic web pages is more costly as compared to static ones.	The designing of static web pages requires meager costs as compared to dynamic ones.
Work required	Less work and complexity required into designing static web pages.	More work and complexity are required to design dynamic web pages.
Rendered data	The data and information in static web pages do not change by own. One needs to make necessary changes on it – making it fixed manually.	The data and information in dynamic web pages preferably stay interoperate at the server-side. Due to this, the data doesn't remain similar on each call – making the data contained in it dynamic.

HYPERTEXT TRANSFER PROTOCOL (HTTP)

HTTP is possibly the most famous application protocol used on the Internet.

- It is an asymmetric request/response client-server protocol. A client sends a request message to an HTTP server. The server, in turn, returns a response message. In other words, HTTP is a pull protocol, and the client pulls information from the server.

- HTTP is a stateless protocol. Generally, the current request does not know what has been done in the previous recommendations.

- HTTP permits negotiating data type and representation to allow systems to be built independently of the transferred data.

- The HTTP is an application-level protocol used as distributed, collaborative information systems. It is a generic protocol which can be used for various tasks beyond the hypertext, such as name servers and distributed object management systems, through the extension of its request methods, error codes, and headers.

When the request reaches the server, the server can take one of these actions:

- The server maps the request into a file under the server document directory and returns the file requested to the client.

- The server maps the request into a program, keeps it in the server, executes the program, and returns its output to the client.

- And the request cannot be satisfied, and the server returns an error message.

UNIFORM RESOURCE LOCATOR

A URL is used to identify a resource over the Web uniquely. URL has the following syntax:

```
protocol://hostname:port/path-and-file-name
```

There are four parts in a URL:

- **Protocol:** This protocol is used by the client and server, for example, HTTP, FTP, and telnet.

- **Hostname:** The server's DNS domain name (e.g., www.nowhere123. com) or IP address (e.g., 192.128.1.2).

- **Port:** The port number on the server is usually listening to for incoming requests from the front-end user.

- **Path-and-file-name:** The name and location of the requested client underneath the server document base manual.

TERMINOLOGY

The HTTP uses several terms to refer to the roles played by participants and objects of the HTTP communication.

Terminology	Description
Connection	The connection is done on a transport layer virtual circuit established between two programs for the purpose of communication.
Message	The basic HTTP communication unit consists of a structured sequence of octets matching the syntax defined in section 4 and transmitted via the connection.
Request	It is an HTTP request message.
Response	It is an HTTP response message.
Resource	It means a network data object or service that a URI and its resources can specify may be available in multiple representations (example: multiple languages, data formats, size, and resolutions) or vary in other ways.
Entity	The information is transferred as the payload of a request or response and it's an entity that consists of metainformation in the form of entity-header fields and content in the form of an entity-body.
Representation	It is an entity which is included with a response that is subject to content negotiation There might be exist multiple representations linked with a particular response status.
Content negotiation	A mechanism for selecting the suitable representation when servicing a request The representation of entities in any response can be negotiated, including error responses.
Variant	It is a resource that may have one, or more than one, representations associated with it at any given instant and each of these representations is termed as 'variant' use of the term 'variant' does not necessarily indicate that the resource is subject to content negotiation.
Client	A client is a user that establishes connections for the purpose of sending some requests.

(Continued)

Terminology	Description
User agent	The client who initiates a request are often browsers, editors, spiders (web-traversing robots), or other end-user tools.
Server	It is an application program that accepts connections in order to serve the requests by sending back responses any given program may capable of both a client and a server, our use of these terms refers only to the role performed by the program for a particular connection, rather than to the program capabilities in general. The server act as an origin server, proxy, gateway, or tunnel, switching behavior is based on the nature of each request.
Origin server	The origin server is which a given resource resides or is to be created.
Proxy	It is an intermediary program that acts as both a server and a client to make requests on behalf of other clients and requests are serviced internally or bypassing them on, with correct translation, to the other servers. A proxy MUST be implemented on both the client and server requirements of this specification.
	A "transparent proxy" is a proxy that doesn't modify the request or response beyond that what is required for proxy authentication and identification. A "non-transparent proxy" means a proxy that changes the request or response in order to provide some added service to the user agent, such as media type transformation, anonymity filtering, group annotation services, protocol reduction but except where either transparent or non-transparent behavior is explicitly noticed, the HTTP proxy requires apply to both types of proxies.
Gateway	It is a server that acts as a middleware for some other server. Unlike a proxy, a gateway acquires requests as if it were the origin server for the requested resource; the requesting client may not be aware that it is communicating with a gateway.
Tunnel	It is an intermediary program which is acting as an arbitrary relay between two connections. Once active, a tunnel is not considered as a party to the HTTP communication, though an HTTP request may have initiated the tunnel. The tunnel ceases exist when both ends of the relayed connections are closed.
Cache	A local store of response messages and the subsystem that controls its message storage, retrieval, and deletion process. A cache stores cacheable responses in order to lower the response time and network bandwidth consumption on equivalent requests and client or server may include a cache, though a cache cannot be used by a server that is acting as a tunnel.

(Continued)

Terminology	Description
Cacheable	It is an HTTP response that can be cached, that is stored to be retrieved and used later, saving a new request to the server. If a cache allows to store a copy of the message (response – the rules for identifying the cacheability of HTTP responses). Even if a resource is cacheable, then there might be extra constraints on whether a cache uses the cached copy for a particular request.
First-hand	A response is first-hand if it comes directly and without unnecessary delay from the origin server, perhaps via one or more proxies. A response is also first-hand if its validity has just been checked directly with the origin server.
Explicit expiration time	The time at which the origin server intends that a cache should no longer return an entity without further validation.
Age	The age of any of the response is the time since it was sent by, or successfully validated with, the origin server.
Freshness lifetime	The max-length of time between the generation of a response and its expiration time.
Fresh	A response fresh if the age has not yet exceeded its freshness lifetime.
Stale	A stale response is an age that has passed its freshness lifetime.
Semantically transparent	A cache behaves in a "semantically transparent" manner, with respect to a particular response, when its use affects neither the requesting client nor the origin server, except to improve performance. When a cache is semantically transparent, the client receives exactly the same response (except for hop-by-hop headers) that it would have received had its request been handled directly by the origin server.
Validator	A response protocol element example, an entity tag, or a Last-Modified time is used to determine whether an entry is a similar copy of an entity.
Upstream/downstream	The response upstream and downstream describes the flow of a message where all messages flow from upstream to downstream.
Inbound/outbound	The response inbound and outbound refer to the request and response paths for messages: "inbound" means "traveling toward the origin server", and "outbound" means "traveling toward the user agent."

OVERALL OPERATION OF HTTP

The HTTP protocol is a request and response protocol. The client sends a request to the server with the various methods, URI, i.e., a URI has two types known as Uniform Resource Locator (URL) and Uniform Resource Name (URN). Most people get confused between URN and URL. URN is a resource name, and URI is an absolute location of a web resource (e.g., http://example.com/home.html).

And protocol version and a message containing request modifiers, users' information, and body content over a connection with any server. Then, the server responds with a status, having the message of the protocol version with a success or error code.

Most HTTP communication is done by a user agent and consists of a request applied to a resource on some origin server. In the same case, this can be performed via a single connection (v) between the user agent (UA) and the origin server (O).

HTTP communication takes place over TCP/IP connections. The default port is TCP 80, and other ports can be used. This does not prevent HTTP from implementing any different protocol on the Internet.

UNIFORM RESOURCE IDENTIFIERS (URIs)

Many names have learned URIs: WWW addresses, Universal Document Identifiers, Universal Resource Identifiers, and Uniform Resource Locators (URL) and Uniform Resource Names (URN). The HTTP is concerned. URIs are simply formatted strings that identify a resource via name, location, or other characteristics.

HTTP GENERAL SYNTAX

HTTP URIs can be represented as absolute form or relative to base URI. The two states are distinguished because absolute URIs always initiate with a scheme name followed by a colon.

For definitive information on URL syntax, see the "Uniform Resource Identifiers (URI): Generic Syntax and Semantics," RFC 2396 [42].

The specification definitions of "URI-reference", "absoluteURI", "relativeURI", "port", "host", "abs_path", "rel_path", and "authority" from that specification.

HTTP URL

The "HTTP" is used to locate network resources via the HTTP protocol and also defines the scheme-specific syntax and semantics for HTTP URLs.

Syntax of HTTP given below,

```
http_URL = "http:" "//" host [ ":" port ] [ abs_path [
"?" query ]]
```

HTTP REQUEST METHODS

The HTTP protocol defines a group of request methods. A client can use these request methods to send a request message to an HTTP server. The methods are:

- **GET:** A user can use the GET request to get a web from the server.

- **HEAD:** A user uses the HEAD request to obtain the header from a GET request. The header section contains the last modified date of the data, and this can use to check against the local cache copy.

- **POST:** It is used to post data up to the webserver.

- **PUT:** It tells the server to store the data.

- **DELETE:** It tells the server to delete the data.

- **TRACE:** It tells the server to return a diagnostic trace of the actions it takes.

- **OPTIONS:** It tells the server to return the list of request methods it supports.

- **CONNECT:** It is used to tell a proxy to connect to another host and reply to the content without attempting to parse or cache it. This is often used to make an SSL connection through the proxy.

GET REQUEST METHOD

It is the most commonly used HTTP request method. A client uses the GET request method to request a piece of data from an HTTP server. A GET request takes the following syntax as given below.

```
GET request-URI HTTP-version
(request headers)
(blank line)
(request body)
```

- The GET keyword is case-sensitive, and it must be in uppercase.

- **Request-URI:** It specifies the path of the requested resource, which should begin with the root "/" of the document base directory.

- **HTTP-version:** It either uses HTTP/1.0 or HTTP/1.1. This client can negotiate the protocol used for the current session. For example, the client can request to use HTTP/1.1. If the server does not support version HTTP/1.1, it may inform the client to use the version HTTP/1.0.

- The client can use the optional request headers to negotiate with the server and ask the server to deliver the preferred contents.

- The GET request message has an optional request body that contains the query string.

RESPONSE STATUS CODE

The status code element in a server response consists of a 3-digit integer where the first digit is for the status code defines the class of response, and the last two digits do not have any role and having five values for the first digit.

These responses are grouped in five classes:

- Informational responses (100–199)

- Successful responses (200–299)

- Redirection messages (300–399)

- Client error responses (400–499)

- Server error responses (500–599)

The first line of the response states that the status line has the response status code returned by the server to indicate the outcome of the request.

Serial Number	Code	Description
1	1xx: Informational	It represents the request has been received and the process is continuing.
2	2xx: Success	It represents the action was successfully received, understood, and accepted.
3	3xx: Redirection	It represents further action must be taken in order to complete the request.
4	4xx: Client Error	It represents the request contains incorrect syntax or cannot be fulfilled.
5	5xx: Server Error	It represents the server failed to fulfill an apparently valid request.

These HTTP status codes are extensible, and applications are not required to understand the meaning of all the registered status codes and below are a list of all the status codes.

There are some Information responses in HTTP with its status code.

- **100 Continue:** This will indicate that one should continue the request or ignore it if it is already finished.

- **101 Switching Protocols:** This code is sent as a response to the upgrade header from the client and indicates the server's protocol.

- **102 Processing (WebDAV):** This indicates that the server has received and is now processing the request, but there is no response available yet.

- **103 Early Hints:** This status code is mainly intended for the Link header and lets the user agent begin preloading resources while the server prepares a response.

There are some Successful responses in HTTP with its status code.

- **200 OK:** It occurred when the request succeeded. The "success" depends on the HTTP method:

  - **GET:** The information has been fetched and transmitted in the message body.

  - **HEAD:** The headers are included in the response without any message body.

  - **PUT or POST:** The resource telling the result of the action is passed on to the message body.

  - **TRACE:** The message body has the request message received by the server.

- **201 Created:** This request succeeded, and a new one was created as a result. This response is sent after POST or PUT requests.

- **202 Accepted:** This request has been received but not acted upon. It is an HTTP request which has no way to send an asynchronous response later indicating the outcome of the appeal. For cases where another process, the server handles the request or batch processing.

- **203 Non-Authoritative Information:** It indicates that the request was successful, but the enclosed payload has been modified, and it is used for mirrors or backups of another resource.

- **204 No Content:** It indicates that a request has succeeded, but the client does not need to navigate away from its current page.

- **205 Reset Content:** It tells the user to reset the document view.

- **206 Partial Content:** It indicates that the request has succeeded, and the body contains the requested ranges of data.

- **207 Multi-Status (WebDAV):** It conveys information about multiple resources for situations.

- **208 Already Reported (WebDAV):** It is used inside a <dav:propstat> response element to avoid repeatedly enumerating.

- **226 IM Used (HTTP Delta Encoding):** The server has to be fulfilled a GET request for the resource, and the response represents the result.

There are some Redirection messages in HTTP with its status code.

- **300 Multiple Choice:** It indicates that the request has more than one possible response. The user should choose one of them. And there is no other way of choosing one of the responses, and this response code is rarely used. It should generate a Location header.

- **301 Moved Permanently:** Its redirect status-response code indicates that the requested resource has been changed permanently, returning the new URL.

- **302 Found:** This response means that the URI of the requested resource has been changed temporarily moved to the URL given by the Location header.

- **303 See Other:** The server sent this response directly to the client and got the requested resource at another URI using the GET request.

- **304 Not Modified:** It indicates that there is no need to retransmit the requested resources.

- **305 Use Proxy:** The HTTP specification indicates that a proxy must access a requested response. It was deprecated due to security concerns regarding the in-band configuration of a proxy.

- **306 Unused:** This code is no longer used. It is just reserved.

- **307 Temporary Redirect:** It indicates that the resource has been moved to the URL given by the Location headers. The original request's method and body are reused to perform the redirected request.

- **308 Permanent Redirect:** This status-response code indicates that the resource requested has been definitively moved to the URL given by the Location headers.

There are some client error responses in HTTP with its status code.

- **400 Bad Request:** It is response status code indicates that the server cannot or will not process the request due to syntax error or something that is sensed to be a client error.

- **401 Unauthorized:** This response means "unauthenticated," and also means that client must authenticate itself to get the response. It indicates that the request has not been completed due to a lack of valid authentication credentials for the requested resource.

- **402 Payment Required:** This code is reserved for future use. The aim of creating this code is to use it for digital payment systems.

- **403 Forbidden:** This means that client does not have access rights to the content; also it is unauthorized, so the server is preventing giving the requested resource.

- **404 Not Found:** This means that server cannot find the requested resource, and also means that URL is not recognized. In API, this means that the endpoint is proper, but the resource itself does not exist.

- **405 Method Not Allowed:** The code means that server knows the request method but is not supported by the resource. For example, the API may not allow DELETE to remove a resource.

- **406 Not Acceptable:** This code response is sent when the web server doesn't find any content that conforms to the criteria given by the user.

- **408 Request Timeout:** It is sent on a single connection by some servers, even without any previous request by the client.

It means that the server likes to shut down this unused connection and is more commonly used browsers, like Chrome, Firefox.

- **409 Conflict:** It indicates a request conflict with the current state of the target resource.

- **410 Gone:** It indicates that access to the target resource is no longer available at the origin server or might be permanent.

- **411 Length Required:** It indicates that the server refuses to accept the request without a defined Content-Length header.

- **412 Precondition Failed:** It indicates that access to the target resource has been denied. And it happens with conditional requests on methods other than GET or HEAD.

- **413 Payload Too Large:** It indicates that the request entity is larger than the limits defined by the server, and the server closes the connection or returns a Retry-After header field.

- **414 URI Too Long:** It indicates that the URI requested by the client is longer than the server is willing to interpret.
  Few conditions when this might occur:

  - When a client has improperly tried to convert a POST request to a GET request.

  - The client has crashed into a loop of redirection.

  - When the server is under attack by a client attempting to exploit security holes.

- **416 Range Not Satisfiable:** It is an error-response code that indicates a server cannot serve the requested ranges, and the reason is that the document does not contain such ranges or the Range-header value.
  This means that the range specified by the Range-header field cannot be fulfilled that the range is outside the size of the target URI's data.
  The response message contains a Content-Range that indicates an unsatisfied range followed by a '/' and the current length of the resource. For example, Content-Range: bytes */12777.

- **417 Expectations Failed:** It means the expectation indicates that they expect the server cannot meet request-header field.

- **421 Misdirected Requests:** It indicates that the directed request cannot produce a response and can be sent by a server that is not configured to produce responses authority that is included in the request URI.

- **422 Unprocessable Entities (WebDAV):** This response status code indicates that the server understands the content type of the request entity, and the syntax of the request entity is correct. Still, it was unable to process the contained instructions.

- **428 Preconditions Required:** It indicates that the server requires the request to be conditional, and it is intended to prevent the 'lost update' problem. A client GETs a resource state, modifies it, and PUTs it back to the server. That means, a third party has modified the state on the server, leading to a conflict.

- **426 Upgrade Required:** It indicates that the server refuses to perform the request using the current protocol but might be willing to do so after the client upgrades to a different protocol. The server sends an Upgrade header in a 426 response to indicate the required protocol(s).

- **429 Too Many Requests:** It represents that the user has sent too many requests in a given time.

- **431 Request-Header Fields Too Large:** It represents that the server is unwilling to process the request because its header fields are too large. The request may be resubmitted after reducing the size of the request-header fields.

- **451 Unavailable for Legal Reasons:** It indicates that the user agent requested a resource that cannot legally be provided such as a government-censored web page.

There are some Client-Server error responses in HTTP with its status code.

- **500 Internal Server Error:** It indicates that the server has encountered a situation that does not know how to handle.

- **501 Not Implemented:** This error code indicates that the server's request method is not supported and cannot be taken. The methods that servers are required to support are GET and HEAD.

- **502 Bad Gateway:** This error indicates that while working as a gateway to get a response needed to handle the request, this error response indicates that the server got an invalid response.

- **503 Service Unavailable:** It indicates that the server is not ready to handle any request.

  This should use for temporary conditions, and the Retry-After HTTP header should, if possible, contain the estimated time for the recovery of the service.

- **504 Gateway Timeout:** This server response code indicates that the server was acting as a gateway or proxy and did not get a response in time from the upstream server needed to complete the request.

- **505 HTTP Version Not Supported:** The code indicates that the server does not support the HTTP version used in the request.

- **506 Variant Also Negotiates:** The server has an internal configuration error configured to engage in transparent content negotiation. It is therefore not an appropriate endpoint in the negotiation process.

- **507 Insufficient Storage (WebDAV):** This method is not be performed on the resource because the server cannot store the representation needed to complete the request.

- **508 Loop Detected (WebDAV):** The server detected an infinite loop while processing the request.

HTTP HEADERS

These headers pass extra information via the request and response header between the clients and the server. All the headers are case-insensitive. A colon (:) separates headers fields, key-value pairs in clear-text string format. An empty field header denotes the end of the header section. There are rare header fields that can contain the comments. And a few headers can have quality (q) key-value pairs separated by an equal sign.

There are four kinds of headers context-wise:

- **General Header:** This type of header is applied both on Request and Response headers but without affecting the database body.

- **Request Header:** This type of header contains information about the fetched request by the client.

- **Response Header:** This type of header contains the location of the source that the client has requested.

- **Entity Header:** This type of header contains the information about the body of the resources such as MIME type, Content-length, and so on.

Headers can be categorized according to how proxies handle them:

- Connection

- Keep-Alive

- Transfer-Encoding

- Proxy-Authenticate

- Proxy-Authorization

- Authentication

There are some General Headers in HTTP.

Cache-Control

This General-header field specifies directives that all the caching systems MUST obey. The syntax is Cache-Control: cache-request-directive|cache-response-directive. It specifies the cache parameters or requests certain kinds of documents from the cache.

Cache Request Directive	Description
no-cache	It means that a cache must not use the response to satisfy a following request without any successful revalidation with the origin server.
no-store	It means that a cache should not store anything related to the client request or server response.
max-age = seconds	It indicates that the client is willing to accept a response whose age is not greater than the specified time in seconds.
max-stale [= seconds]	It indicates that the client is ready to accept a response that has exceeded its expiration time and the time is given in seconds, which means that it must not be expired by more than that time.
min-fresh = seconds	It indicates that the client is willing to accept a response whose freshness lifetime is no less than its current age plus the specified time in seconds.

(Continued)

Cache Request Directive	Description
no-transform	It does not convert the entity-body.
only-if-cached	It does not retrieve any new data, and the cache can be sent a document only if it is in the cache, and should not contact the origin server to see if a newer copy exists.
Public	It indicates that any cache may cache the response.
private	It indicates that all or part of the response message is intended for a single user and must not be cached by a shared cache.
proxy-revalidate	The proxy-revalidate directive has the similar meaning as the must-validate directive, except it does not apply to private user agent caches.
must-revalidate	It means that must-revalidate (directive) is used to tell a cache that it must first revalidate an asset with the origin after it becomes stale and the cache must verify the status of the stale documents before using it and expired ones should not be used.
s-maxage = seconds	The maximum age defined by this directive overrides the maximum age specified by either the maximum age directive or by the Expires header and the s-maxage directive is always ignored by a private cache.

GENERAL HEADERS

Connection

The connection field allows the sender to specify options for that connection and must not be communicated by proxies over further connections. The following is the simple syntax for using connection header:

```
Connection : "Connection"
```

It defines the "close" connection option for the sender to signal that the connection will close after completing the response.

Example:

```
Connection: close
```

If the client wishes to use persistent connections, it uses the keep-alive parameter as follows:

```
Connection: keep-alive
```

Date

All HTTP date-time stamps must be represented in Greenwich Mean Time (GMT), without exception.

Pragma

The Pragma field is used to include implementation-specific directives that might apply to any recipient along the request/response chain.

Example:

```
Pragma: no-cache
```

Trailer

The Trailer field value indicates that the given header fields are present in the trailer of a message encoded with transfer-coding. The syntax of the Trailer header field:

```
Trailer: field-name
```

The message header fields listed in the Trailer header field do not include the following header fields:

- Transfer-Encoding

- Content-Length

- Trailer

Transfer-Encoding

The Transfer-Encoding field indicates the type of transformation applied to the message body to safely transfer it between the sender and the recipient. All transfer-coding values are case-insensitive.

This is not the same as content-encoding because transfer-encodings are a property of the message, not of the entity-body. The syntax of the Transfer-Encoding header field is as follows:

```
Transfer-Encoding: chunked
```

Upgrade

This general header allows the client to specify what additional communication protocols it supports and uses if the server finds it fit to switch protocol.

Via

The Via general header must be used by gateways and proxies to indicate the intermediate protocols and recipients.

Warning

This general header carries extra information about the status or transformation of a message that is not reflected in the message.

CLIENT REQUEST HEADERS

Accept

This Request-header field specifies certain media types that are acceptable for the response. The general syntax is as follows:

```
Accept: type/subtype [q=qvalue]
```

Accept-Charset

The Accept-Charset Request-header field can indicate what character sets are acceptable for the response. Following is the general syntax:

```
Accept-Charset: character_set [q=qvalue]
```

Accept-Encoding

The Request-header field is the same as Accept but restricts the content-codings acceptable in the response. The general syntax is:

```
Accept-Encoding: encoding types
```

Accept-Language

The Request-header field is the same as About restricts the natural languages preferred to respond to the request. The general syntax is:

```
Accept-Language: language [q=qvalue]
```

Authorization

This Request-header field consists of credentials containing the authentication information of the user agent of the resource being requested. The following syntax is:

```
Authorization: credentials
```

Cookie

This Request-header field contains a name-value pair of information stored for that URL. The following is the syntax:

```
Cookie: name=value
```

Expect

This field indicates that the client requires a particular set of server behaviors. The general syntax is:

```
Expect : 100-continue | expectation-extension
```

From

This field contains an email address for the user who controls the requesting user agent. The following is a simple example:

```
From: web_master@w3.org
```

Host

This field specifies the Internet host and the port number of the requested resource. The general syntax is:

```
Host : "Host" ":" host [ ":" port ] ;
```

Proxy-Authorization

This Request-header field allows the client to identify itself to a proxy that requires authentication. Here is the syntax:

```
Proxy-Authorization: credentials
```

The field value consists of credentials containing the user's authentication information for the proxy and the realm of the resource requested.

Range

The Range field specifies the partial range of the content requested from the document. The general syntax is:

```
Range: bytes-unit=first-byte-pos "-" [last-byte-pos]
```

SERVER RESPONSE HEADERS

Accept-Ranges

The Accept-Ranges field allows the server to indicate its acceptance of range requests for a resource. The syntax is:

```
Accept-Ranges: range-unit | none
```

Location

The Location field redirects the recipient to a location other than the Request-URI for completion. The syntax is:

```
Location : absoluteURI
```

Proxy-Authenticate

The Proxy-Authenticate field must be included as a part of a 407 response. The syntax is:

```
Proxy-Authenticate: challenge
```

HTTP

HTTPS (HyperText transfer protocol secure) is the secure version of HTTP, the primary protocol used to send data between a web browser and a website. HTTPS is encrypted to increase the security of data transfer. And this is especially important when users transmit sensitive data by logging into a bank account, email service, or health insurance provider.

How Does HTTPS Work?

It uses an encryption protocol to encrypt communications. The protocol is called Transport Layer Security (in short, TLS), although formerly known as Secure Sockets Layer (in short, SSL). This is used as the protocol to secure the communications by using what is known as an asymmetric public key infrastructure, and this type of security system uses two separate keys to encrypt communications between two parties.

The owner of a particular website controls the private key, and it's kept, as the reader may have speculated, private, and this key lives on a web server and is used to decrypt information encrypted by the public key.

The public key is available to everyone who wants to interact with the server securely. The private key can only decrypt information encrypted by the public key.

What Does HTTPS Do?

The HTTPS connection ensures three things:

- Confidentiality

- Authenticity

- Integrity

What Information Does HTTPS Protect?

It encrypts all information sent between a client and a web service. Suppose an unencrypted HTTP request reveals not just the body of the request, but the full URL, query-string, and various HTTP headers about the client and request.

CHAPTER SUMMARY

In this chapter, we have covered the basics of HTTP, Web, Web servers, HTTP structure, Static and Dynamic web pages, HTTP URL, General Headers, Client Request Headers, HTTPS and how it works, as well as an HTTP vs. HTTPS comparison.

CHAPTER 7

Data Persistence

IN THIS CHAPTER

➢ File system functions

➢ Database

➢ GUI clients

➢ MySQL connection using PHP script

In the previous chapter, we have covered the basics of HTTP, its structure, Static and Dynamic web pages, HTTPS with its workings, etc.

WEB SERVER

The web server can access only files located under the root folder/directory. On the other hand, PHP can access a file from any file system. If the file permissions are set correctly, include_path is also set correctly.

In the file-manipulation process, following tasks can be included:

- We can open files for reading and writing
- We can close the file
- We can perform operations on file
- We can write results

With PHP, we can handle files easily. There are various inbuilt functions available for file handling in PHP. We can perform open, create, upload, and edit files using file handling. In PHP, we must open the file first using the fopen() function before working with the file. The fopen() function is used in the following manner to perform the various task:

Example:

```
<?PHP
 $fp=fopen(<the filename to be opened with path
 location>, <the mode in which file is to be opened>);
 ?>
```

We have used two parameters in the given code while using the fopen() function: Filename to be opened. The mode in which the file is used is to be opened.

This function will return a file pointer if the file is successfully opened. Otherwise, it will return false or zero.

Various modes are used in file handling in PHP:

Mode	Description
r	Read-only mode, the file pointer sets at the starting position of the file.
r+	Read and write mode, the file pointer sets at the starting of the file.
w	Write mode only, and if the file exists, it will open. Otherwise a new file will be created. If the file already exists, earlier contents will be overwritten.
w+	Write and read mode, and if the file exists, contents will be overwritten; otherwise, a new file will be created.
a	Append file, and if file exists, it will open and file pointer will set at the end of the file. If it doesn't exist, a new file will be created.
a+	Read and append mode, and if the file exists, the pointer will set at the end of the file. Otherwise, a new file will be created.
X	It is used to create and open a file only for writing purposes. If the file exists, this mode returns false and will display an error, and if file does not exists, it will simply create a file.
x+	Read/Write. Creates a new file. Returns FALSE and an error if the file already exists.

There are four types of file connections that can be made in PHP:

- HTTP
- FTP
- Standard I/O
- Filesystem

File Read

For the reading purpose of a file, in the PHP, fread() function can be used and it takes a file pointer and a file size in bytes as parameters. If the file size is not apparent, we can use the filesize() function as a parameter, like:

```php
<?php
$fstring= fread($fd, filesize($filename));
?>
```

File Write

In PHP, the file writing method can be done with the fwrite() function, which takes a file pointer and a string with an optional length in bytes. The way to write the fwrite() function is:

```php
<?php
        $fout=fwrite($fp,$fstring);
if($fout!=strlen($fstring))
{
{
     echo "file write failed!";
}
```

File Close

In PHP, the file closing method can be done using fclose(). The syntax of file close is: fclose($fd).

Example:

```php
<?php
$file = fopen("test.txt", "r");
fclose($file);
?>
```

fclose() function doesn't require assignment in any variable.

```
     echo "file write failed!";
}
?>
```

feof() Function

In PHP, to check the "end-of-file" (EOF) we can use the fclose() function. The syntax of feof() is: feof($filename).

Example:

```php
<?php
$filename= fopen("test.txt", "r");

//Output lines until EOF is reached
while(! feof($filename)) {
 $line = fgets($filename);
   echo $line. "<br>";
}
fclose($filename);
?>
```

fflush() Function

The function fflush() can write all buffered output to an open file. The syntax of fflush() is: flush($filename).

Example:

```php
<?php
$filename = fopen("test.txt","r+");
rewind($filename );
fwrite($filename,  'Hello PHP');
fflush($filename );
fclose($filename );
?>
```

PHP fgetc() Function

The fgetc() function produces a single character from an open file. The working of this function is slow and should not be used for large files. If you would like to read a single character at a single time from a big file, you can use fgets() to read data one line at a time and then process the line a single character at a time using fgetc(). The syntax of fgetc() is: fclose($filename).

Example:

```php
<?php
$filename = fopen("test.txt","r");
echo fgetc($filename );
fclose($filename );
?>
```

fgets() Function

The fgets() function returns a line from an open file. The syntax of the gets() is: fgets(file, length).

Example:

```php
<?php
$filename = fopen("test.txt","r");
echo fgets($filename );
fclose($filename );
?>
```

fgetcsv() Function

The function fgetcsv() parses a line from an open file, checking for CSV fields. The syntax of fgetcsv() is: fgetcsv($filename).

Example: It reads and outputs one line from the open CSV file:

```php
<?php
$filename= fopen("contacts.csv","r");
print_r(fgetcsv($file$filename));
fclose($filename);
?>
```

fgetss() Function

The function gets() returns a line from an open file – stripped from HTML and PHP tags. But this function is deprecated from PHP 7.3. The syntax of the fgetss() is: fgetss(file, length, tags).

Example:

```php
<?php
$filename = fopen("test.htm","r");
echo fgetss($filename );
fclose($filename );
?>
```

fgetss() Function

The function file() reads a file into an array form. The syntax of the file() is: file(filename, flag, context).

Every array element contains a line from the file, with the newline character still attached.

Example:
```
<?php
print_r(file("test.txt"));
?>
```

The flag is optional. It can be one or more of the following constants:

- **FILE_USE_INCLUDE_PATH:** It searches for the file in the include_ path (in php.ini)

- **FILE_IGNORE_NEW_LINES:** It skips the newline at the end of each array element

- **FILE_SKIP_EMPTY_LINES:** It skip empty lines in the file

file_exists() Function
The function file_exists() used to check whether a file or directory exists or not. The syntax of file_exists() is: file_exists(path).

Example:
```
<?php
echo file_exists("test.txt");
?>
```

file_exists() Function
The function file_get_contents() can read a file into a string, and this function is the preferred way to read the contents of a file into a string. If the server supports this, it will use memory mapping techniques to enhance performance. The syntax of file_get_contents() is: file_get_contents(path, include_path, context, start, max_length).

The parameter values:

- **path:** It is a required parameter that specifies the way to the file to read.

- **include_path:** It is an optional parameter, and it sets this parameter to '1' if you want to search for the file in the include_path as well.

- **context:** It is an optional parameter that specifies the context of the filehandle. The context is a collection of options that can modify the behavior of a stream. It can be skipped by using NULL.

- **start:** It is an optional parameter that specifies the file to start reading. Negative values count from the end of the file.

- **max_length:** It is an optional parameter that specifies the maximum length of data read. Default is read to EOF.

file_put_contents() Function

The function file_put_contents() writes data to a file.
This follows these rules when accessing a file:

- If FILE_USE_INCLUDE_PATH is set, check the include path for a copy of the filename.

- file_put_contents() help users to create the file if it does not exist.

- It opens the file.

- It locks the file if LOCK_EX is set.

- If FILE_APPEND is set, move to the end of the file. Otherwise, clear the file content.

- It writes the data into the file.

- file_put_contents() closes the file and releases any locks.

Note: Always use FILE_APPEND to avoid deleting the existing content of the file.

The syntax of the following function is: file_put_contents(filename, data, mode, context).

Example:

```php
<?PHP
echo file_put_contents("test.txt","Hello PHP.
Testing!");
?>
```

fileatime() Function

The fileatime() returns the last access time of the specified file. The result of this function is cached. To clear the cache, use the clearstatcache() function.

Note: The time of a file change each time the file's data is read. This can decrease the performance of an application that accesses a large number of files or directories. Some Unix systems have access time updates disabled to increase performance. In this case, this function is useless.

The syntax of the following fileatime() is: ileatime(filename).

Example:

```php
<?php
echo fileatime("text.txt");
echo "<br>";
echo "Previous access: ".date("F d Y H:i:s.",
fileatime("text.txt"));
?>
```

filectime() Function

The filectime() returns the last time a file was changed. This function checks for inode changes as well as regular changes. Inode changes is when permissions, owner, group, or other metadata is changed and use the filemtime() function to return the last time the file content was changed.

The result is cached. To clear the cache, use the clearstatcache() function. The syntax of the filectime() is: filectime(filename).

Example:

```php
<?php
echo fileatime("text.txt");
echo "<br>";
echo "Last change: ".date("F d Y H:i:s.",
filectime("text.txt"));
?>
```

filegroup() Function

The filegroup() function returns the group ID of a file and uses the posix_getgrgid() function to convert the group ID to a group name.

The result is cached and uses clearstatcache() to clear the cache. The syntax of the filegroup() is: filegroup(filename).

Example:
```
<?php
echo filegroup("test.txt");
?>
```

filesize() Function

The filesize() function returns the size of a file. The result is cached. To clear the cache, use the clearstatcache() function. The syntax of the filesize() is: filesize(filename).

Example:
```
<?php
echo filesize("test.txt");
?>
```

The filetype() function returns the file type of a file.
The possible return values are given below:

- fifo
- char
- dir
- block
- link
- file
- socket
- unknown

Example:
```
<?PHP
echo filetype("test.txt");
?>
```

The result is cached. To clear the cache, use the clearstatcache() function.

fileinode() Function

The function fileinode() returns the inode of the specified file. The syntax of the fileinode() is: fileinode($filename).

Example:

```
<?php
echo fileinode ("test.txt");
?>
```

filemtime() Function

The function filemtime() returns the last time the file content was modified. The syntax of the following function is: filemtime(filename).

Example:

```
<?php
echo filemtime ("text.txt");
echo "<br>";
echo "Last content changed: ".date ("F d Y H:i:s.",
filemtime ("text.txt"));
?>
```

fileowner() Function

The file owner() returns the user ID of the specified file and uses the posix_getpwuid() to convert the user ID to a username. The syntax of the following function is: fileowner(filename).

Example:

```
<?php
echo fileowner ("test.txt");
?>
```

fileperms() Function

The fileperms() function returns the permissions for a file. The syntax of the following function is: fileperms(filename).

Example:

```
<?php
echo fileperms ("test.txt");
?>
```

fpassthru() Function

The fpassthru() reads from the current position in a file until EOF, then writes the result to the output buffer and uses fpassthru() on a binary file on Windows. Remember to open the file in binary mode. Invoke rewind() to fix the pointer to the beginning of the file.

Dump the contents of a file to the output buffer, use the readfile() function instead. The syntax of the fpassthru() is: fpassthru(file).

```php
<?php
$filename = fopen("test.txt", "r"); //file name is
text.txt and mode is read.
// It reads first line
fgets($filename);
// It read from the current position - until EOF, and
then write the result to the output buffer
echo fpassthru($filename);
fclose($filename);
?>
```

fputcsv() Function

The fputcsv() formats a line as a CSV file and writes it to an open file. The syntax of the following function is: fputcsv(file, fields, separator, enclosure, escape).

There are the following parameters of this function:

- **file:** It is required filed, and it specifies the open file to write to.

- **fields:** It is required filed and specifies which array to get the data from.

- **separator:** This field is optional that specifies the field separator. Default is comma (,).

- **enclosure:** This field is optional that specifies the field enclosure character default is ".

- **escape:** This field is optional that specifies the escape character, and the default is "\\." It can also be an empty string ("") which disables the escape mechanism.

mkdir() Function

The mkdir() function makes a directory specified by a pathname. The syntax of the following function is: mkdir(path, mode, recursive, context).

Example:

```php
<?php
mkdir("test");
?>
```

move_uploaded_file() Function

The function move_uploaded_file() moves an uploaded file to a new destination and it works on files uploaded through the PHP HTTP POST upload mechanism. The syntax of the following function is: move_uploaded_file(file, dest).

When the destination file already exists, it will be overwritten.

```php
<?php
    if (move_uploaded_file($_FILES['file_name']['tmp_name'], "/documents/new/location")) {
        print "successfully uploading !";
    } else {
        print "failed uploading !";
    }
?>
```

popen() Function

The popen() opens a pipe and can be used with fgets(), fgetss(), and fwrite(). The file pointer initiated by the popen() function must be closed with pclose(). The syntax of the following function is: popen(command, mode).

The following parameters are:

- **command:** It sets the command to be executed.

- **mode:** It sets the mode such as "r", "w", etc.

popen() Function

This function closes an opened pipe by popen() and returns the termination status of the process. In case of any errors, it will return -1 as result. The syntax of the pclose() is: pclose(file_pointer).

```php
<?php
    // opening a pipe
    $file_pointer = popen("/file_path", "r");
```

```
//some code to be executed
   pclose($file_pointer);
?>
```

readfile() Function

The readfile() reads a file and writes it to the output buffer. The syntax of the following function is: readfile(file_path, include_path, context).
The following parameters are:

- **file_path:** It represents the path of the file.

- **include_path:** It sets this parameter to TRUE if you want to search for the file in the include_path.

- **context:** It specifies the behavior of the stream, and it returns the number of bytes read from the file.

Example:

```
<?php
   echo readfile("one.txt");
?>
```

readlink() Function

The readlink() returns the target of a symbolic link, and this function can return the target of a link on success or false on failure. The syntax of the following function is: string readlink (string $path).
The function does the same as the readlink() function in C.

Example:

```
<?PHP
   echo readlink("/Php/code");
?>
```

realpath() Function

The realpath() function returns the absolute pathname. This function removes all symbolic links using '/./', '/../' and extra '/' and it returns the absolute pathname. This function can return false on failure. The syntax of the following function is: string realpath (string $path).
It can expand all symbolic links and resolve references to /./, /../, and extra / characters in an input path and return an absolute pathname.

Example:

```php
<?php
    echo $pathname = realpath("C:/Php_Project/
index_file.php");
?>
```

clearstatcache() Function

When you operate some filesystem functions, such as fileatime(), file-group(), or any of the other parts listed above in the functions list, PHP caches the information to provide a faster performance to return some values. However, if you want to clear the cached data in specific cases. For example, if the same file is checked several times within a script, that file is in danger. You can clear the status cache. In those cases, you can use the clearstatcache() function to clear caches regarding a file.

The syntax of the following function is: clearstatcache (bool $clear_real-path_cache = false, string $filename = "")

The following parameters are:

- **clear_realpath_cache:** It is used to clear the realpath cache or not.

- **filename:** It clears the real path and stats cache for a specific filename only; only used if clear_realpath_cache is true.

The cached created by the following function are listed such as filectime(), fileatime(), filemtime(), fileinode(), filegroup(), fileowner(), filesize(), filetype(), and fileperms()stat(), lstat(), file_exists(), is_writable(), is_read-able(), is_executable(), is_file(), is_dir(), is_link().

Also include stat(), lstat(), file_exists(), is_writable(), is_readable(), is_executable(), is_file(), is_dir(), is_link(), filectime(), fileatime(), filem-time(), fileinode(), filegroup(), fileowner(), filesize(), filetype(), and fileperms().

basename() Function

It operates naively on the input string and is unaware of the actual filesys-tem or path components such as "..". It returns the base name of the given path. The syntax of the following function is: basename(string $path, string $suffix = ""): string.

Note: If the path contains an invalid character for the current locale, the behavior basename() will be undefined.

Example:

```php
<?php
echo basename("/file").PHP_EOL;
echo basename(".");
?>
```

The output will be,

```
file
```

.

copy() Function

It is used to make copies of the file source to destination. The syntax of the function is: copy(string $source, string $dest, resource $context = ?). It returns the true on success or false on failure.

The following parameters are:

- **source:** It is the path to the source file.

- **dest:** It is the destination path.

- **context:** A valid context resource created with stream_context_ create().

Note: If the destination file already exists, it will be overwritten.

Example:

```php
<?php
$file = 'text.txt';
$newfile = 'example.txt.';
if (!copy($file, $newfile)) {
    echo "failed to copy $file...\n";
}
?>
```

dirname() Function

The dirname() function returns the path of the parent directory. The syntax of the following function is: dirname(path, levels).

Example:

```php
<?php
echo dirname("c:/php/home.php") . "<br />";
echo dirname("/php/home.php");
?>
```

rename() Function

It is used to rename the file or folder(directory).The syntax of the following function is: rename(string $oldname, string $newname, resource $context = ?).

Attempts to rename old_name to new_name, moving it between directories if necessary. If renaming a file and new_name exists, it will be overwritten. If renaming a directory and new_name exists, this function will emit a warning.

The following parameters are:

- **oldname:** The old name of the file.

    If the wrapper used in old_name, it should match the wrapper used in new_name.

- **newname:** The new name of the file.

Note: On Windows, if new_name already exists, it must be writable. Otherwise rename() fails and creates E_WARNING.

- **context:** A context stream resource.

is_writable() Function

It tells whether the filename is writable or not. The syntax of the following function is: is_writable(string $filename): bool.

Explanation: It returns true if the filename exists and is writable. The filename argument is a directory name to check if a directory is writable or not. Remember that PHP may be accessing the file as the user ID that the web server runs. It is true if the filename exists and is writable otherwise false.

```php
<?php
$filename = 'text.txt';
if (is_writable($filename)) {
    echo 'The file is writable';
} else {
    echo 'The file is not writable';
}
?>
```

is_dir() Function

It is an inbuilt function which is used to tell whether the filename is a directory. The syntax of the following function is: is_dir(string $filename): bool.

Explanation: It tells whether the given filename is a directory.

The following parameters are:

- **filename:** It is the path to the file. If the filename is relative, it will be checked relative to the current working directory. If the filename is a symbolic or hard link, the link will be resolved and checked. If you have enabled open_basedir, further restrictions may apply.

It returns true if the filename exists and is a directory, false otherwise.

Example:
```php
<?php
var_dump(is_dir('file.txt'));
var_dump(is_dir('dir/abc'));
var_dump(is_dir('..')); //one dir up
?>
```

is_executable Function

It is used to tell whether the filename is executable. The syntax of the following function is: is_executable(string $filename): bool.

The following parameters are:

- **filename:** It gives the path to the file.

- **Return Values:** Its return is true when filename exists and is executable, otherwise false on error.

Example:
```php
<?php
$file = '/php/executable.sh';
if (is_executable($file)) {
    echo $file.' is executable';
} else {
    echo $file.' is not executable';
}
?>
```

is_file() Function

It is used to tell whether the filename is a regular file. The syntax of the following function is: is_file(string $filename): bool.

The following parameters are:

- **filename:** It is the path to the file.

- **Return Values:** Its return value is true when the filename exists and is a regular file, false otherwise.

- **Errors/Exceptions:** When failure occurs, an E_WARNING is emitted.

Example:

```php
<?php
var_dump(is_file('a_file.txt')) . "\n";
var_dump(is_file('/usr/bin/')) . "\n";
?>
```

is_link() Function

It is used to tell whether the filename is a symbolic link. The syntax of the following function is: is_link(string $filename): bool.

The following parameters are:

- **filename:** It is the path to the file.

- **Return Values:** Its return value is true when the filename exists and is a regular file, false otherwise.

- **Errors/Exceptions:** When failure occurs, an E_WARNING is emitted.

Example:

```php
<?php
$link = 'upds';
if (is_link($link)) {
    echo(readlink($link));
} else {
    symlink('upds.php', $link);
}
?>
```

is_readable() Function

It tells whether a file exists and is readable. The syntax of the following function is: is_readable(string $filename): bool.

The following parameters are:

- **filename:** It is the path to the file.

- **Return Values:** Its return value is true when the filename exists and is a regular file, false otherwise.

- **Errors/Exceptions:** When failure occurs, an E_WARNING is emitted.

Example:

```php
<?php
$filename = 'text.txt';
if (is_readable($filename)) {
    echo 'The file is readable';
} else {
    echo 'The file is not readable';
}
?>
```

is_uploaded_file() Function

It tells whether the file was uploaded via HTTP POST. The syntax of the following function is: is_uploaded_file(string $filename): bool.

It returns true if the file named by filename was uploaded via HTTP POST, and it ensures that a malicious user does not try to trick the script into working upon files that should not be working.

It is essential if there is any chance that anything done with uploaded files could reveal their contents to the user or even to other users on the same system.

For proper working, the function is_uploaded_file() needs an argument like $_FILES['userfile']['tmp_name'], – the name of the uploaded file on the client's machine $_FILES['userfile']['name'] does not work.

The following parameters are:

- **filename:** It is the path to the file.

- **Return Values:** Its return value is true when the filename exists and is a regular file, false otherwise.

Example:

```php
<?php
if (is_uploaded_file($_FILES['file_name']['tmp_
name'])) {
```

```php
    echo "File ". $_FILES['file_name']['name'] ."
uploaded successfully.\n";
    echo "Displaying contents\n";
    readfile($_FILES['file_name']['tmp_name']);
} else {
    echo "Possible file upload attack: ";
    echo "filename '". $_FILES['file_name']['tmp_
name'] . "'.";
}
?>
```

is_writable() Function

It tells whether the filename is writable. The syntax of the following function is: is_writable(string $filename): bool.

It returns true if the filename exists and is writable, and the filename argument may be a directory name allowing you to check if a directory is writable.

The following parameters are:

- **filename:** It tells the path to the file.

- **Return Values:** Its return value is true if the filename exists and is writable. It is false otherwise.

- **Errors/Exceptions:** When failure occurs, an E_WARNING is emitted.

Example:

```php
<?php
$file_name = 'tect.txt';
if (is_writable($file_name)) {
    echo 'The file is writable';
} else {
    echo 'The file is not writable';
}
?>
```

chgrp( ) Function

The function in PHP is an inbuilt function used to change the user group of the specified file and returns true on success and false on failure. Only the superuser has the right to arbitrarily change the group of a file. The syntax of the following function is: bool chgrp ($filename, $group).

This function accepts two parameters: filename and user.

- **$filename:** It specifies the file's user group you want to change.

- **$group:** It specifies the new user group. It can be a group name or a number.

Errors and Exceptions: The function doesn't work for remote files but only on files accessible by the server's filesystem.

Example:

```
<?PHP
// changes the file group to administrator
chgrp("text.txt", "administrator")
?>
```

chmod( ) Function

The function in PHP is an inbuilt function used to change the mode of a specified file to a specific way given by the user.

The function changes the permissions of the specified file and returns true on success and false on failure. The syntax of the following function is: bool chmod (string $filename, int $mode).

This function accepts two parameters: filename and user.

- **$filename:** It specifies the file whose permissions need to be changed.

- **$mode:** It is used to identify the new permissions.

The $mode parameters consist of four numeric values. The first value is always zero. The second value specifies permissions for the owner, the third value specifies permissions for the owner's user group, and the fourth value specifies permissions for everybody else.

There are three possible values, and to set multiple permissions, the following values can be added.

1 to execute permissions, 2 for write permissions, and 4 for read permissions

- **Return Value:** It returns true on successful code execution and otherwise false on failure.

Errors and Exceptions: The function doesn't work for remote files. It only works on files that are accessible by the server's filesystem.

Example:

```php
<?PHP
// Read and write permission to owner
chmod("txt.txt", 0600);
?>
```

chown( ) Function

The function in PHP is an inbuilt function that is used to change the owner of the specified file, and it returns true on success and false on failure and only the superuser has the right to change the owner of a file.

The syntax of the following function is: bool bool chown ($filename, $user).

The following parameters: This function accepts two parameters: filename and user.

- **$filename:** It specifies the file whose owner you want to change.
- **$mode:** It specifies the new owner. It can be a username or a user ID.
- **Return Value:** It returns true on successful code execution and otherwise false on failure.

Errors and Exceptions: The function doesn't work for remote files. It only works on files that are accessible by the server's filesystem.

Example:

```php
<?php
// Sets root as owner of the file "file.php"
$path = "/usr/Desktop/PHP/file.php";
$user_name = "root";
chown($path, $user_name);
?>
```

DATABASES

It is an essential part of our coding section. We can encounter several activities involving our interaction with databases such as in the school, in the railway station, in any store, etc. These are the examples where we need to store a large amount of data in one place and fetch these data efficiently.

A database is a group of organized data, also known as structured data. It can access or store in a system. It can manage through a Database Management System (DBMS), software used to collect data. It is related data in a structured form.

The data is organized into tables consisting of rows and columns and indexed, so that data can be updated, expanded, and deleted quickly. Different databases range from the most general approach, the relational database, to a distributed database, cloud database, and NoSQL databases.

- **Relational Database:** A relational database comprises a group of tables with data.

- **Distributed Database:** It is a database in which portions are stored in multiple physical locations.

- **Cloud Database:** It is a database that typically runs on a cloud computing platform. Database service provides access to the database. Database services make the underlying software stack transparent to the user.

GUI CLIENTS

MySQL GUI Clients and Tools

It makes it easy to manage MySQL databases without manually typing SQL commands. These GUI tools allow you to design, manage, and administer MySQL databases using a graphical interface. Here is a list of the GUI tools for database developers and administrators.

Here are the five best MySQL GUI tools for Windows, Linux, and Mac. MySQL GUI tools are,

MySQL Workbench

It is a popular MySQL GUI tool available for Windows, Linux, and Mac.

It is designed for database designers and architects, developers, and administrators. MySQL Workbench is available in three versions: Community, Standard, and Enterprise.

While the Community Edition is the free version, the Standard and Enterprise Editions are commercial versions.

Its workbench allows you to monitor MySQL server health via dashboards. It even allows you to design database schema and run SQL queries graphically.

It allows you to import or export data to/from your databases.

dbForge Studio

One of the best MySQL GUI clients allows you to create, develop, and manage databases easily. You can create and execute SQL queries, build and debug stored procedures and routines. You can even automate database management and analyze data.

It enables you to easily convert one or more SQL queries into portable scripts. It also provides a rich-formatting code interface to write and debug SQL queries quickly.

PHPMyAdmin

It is the most popular web-based MySQL Administration tool. It is straightforward to install and use and is completely free.

It lacks advanced features available in other MySQL GUI tools, and it is more than enough for small-medium databases.

PHPMyAdmin is web-based. It can access from any system. Moreover, it is available in 80+ languages.

HeidiSQL

It is a simple, easy-to-use GUI client for databases. A free GUI makes it easy to create, edit, and manage database tables.

It allows you to manage users, automate tasks, and connect to your database via SSH tunneling and support batch insertion of ASCII and binary files into database tables.

It is available for Windows and Linux and is a portable version that does not require any installation.

Toad Edge

It is a database management tool that provides tons of database development and administration features.

It supports schema comparison, database synchronization, import and export, SQL query monitor, and even JSON editor.

Its feature of session monitoring allows the administrators to monitor and terminate sessions or even cancel the queries. It is available for Windows and macOS.

MySQL

It is a popular relational DBMS. Before explaining the introduction to MySql, we will see the basic concepts related to the database.

It is (database) used to store the data; that is, the database is an application that keeps the collection of related data. The other source of storing the data can be flat files, but the problem is to store, manage, and access the data not fast, and it is difficult; therefore, the excellent option is to use the DBMS. There are various DBMSs, and each uses other APIs to store and manage the data.

Types of Database Management Systems

Other types of DBMSs based on the data models are as follows,

- Relational Database Management Systems

- Hierarchical Database Management Systems

- Network Database Management Systems

- Object-oriented Database Management Systems

A Relational Database Management System (RDBMS) is software that –

- It enables you to implement a database with tables, columns, and indexes.

- It guarantees the integrity between rows of various tables.

- It updates the indexes automatically.

- It interprets an SQL query and combines information from various tables.

RDBMS Terminology

Before we explain the MySQL database system, let us revise a few definitions related to the database.

- **Database:** A database is a collection of tables with related data.

- **Table:** It contains data, and it looks like a simple spreadsheet.

- **Column:** A column contains data of the same kind, for example, the column postcode.

- **Row:** A row or tuple is a group of related data such as one subscription.

- Redundancy stores data twice, redundantly, to make the system faster.

- **Primary key:** It is unique, and its value cannot occur twice in one table. With a key, you can only find one row.

- **Foreign key:** A foreign key is a linking pin between two tables.

- **Compound key:** A compound key (composite key) is a key that consists of multiple columns because one column is not sufficiently unique.

- **Index:** An index in a database corresponds to an index at the back of a book.

- **Referential integrity:** It makes that a foreign key value always points to an existing row.

MySQL Database (RDBMS)
- MySQL is a fast, easy-to-use used for small and big businesses. MySQL is developed, marketed, and supported by MySQL AB, a Swedish company. It is becoming so popular because of good reasons.

- It was released under an open-source license.

- MySQL is a powerful program that handles a large subset of the functionality and is friendly to PHP language.

- It uses a standard form of the SQL data language.

- It works on many operating systems and languages, including C, C++, PHP, PERL, JAVA, etc.

- It works quickly and well with large data sets and supports large databases.

- It is customizable. The open-source GPL license allows programmers to modify MySQL.

MySQL CONNECTION USING PHP SCRIPT

PHP provides function named mysqli contruct or mysqli_connect() to make a database connection. It has six parameters and returns a MySQL link identifier on success or FALSE on failure.

Syntax:

```
$mysqli = new mysqli($host_name, $user_name,
$password, $database_name, $port, $socket);
```

- **$host:** The hostname running the database server, e.g., localhost. If it is not given, then the default value will be localhost:3306.

- **$user_name:** It is optional. The username accesses the database. If it is not specified, the default will be the user's name that owns the server process.

- **$password:** It is optional. The password is used to secure access to the database. If not specified, then the default will be an empty password.

- **$databas_name:** It is the database name on which query is performed.

- **$port:** It defines the port number to connect to the MySQL server.

- **$socket:** It is a socket or named pipe that should be used, and it is optional.

You can disconnect from the database anytime using PHP function close().

Syntax:

```
$mysqli->close();
```

Example: Try the following example to connect to a MySQL server –

Copy and paste the following example as mysql_connection.php –

```
<html>
   <head>
      <title>Connecting MySQL Server</title>
   </head>
```

```
<body>
    <?php
        $dbhost = 'localhost';
        $dbuser = 'admin';
        $dbpass = 'root';
        $mysqli = new mysqli($dbhost, $dbuser,
$dbpass);

        if($mysqli->connect_errno ) {
            printf("Connect failed: %s<br />",
$mysqli->connect_error);
            exit();
        }
        printf('Connected successfully.<br />');
        $mysqli->close();
    ?>
</body>
</html>
```

CREATE A DATABASE USING PHP SCRIPT

The function MySQL query() or mysql_query() to create or delete a MySQL database and this function takes two parameters and returns TRUE on success or FALSE on failure.

Syntax:

```
$mysqli->query($sql,$result_mode)
```

- **$sql:** It is required to file for SQL query to create a MySQL database.

- **$result_mode:** It is either the constant MYSQLI_USE_RESULT or MYSQLI_STORE_RESULT, depending on the desired behavior. By default, MYSQLI_STORE_RESULT is used.

The following example of creating a database in MySQL PHP

```
<html>
    <head><title>Creating MySQL Database</title></head>
    <body>
        <?php
            $dbhost = 'localhost';
            $dbuser = 'admin';
```

```
        $dbpass = 'root';
        $mysqli = new mysqli($dbhost, $dbuser, $dbpass);

        if($mysqli->connect_errno ) {
            printf("Connect failed: %s<br />",
$mysqli->connect_error);
            exit();
        }
        printf('Connected successfully.<br />');

        if ($mysqli->query("CREATE DATABASE
TUTORIALS")) {
            printf("Database TUTORIALS created
successfully.<br />");
        }
        if ($mysqli->errno) {
            printf("Could not create database:
%s<br />", $mysqli->error);
        }
        $mysqli->close();
    ?>
  </body>
</html>
```

To create an in MySQL, the table creation command requires the following details –

- Name of the table

- Name of the fields

- Definitions for each field

Here is SQL syntax to create a MySQL table:

The SQL query is CREATE TABLE table_name (column_name column_type).

It will create the following table in the database.

The example of SQL query given below,

```
create table Student(
   student_id INT NOT NULL AUTO_INCREMENT,
    student_name VARCHAR(100) NOT NULL,
    PRIMARY KEY ( student_id )
);
```

Here, a few terms need explanation –

The attribute NOT NULL is used because we do not want this field to be NULL (empty). So, when a user tries to create a record with a NULL value, it will raise an error.

The attribute AUTO_INCREMENT means MySQL to go ahead and add the following available number to the particular field.

The PRIMARY KEY is used to define a column as a primary key. You can use numerous columns separated by a comma to determine a primary key.

MySQL INSERT

It is a process of inserting information into a MySQL table. So, you first create the table using create table query. It must have column(s) of the same type as the content you would like to add to the database.

Here is the MySQL Insert query syntax, INSERT INTO table_name (col_1, col_2) VALUES('data_1', 'data_2').

An example of how to INSERT data in a MySQL table:

```
INSERT INTO phonebook(phone, first_name, last_name,
address) VALUES('+1 123 456 7890', 'John', 'Swift','
USA')
<?php
// Connects to your Database
mysql_connect("localhost", "db_user", "db_passwd") or
die(mysql_error());
mysql_select_db("db_name") or die(mysql_error());
?>
```

FETCHING DATA

The SQL SELECT query is used to fetch data from the database.

Syntax: Here is the generic SQL syntax of the SELECT command to fetch data from the MySQL table:

```
SELECT field_1, field_2,... field_N
FROM table_1, table_2...
[WHERE Clause]
[OFFSET M ] [LIMIT N]
```

Points to remember:

- You can use more tables separated by comma (,) to include various conditions using a WHERE clause, but the WHERE clause is optional for the SELECT query.

- You can fetch more fields in a single SELECT command.

- You can specify any condition using the WHERE clause.

- You can specify star (*) in place of fields. The SELECT will return all the fields and use OFFSET from where SELECT will start producing records. By default, the offset starts at zero.

- Limit the number of returns using the LIMIT attribute.

UPDATING DATA

You can utilize the SQL UPDATE command to modify any field value of any MySQL table.

Syntax: The following code has a generic SQL syntax of the UPDATE command to modify the data in the MySQL table:

```
UPDATE table_name SET field_1 = new_1, field_2 =
new_2
[WHERE Clause]
```

Points to remember:

- You can update more than one field altogether and specify any condition using the WHERE clause.

- You can update the values in a table at a time.

- The WHERE clause is helpful when you want to select rows in a table.

DELETING DATA

If you like to delete a record from the MySQL table, you can use the SQL command DELETE. The function MySQL query() or mysql_query() to delete records in a MySQL table. This function accepts two parameters and returns TRUE on success or FALSE on failure.

Syntax:

```
$mysqli->query($sql,$resul_tmode)
```

The following code has a generic SQL syntax of the DELETE query to delete data from a MySQL table:

```
DELETE FROM table_name [WHERE Clause]
```

The WHERE clause is handy when deleting selected rows in a table. If it is not specified, then all records will be deleted from the given MySQL table.

What Is SQL Injection in PHP?

SQL injection, also known as SQLI, is a common attack vector that uses malicious SQL code for back-end database manipulation to access information that was not intended to be displayed. The error-based SQLI technique seeks to retrieve information about the structure of the database using error messages returned by the database server. The information includes any number of items, including sensitive company data, user lists, or private customer details. Using this technique, an attacker can retrieve valuable information about the database, such as if a given table exists in the database or not.

The Basis of an SQL Injection Attack

The receiving program processes especially user input to allow the information to exit a data context and enter a command context. This allows the attacker to change the structure of the SQL statement which is executed.

Which Function Can Be Used to Avoid SQL Injection?

```
mysql_real_escape_string
```

This function is to prevent these attacks. mysql_real_escape_string takes a string that will be used in a MySQL query and returns the same string with all SQL injection attempts safely escaped.

PREPARED STATEMENTS AND BOUND PARAMETERS

A prepared statement is a feature used to execute the same SQL statements with high efficiency repeatedly.

Prepared statements work like this:

- **Prepare:** An SQL template is created and sent to the database. Specific values are unspecified, called parameters (labeled "?"). Example: INSERT INTO table_name VALUES(??, ?).

- The database compiles, parses, and performs query optimization on the SQL statement template and stores the result without executing it.

- **Execute:** Later, the application wraps the values to the parameters, and the database executes the statement. The application may run the statement multiple times with other values.

```
// prepare and bind
$stmt = $conn->prepare("INSERT INTO table_name(first_
name, last_name, email) VALUES (?, ?, ?)");
$stmt->bind_param("aaa", $firstname, $lastname,
$email);
```

It ensures that a class has one instance and provides a global point to access it. It ensures that only one object is available across the application in a controlled state. Singleton pattern offers a way to access its only object that can be accessed directly without instantiating the class object.

CHAPTER SUMMARY

In this chapter, we have learned file systems in PHP with their functions, like is_dir(), is_writeable(), is_link(), is_readable() and also some permission functions like chown(), chgrp(), other file system functions like filesize(), fflush(), fgetc(), fgets(), fgetss(), fgetss(), file_exists(), file_exists(), and many more functions.

CHAPTER 8

Error Handling in PHP

IN THIS CHAPTER

➤ Error handling

➤ Methods

➤ PHP error

➤ Exceptional handling

➤ Try, catch, finally block

In the previous chapter, we learned file systems in PHP with their different functions like is_dir() and is_writeable(), some permission functions like chown() and chgrp(), and many more functions.

In this chapter, you will learn about various errors, including error logs, handling and handling functions, and other PHP framework errors. Let's define the difference between "error" and "exception" and other standard terms in PHP.

PHP language is free to use, and many web developers use this programming language to make web applications. The most popular content management systems (CMSs) are based on this programming language. The error handling in PHP is almost the same as error handling in other programming languages. But when a user is new to the language, catching all the mistakes for the very first time can be scary and irritating. Below is an example.

DOI: 10.1201/9781003308669-8

These are some functions that deal with error handling and logging in code. They allow you to define your custom error handling rules and modify how the errors can be logged. This will enable you to change and enhance error reporting as per your needs.

Using the logging functions, you can send messages directly to other machines, email (or email to pager gateway!), system logs, etc., so you can selectively log and monitor the essential parts of your applications and websites.

The error functions allow you to modify the level and kind of error feedback, ranging from simple notices to customized parts returned during errors.

ERROR HANDLING

The concept of error handling is very simple in PHP. An error is like a message with a filename, line number, and a message that describes the error sent to the browser.

When we create scripts and web applications, error handling is critical. If your code lacks error checking, your code may look unprofessional and may be open to security risks.

This chapter contains some of the common error-checking methods in PHP. We will show the following different error handling methods:

- Simple "die()" statements

- Custom errors

- Error triggers

- Error reporting

BASIC ERROR HANDLING

Use of the die() Function

The following example shows a simple script that opens a text file:

```php
<?php
$file=fopen("text.txt","r");
?>
```

If the file does not present, you get an error like this:

```
Warning: fopen(text.txt) [function.fopen]: failed to
open stream:
```

No such file or directory in C:\folder\text.php on line 3

To get rid over this error message like the one above, we test whether the file exists before we try to access it:

Example:

```php
<?php
if(file_exists("text.txt")) {
  $file = fopen("text.txt", "r");
} else {
  die("Error: The file does not exist.");
}
?>
```

When the file does not exist, you will get an error message like this: Error: Does not exist.

This code is much efficient than the previous code because it displays a simple error handling concept to stop the script after the error.

However, stopping the script is not always the right way to go. Let's have a look at various PHP functions for handling errors.

CUSTOM ERROR HANDLER

By creating a custom error handler is simple. We make a particular function called when an error occurs in PHP.

This function must handle a minimum of two parameters (error level and error message). Still, it can accept up to five parameters (optionally: file, line-number, and the error context).

You can create your error handler function to deal with the run-time error generated by the PHP engine. The error handler provides you superb flexibility and finer control over the errors, and it can inspect the error, decide what to do with the error; it displays a message to the user, logs the error in a file or database or sends it by email, attempts to fix the problem and carries on, exits the execution of the script or ignores the error altogether.

The custom error handler function must handle at least two parameters (err_no and err_str). However, it can optionally accept additional three parameters (err_file, err_line, and err_context), as described below:

- **err_no:** It specifies the level of the error as an integer, corresponds to the appropriate error level constant (E_ERROR, E_WARNING, and so on).

- **err_str:** It specifies the error message as a string.

The following parameters are optional:

- **err_file:** It specifies the filename of the script file in which the error occurred, as a string.

- **err_line:** It defines the line number on which the error occurred as a string.

- **err_context:** It specifies an array containing all the variables and their values that existed when the error occurred. Useful for debugging.

UNDERSTANDING ERROR LEVELS

Usually, when a problem stops a script from running accurately, the PHP engine activates an error. Each error is defined by an integer value and an associated constant. The following table lists some of the standard error levels:

Parameter	Description
error_level	It is a required field and specifies the error report level for the user-defined error. It must be a value number. There are various error_level used in the error handler.
error_message	It is the required field and specifies the error message for the user-defined error.
error_file	It is an optional field and specifies the filename in which the error occurred.
error_line	It is an optional field and specifies the line number in which the error occurred.
error_context	It is an optional field and identifies an array containing every variable, and their values, in use when the error occurred.

ERROR REPORT LEVELS

These error report levels are the various types of errors; the user-defined error handler can be used for some purposes. Let's discuss some error handlers of error_level in PHP.

Constant	Description
E_ERROR	It is a fatal run-time error, and the execution of the script is stopped. Its value is 1.
E_WARNING	It is a non-fatal run-time error, and the execution of the script is not stopped. Its value is 2.

(Continued)

Constant	Description
E_NOTICE	It is a run-time notice. The script returns something that might be an error but could also happen when running a script normally. Its value is 8.
E_USER_ERROR	A fatal user-generated error like an E_ERROR, except it, is generated by the PHP script using the function trigger_error(). Its value is 256.
E_USER_WARNING	It is a non-fatal user-generated warning like an E_WARNING, except it is generated by the PHP script using the function trigger_error(). Its value is 512.
E_USER_NOTICE	It is user-generated like an E_NOTICE, except it is generated by the PHP script using the function trigger_error(). Its value is 1024.
E_ALL	All the warnings and errors. Its value is 8191.
E_STRICT	It is not a strict error. Its value is 2048.

SET ERROR HANDLER

The default handler for PHP is the built-in error handler. We will make the function above the default error handler for the duration of the script.

To change the error handler to apply only for some errors that can handle different errors in different ways. Now we are going to use a custom error handler for all errors:

```
set_error_handler("custom error");
```

If we want our custom function to handle all errors, the set_error_handler() only needs a single parameter. A second parameter adds to specify an error level.

Way to Trigger an Error

In a code where users can input data, it is good to trigger errors when an invalid input occurs. In PHP, this is done by the trigger_error() function.

An error can be triggered anywhere in a script. You can specify what error level is triggered by adding a second parameter.

Possible error types are:

- **E_USER_ERROR:** It is a fatal user-generated run-time error that cannot be recovered from. Execution of the script is halted.

- **E_USER_WARNING:** It is a non-fatal user-generated run-time warning and the execution of the script is not halted.

- **E_USER_NOTICE:** It is the default. The user-generated run-time notice. The script found something that might be an error but could also happen when running a script normally.

Example:

```php
<?php
function Division($dnd, $dvsr){
    if($dvsr == 0){
        trigger_error("It cannot be zero",
E_USER_WARNING);
        return false;
    } else{
        return ($dnd/ $dvsr);
    }
}

// Calling the function
echo Division(5, 0);
?>
```

LOGGING ERROR

By default, PHP helps to send an error log to the server's logging system or a file, depending on how the error_log configuration is set in the php. ini file. Using the error_log() function, you can also send error logs to a particular file or a remote destination.

Sending error messages by email can be a good method of getting informed of distinct errors.

Four Different Types of Errors in PHP

Introduction

An error in PHP code only occurs when something is wrong. The error can be as simple as a missing semicolon or as complex as calling an incorrect variable. An error is a mistake in a program that may be caused by writing incorrect syntax or incorrect code. The error message is displayed on your browser containing the filename and location, a message describing the error, and the line number in which the error occurred.

To efficiently fix a PHP issue in a script, you must understand what problem occurs.

The four types of PHP errors are:

- Warning Error

- Notice Error

- Parse Error or Syntax Error

- Fatal Error

1. **Warning Error:** This error does not stop the script from running and warns you that a problem is likely to cause issues in the future. The main reason for warning errors is including a missing file.

   The most common causes of warning errors are: by invoking an external file that does not exist in the directory. Wrong parameters in a function.

   Example:
   ```php
   <?php
     $x = "Warning error";
     include ("other_file.php");
     echo $x . "This is demo text";
   ?>
   ```
   Error: PHP Warning: include(other_file.php): failed to open stream: No such file or directory in/home/other_file.php on line 3.

   There is no "other_file," the output displays a message notifying it failed to include it. Still, it does not stop executing the script.

   The common causes of warning errors are:

   - While calling an external file that does not present in the directory.

   - Defining wrong parameters in a function.

2. **Notice Error:** These are minor errors similar to warning errors, as they also do not stop code execution. The system is often unsure whether it is an actual error or a regular code. Notice errors usually occur if the script requires an undefined variable.

   It means that the code contains something wrong, but it allows the further execution of the script.

Example:

```php
<?php
     /*------------------notice
error------------------*/
  $x = "Notice Error";
  echo $x;
  echo $y;
?>
```

Error: PHP Notice: Undefined variable: y in /php/home.php on line 5. It means that the program contains something wrong, but it allows the execution of the script.

3. **Fatal Error:** This error is the type of error that occurs due to an undefined method or variable. The PHP compiler can easily understand the code and recognize the unclear function. The PHP compiler generates this fatal error when a function is called without providing its definition.

   A fatal error is caused when a function is called without its definition. See the below example containing the fatal error.

   Example of calling undefined function in PHP:

```php
<?php
     /*------------------fatal
error------------------*/
     function addition ($f1, $f2) {
          $sum = $f1 + $f2;
          echo "Addition of two number is:" . $sum;
     }

     $f1 = 23;
     $f2 = 56;

     //call the function that is not defined
     //Generate fatal error
     catch_fatal_error();
     //echo "Fatal Error";
?>
```

There are three types of fatal errors:

- Startup fatal error (it occurs when the system cannot run the code at installation)

- Compile-time fatal error (it occurs when a programmer attempts to use nonexistent data)

- Runtime fatal error (it occurs when the program is running, causing the code to stop performing thoroughly)

4. **Parse Error or Syntax Error:** It is a mistake in the syntax of source code, which programmers can do due to their lack of concern or knowledge. It is also known as Parse error. The compiler is used to catch the syntax error at compile time. The syntax error stops the execution of the code when it occurs.

These errors can only occur for common reasons like unclosed quotes, missing semicolons, extra or missing parentheses, unclosed brackets, and many more. While compiling the program, syntax errors can catch by the compiler. It gives a parse or syntax error message.

Example of missing semicolon:

```
<?php
    /*-----------------syntax
error------------------*/
    echo "A syntax error is a mistake in the
syntax of source code.</br>";
    echo "Compiler is used to catch the syntax
error at compile time"
    echo "These errors can occur due to these
common reasons";
?>
```

Parse errors are caused by:

- Missing unclosed brackets or quotes

- Missing or extra semicolons or parentheses

- Misspellings

PHP ERROR

These functions are used to deal with error handling and logging and allow us to define our own error handling rules and modify how the errors can be logged.

The logging functions allow us to send messages directly to other machines, emails, or system logs.

The error reporting functions allow customizing the level and kind of error feedback are given. The error functions are part of the core PHP, and there is no installation required to use these functions.

Runtime Configuration

The behavior of the functions is affected by settings in php.ini. Errors and logging configuration and their options:

Name	Default	Description
error_reporting	NULL	It sets the error reporting level.
display_errors	"1"	It specifies whether errors should be printed to the screen, or if they should be hidden from the user and never be used on production systems.
display_startup_errors	"0"	When display_errors turns on, errors that occur during PHP's startup sequence are not displayed and strongly recommended to keep display_startup_errors off, except for debugging.
ignore_repeated_errors	"0"	It specifies whether to log repeated error messages and when it sets to "1" it will not log errors with repeated errors from the same file on the same line.
log_errors_max_len	"1024"	It sets the maximum length of log_errors in bytes and its value "0" can be used not to apply any maximum length at all. This length is applied to logged errors, displayed errors, and also to $php_errormsg.
log_errors	"0"	It defines whether script error messages should be logged to the server's error log or error_log and is strongly advised to use error logging instead of error displaying on production web sites.
ignore_repeated_source	"0"	It specifies whether to log repeated error messages and when it sets to "1" it will not log errors with repeated errors from different files or source lines.
report_memleaks	"1"	If set to "1" (by default), this parameter shows a report of memory leaks detected by the Zend memory manager.
track_errors	"0"	If set to "1", the last error message always be present in the variable $php_errormsg.
html_errors	"1"	It turns off HTML tags in error messages.
xmlrpc_errors	"0"	It turns off normal error reporting and formats errors as XML-RPC error message.
xmlrpc_error_number	"0"	It is used as the value of the XML-RPC faultCode element.
error_prepend_string	NULL	It specifies a string to output before an error message

(Continued)

Name	Default	Description
error_append_string	NULL	It specifies a string to output after an error message.
error_log	NULL	It specifies the name of the file where script errors should be logged. The file should be writable by the web server's user. If the special value Syslog is used, the errors are sent to the system logger instead.

PHP ERROR AND LOGGING FUNCTIONS

debug_backtrace() Function

It is used to generate a backtrace. It displays data from the code that led up to the debug_backtrace() function. It returns an array of associative arrays. The possible returned elements are:

The syntax is debug_backtrace(options, limit).

1. function (the type is a string and returns the current function name)

2. line (the type is an integer and returns the current line number)

3. file (the type is a string and returns the current file name)

4. class (the type is a string and returns the current class name)

5. object (the type is a string and returns the current object)

6. type (the type is a string and returns the current call type, it also returns method call, static method call, and function call)

7. args (the type is array and it accepts argument functions)

There are two parameters of this function:

1. **options:** It is an optional field, and it specifies a bitmask for the following options: DEBUG_BACKTRACE_PROVIDE_OBJECT.

2. **limit:** It is an optional field, limiting the number of stack frames printed. By default (limit=0), it prints all stack frames.

debug_print_backtrace() Function

The debug_print_backtrace() function prints a PHP backtrace and displays it data from the code that led up to the debug_print_backtrace() function.

The syntax is debug_print_backtrace(options, limit).

There are two parameters of this function:

1. **options:** It is an optional field and it specifies a bitmask for the following options: DEBUG_BACKTRACE_PROVIDE_OBJECT.

2. **limit:** It is an optional field, limiting the number of stack frames printed. By default (limit=0), it prints all stack frames.

error_get_last() Function

Explaination: This function returns the last error that occurred as an associative array.

The syntax is error_get_last().
The array contains four keys:

1. **[type]:** It describes the error type

2. **[message]:** It describes the error message

3. **[file]:** It describes the file where the error occurred

4. **[line]:** It describes the line where the error occurred

Example:

```php
<?php
echo $test;
print_r(error_get_last());
?>
```

It returns the last error that occurred.

error_log() Function

This function sends an error message to a log, file, or mail account. The syntax is error_log(message, type, destination, headers).

These are the following parameters:

1. **Message:** It is a required field, and it specifies the error message to log.

2. **Type:** It is an optional field, and it specifies where the error message should go, where 0 is the default value. The message is sent to a PHP system logger, using the OS logging mechanism or a file. 1 means it is sent by email to the address in the destination parameter. 3 means

it is no longer used. 4 means the message is sent directly to the SAPI logging handler.

3. **Destination:** It is optional but specifies the destination of the error message, and its value depends on the value of the type parameter.

4. **Header:** It is optional and only used if the type parameter is set to 1 and specifies additional headers, like From, Cc, and Bcc.

Example:

```php
<?php
// This php code for logging error into a given file
    // The error message to be logged
$error_message = "This is an error message!";
    // The path of the log file where errors need to be logged
$log_file = "./my-errors.log";
    // logging error message to given log file
error_log($error_message, 3, $log_file);
 ?>
```

error_reporting() Function

This function specifies which errors are reported. It has many levels of errors and using this function sets that level for the current script. The syntax is error_reporting(level).

There is only one parameter that is,

- **level:** It is an optional field, and it specifies the error-report level for the current script. Error numbers and named constants are accepted. Key to remember that named constants are recommended to ensure compatibility for future PHP versions.

Example:

```php
<?PHP
// Report all errors
error_reporting(E_ALL);

// It is same as error_reporting(E_ALL);
ini_set("error_reporting", E_ALL);
```

```php
    // It reports all errors except E_NOTICE
    error_reporting(E_ALL & ~E_NOTICE);
        // It turns off error reporting
        error_reporting(0);

        // It reports runtime errors like parse.
        error_reporting(E_ERROR | E_WARNING | E_PARSE);
    ?>
```

restore_error_handler() Function

This function can be used to restore the previous error handler and also used to restore the previous error handler after changing it with the sct_error_handler() function.

The syntax is restore_error_handler().

Example:

```php
<?php
    function unserialize_handler($errno, $errstr) {
        echo "Invalid hello value.\n";
    }

    $hello = 'abc';
    set_error_handler('unserialize_handler');

    $original = unserialize($hello);
    restore_error_handler();
?>
```

restore_exception_handler() Function

This function restores the previously defined exception handler function and it is used after changing the exception handler function using set_exception_handler(), to revert to the previous exception handler.

The syntax is restore_exception_handler().

Example:

```php
<?php
//The two user-defined exception handler functions
function myException1($e) {
  echo "[".__FUNCTION__ ."]: ".$e->getMessage();
}
```

```
function myException2($e) {
  echo "[".__FUNCTION__."]: ".$e->getMessage();
}

//It sets myException1 as exception handler
function
set_exception_handler("myException1");
//It sets myException2 as exception handler
function
set_exception_handler("myException2");
//restore the previous exception handler function
//which is myException1
restore_exception_handler();

//It throws an exception
throw new Exception("This triggers the exception
handler");
?>
```

set_error_handler() Function

This function sets a user-defined error function to handle errors in a script.

This function is used to define the method of handling errors during runtime by the user, for instance, in applications in which you need to do cleanup of data/files when a critical error happens or when you need to trigger an error under certain conditions.

The standard PHP error handler is completely avoided for the error types specified by error_levels unless the callback function returns false. If required, the user-defined error handler must end the script using die(), error_reporting() settings will not affect this function be called regardless. However, the user will always be able to read the current value of error_reporting and act appropriately.

The following error types cannot be handled with a user-defined function:

1. E_ERROR

2. E_PARSE

3. E_CORE_ERROR

4. E_CORE_WARNING

5. E_COMPILE_ERROR

6. E_COMPILE_WARNING

If errors are made before the script is executed, the custom error handler cannot be called since it is not registered at that time.

The syntax is set_error_handler(callback, error_levels).

This function has various parameters:

- **callback:** It requires a field that identifies the function with the following signature. Null may be passed instead to reset this handler to its default state. Instead of a function name, an array holding an object reference and a method name can also be used.

  The syntax is handler(errno, errstr, errfile, errline, errcontext).

  The following parameter explanations are:

  i. **err_no:** The first parameter is err_no, which will be passed the error level raised as an integer.

  ii. **err_str:** The second parameter is err_str, which will be passed the error message as a string.

  iii. **err_file:** If the callback accepts a third parameter, err_file, it will be passed the filename that the error was raised in as a string.

  iv. **err_line:** If the callback accepts a fourth parameter, err_line, it will be passed the line number where the error was raised as an integer.

  v. **err_context:** If the callback accepts a fifth parameter, err_context, it will be passed an array that points to the active symbol table when the error occurs. In other words, err_context will contain a variety of every variable that existed in the scope the error was triggered in.

- **error_level:** It is optional but specifies the error_reporting level for the active script and takes on either a bitmask or named constants described in the predefined constants, and using named constants is recommended to ensure compatibility for future versions. By default is "E_ALL."

- It returns the previously defined error handler. If the built-in handler is used, null will return. If the previous error handler were a class method, this function would return an indexed array with the class and the method name.

Example:

```php
<?php
//a user-defined error handler function
function myErrorHandler($err_no, $err_str, $err_
file, $err_line) {
    echo "<b>My ERROR</b> [$err_no]
$err_str<br>\n";
    echo "Error on line $err_line in file
$err_file<br>\n";
    echo "Aborting...<br>\n";
}

//It setting the user-defined error handler
function
set_error_handler("ErrorHandler");

$test = 50;

//It triggering user-defined handler function
if ($test==50) {
    trigger_error("A error has been triggered");
}
?>
```

set_exception_handler() Function

This function sets a user-defined exception handler function, and the script stops executing after the exception handler is called. The syntax is set_exception_handler(callback).

This function has various parameters:

- **callback:** It is a required field that specifies the function's name to be called when an uncaught exception occurs. It requires one parameter, which is the exception object that is thrown. The signature of this handler function is: handler(Exception $ex): void

- In PHP 7, most errors are reported by throwing Error exceptions, which the handler caught. Both Error and Exception implement the Throwable interface. The signature of this handler function is: handler(Throwable $ex): void.

- NULL can be passed to reset this handler to its default state. It returns the previously defined exception handler or null on error. If there is no previous handler specified, null is also returned.

Example:

```php
<?php
// user-defined exception handler functions
function myException($e) {
  echo "Exception: ".$e->getMessage();
}

//It sets user-defined exception handler function
set_exception_handler("myException");

//It throws an exception
throw new Exception("Uncaught exception
occurred!");
echo "This will not be executed.\n";
?>
```

trigger_error() Function

This function triggers a user-defined error condition and generates a user-level error/warning/notice message. It is used with the built-in error handler or with a user-defined error handler function set by the set_error_handler() function. The syntax is trigger_error(message, error_level).

The following parameters are:

- **message:** It is a required field that specifies the error message for this error. It is limited to 1024 bytes in length, and any additional characters beyond 1024 bytes will be truncated.

- **error_level:** It is an optional field that specifies the error type for this error. It can take values from the E_USER family of constants which are:

  - E_USER_ERROR

  - E_USER_WARNING

  - E_USER_NOTICE (default)

  - E_USER_DEPRECATED

Return Value: It returns false if wrong error_level is specified, otherwise true.

The following example shows the usage of trigger_error() function:

```php
<?php
$dvnd= 100;
$dvsr = 0;

if ($dvsr  == 0) {
  trigger_error("Cannot divide by zero",
E_USER_ERROR);
} else {
  echo ($dvnd= /$dvsr );
}
?>
```

user_error() Function

This function triggers a user-defined error condition and generates a user-level error/warning/notice message. It can be used with the built-in error handler or with a user-defined error handler function set by the set_error_handler() function. This function is an alias of trigger_error() function.

The syntax is user_error(message, error_level).

These are the following parameters:

1. **message:** It is a required field, and it specifies the error message for this error. It is limited to 1024 bytes in length. Any additional characters beyond 1024 bytes will be truncated.

2. **error_level:** It is optional and specifies the error type for this error. It can take values from the E_USER family of constants which are:

   - E_USER_ERROR

   - E_USER_WARNING

   - E_USER_NOTICE (default)

   - E_USER_DEPRECATED

Return Value: It returns false if the wrong error_level is specified. True otherwise.

The following example shows the usage of the user_error() function:

```php
<?php
$dvnd= 100;
$dvsr = 0;

if ($dvsr  == 0) {
  user_error("Cannot divide by zero", E_USER_ERROR);
} else {
  echo ($dvnd= /$dvsr );
}
?>
```

Error Handling

It is the process of getting errors raised by your program and then taking appropriate action. If you would handle errors properly, it may lead to many unforeseen consequences.

It's straightforward in PHP to handle errors.

Using the die() Function

During writing PHP program, you should review all likely error states before going forward and take suitable action when required.

Try the following example:

```php
<?php
  if(!file_exists("/folder/text.txt")) {
      die("File does not found");
  }else {
      $file = fopen("/folder/text.txt","r");
      print "Opened sucessfully";
  }
  //The test of the code here.
?>
```

Using the above method, you can stop your code whenever it errors out and display a more meaningful and user-friendly message when you write efficient code.

EXCEPTION HANDLING IN PHP

PHP language has an exception model equivalent to that of other programming languages. The concept of exceptions is essential and provides better control over error handling. It is a powerful mechanism used to handle runtime errors called exceptions so that the usual flow of the application can be maintained.

The primary purpose of exception handling is to maintain the application's normal execution.

WHAT IS AN EXCEPTION?

It is an invalid outcome of a program, which the program itself can handle. It disturbs the normal flow of the code. It is different from an error, and it can be managed, whereas the program itself cannot handle an error.

In other words, "An invalid result of a program is an exception, which the program itself can handle." Exceptions can be thrown and caught in other languages, as in PHP.

Let us explain their new keyword related to exceptions.

THE EXCEPTION OBJECT

The exception object contains the information related to the error or unexpected behavior that the function encountered.

The syntax is the new exception (message, code, previous):

- **message:** It is optional and a string describing why the exception was thrown

- **code:** It is optional. An integer can easily distinguish this exception from others of the same type.

- **previous:** It is optional. If this exception throws in a catch block of another exception, it is recommended to pass it into this parameter.

WHY DO WE NEED EXCEPTION HANDLING?

PHP language provides a mechanism named exception handling. It allows handling runtime errors such as IOException, SQLException, ClassNotFoundException, and more. A most famous example of exception handling is dividing by zero exception, an arithmetic exception.

Exception handling is similar in all the other programming languages. It changes the flow of the program when a particular error condition occurs, and this condition is known as an exception. PHP language offers the following keywords for this purpose:

- **try:** The try contains the code with an exception where an exception can arise. When any exception occurs inside the try block during the code runtime, it is caught and resolved in the catch block.

The try block followed by catch or finally block. A try block can be followed by a minimum one and the maximum number of catch blocks.

- **catch:** The catch block contains the code executed when a specified exception is thrown. It is always used with a try block, not alone. When an exception occurs, PHP finds the matching catch block.

- **throw:** It is a keyword used to throw an exception. It also helps to list all the exceptions that a function throws but does not handle itself.

- **finally:** The final block contains a code used for cleanup activity in PHP languages. It executes the necessary code of the program.

Here is an example of an introductory PHP try-catch statement:

```
try {
    // it runs your code here
}
catch (exception $error) {
    //code to handle the exception
}
finally {
    //It is optional code that always runs
}
```

PHP Try-Catch with Multiple Exception Types

PHP supports using multiple catch blocks within try-catch, which allows us to customize code based on the thrown type of exception. It helps customize how you display an error message to a user or if you should potentially retry something that failed for the first time.

```
try {
    // run your code here
}
catch (Exception $error) {
    echo $error->getMessage();
}
catch (InvalidArgumentException $error) {
    echo $error->getMessage();
}
```

When to Use Try-Catch-Finally

The finally block was added in the error handling flow. Suppose you want to use a final section in your PHP error handling code, it is useful more than just exception handling and is used to perform cleanup code such as closing a file, closing a database connection, etc.

The finally block executes when the try-catch block exits. It ensures that the finally block is executed even if an unexpected exception occurs.

Examples for try catch-finally:

```
try {
    print "this is our try block n";
    throw new Exception();
} catch (Exception $e) {
    print "something went wrong, caught ! n";
} finally {
    print "this part always executed n";
}
```

CREATING CUSTOM PHP EXCEPTION TYPES

PHP also allows creating custom exception types, and it helps make custom exceptions in your application that you can have special exception handling around and to create a custom exception handler, we must create a particular class with functions that can be called when an exception occurs.

```
class DivideByZeroException extends Exception {};
```

The class inherits the properties from the Exception class, and you can add custom functions to it. You may not want to display all the details of an exception to the user or display a user-friendly message and log the error message internally for monitoring.

GLOBAL PHP EXCEPTION HANDLING

Your code will do proper exception handling. You can configure a global PHP exception handler as a best practice. It will call if an unhandled exception occurs that was not named in a proper PHP try-catch block.

To configure a global PHP exception handler, we will use the set_exception_handler() function to set a user-defined function to handle all uncaught exceptions:

```
function our_global_exception_handler($exception) {
    //this code should log the exception to disk and
an error tracking system
```

```
    echo "Exception:" . $exception->getMessage();
}
set_exception_handler('our_global_exception_handler');
```

WHAT HAPPENS WHEN AN EXCEPTION IS TRIGGERED?

- The current state of code is saved.

- The execution of the code is switched to a predefined exception handler function.

- The handler can halt the program's execution, resume the execution from the saved code state, or continue the execution of the code from another location in the code.

WHY HANDLE AN EXCEPTION?

It is to avoid unexpected results on our pages which can be annoying.

It improves the security of our applications by not exposing information that malicious users may use to attack our applications.

The exceptions are used to change the normal flow if any predictable error occurs.

PHP ERROR HANDLING

When an error occurs, it depends on your configuration settings; PHP displays the error message in the web browser with information relating to the error that occurred.

PHP Offers Several Methods to Handle Errors

The three commonly used methods;

Die Statement

The die function merges the echo and exits function in one. It is beneficial to output a message and stop the script execution when an error occurs.

Custom error handlers are user-defined functions that are called whenever an error occurs.

How to Use Try-Catch with MySQL

The libraries for MySQL, PDO, and mysqli have various modes for error handling. If you do not have exceptions enabled for those libraries, you cannot use try-catch blocks. The error handling differences are more complicated.

PDO

In PDO, you need to enable ERRMODE_EXCEPTION when you create the connection.

```
// connect to MySQL
$conn = new PDO('mysql:host=localhost;dbname=db;charse
t=utf8mb4', 'username', 'password');
//PDO error mode to exception
$conn->setAttribute(PDO::ATTR_ERRMODE,
PDO::ERRMODE_EXCEPTION);
mysqli_report(MYSQLI_RPT_ERROR |MYSQLI_RPT_STRICT);
```

PHP ERROR REPORTING

The error message depends on your PHP error reporting settings. This method is beneficial in development when you have no idea what caused the error, and the information displayed can help you debug your application.

Method	Description
getMessage()	It returns a string describing why the exception was thrown.
getPrevious()	If another one triggered this exception, this method returns the previous exception. If not, then it returns null.
getCode()	It is used to return the exception code.
getFile()	It is used to return the full path of the file in which the exception was thrown.
getLine()	It is used to return the line number of the line of code which threw the exception.

CHAPTER SUMMARY

In this chapter, we have discussed the basics of error handling in PHP with their function and methods debug_backtrace(), error_log(), error_get_last(), error_reporting(), and restore_error_handler(). We also learned about PHP errors, and exceptional handling using try-catch and try-catch-finally block.

CHAPTER 9

Working with Composer

IN THIS CHAPTER

> What is a dependency manager?

> What is PHP composer?

> Installation (locally or globally)

> Pre-request of composer

> Packagist

> Autoloading

> VCS versioning

In the previous chapter, we have discussed basics of error handling in PHP with their function and methods debug_backtrace(), restore_error_handler() and so on. We also learned about PHP error and exceptional handling using blocks.

Here, we discuss one of the necessary tools in PHP language: the dependency manager Composer. In this chapter, we will look at the input and output of Composer and also how to install it and use it in simple PHP development.

If you code HP for some time, you will know how PHP libraries can help save work and make code reusable. Previously, it was not easy to add libraries to PHP, which led to many reinventing the wheel for standard features. For example, a database abstraction layer (DAL) is a must-have

DOI: 10.1201/9781003308669-9

for any PHP application. Still, there was no standard library or package, so many people ended up developing their own.

Indeed, there were a lot of options available at that time, but it was challenging to add dependencies, keep track of them, and manage your application in the long run. That's where a dependency manager like Composer comes in. In fact, before Composer, a popular tool called PEAR was used to manage PHP extensions and libraries. But it had its limitations, which Composer was created to address. We need a tool that can be utilized to install libraries and manage application dependencies. The Composer does a wonderful job of this. It is an application-level package manager for PHP that has gained immense popularity and become the de facto standard for managing dependencies in PHP applications.

Programmers who regularly work with PHP and its different scripts understand how tedious it becomes to replicate the same process to perform essential tasks. However, a dependency manager can help resolve this type of issue. This chapter will learn what a dependency manager is and how PHP Composer helps PHP developers' workflow.

WHAT IS A DEPENDENCY MANAGER?

A dependency manager is defined as a software tool to manage, install, upgrade, configure, and remove the various types of libraries needed for a project in a logical and significant way.

Or

It is an external standalone program (library) module that can be as small as a single file or as large as a collection of files and folders organized into packages that perform a specific task.

WHAT IS PHP COMPOSER?

It can be defined as a dependency manager or dependency management tool built explicitly for PHP. By using Composer, you can easily download and incorporate valuable and essential packages into your project via the terminal.

Dependency Management

Composer is not a package manager, same as Yum or Apt, and it deals with packages or libraries. Still, it manages on a per-project basis by installing them in a directory inside your PHP project. By default, it does not install globally. Hence, it is a dependency manager. It supports a "global" project for convenience via the global command.

DOWNLOADING THE COMPOSER EXECUTABLE

PHP Composer Installation on the Windows Operating System

If you are currently working on a Windows system, then download the setup file from getcomposer.org and install the PHP Composer. This process is quite self-explanatory. Simply remember to set your PATH environment variable so that you can call Composer from any directory.

Composer offers a convenient installer to execute directly from the command prompt. Download this file and know more about the inner workings of the installer review Github.

There are two ways to install Composer: locally or globally as a system-wide executable.

System Requirements

For installing the Composer, the system requires PHP 5.3.2 or later to use. Some sensitive PHP settings and compile flags are needed, but you will be alerted about any incompatibilities when using the installer.

Now, install packages from sources instead of zip archives. It depends on how the box is version controlled, and you will need git, svn, fossil, or hg. The Composer is multi cross-platform, and we make it run equally well on Windows, Linux, and macOS.

Locally

To install it locally, run the installer in your working directory. See the Download page for instructions.

The installer may check a few PHP settings and then download Composer.phar to your working directory. This file is the Composer binary. It is a PHAR, an archive format for PHP that can be run on the command line, amongst other things.

Now run PHP composer.phar to run Composer.

You can install the Composer into a specific directory by using the –install-dir option and (re)name it using the option –filename and when running the installer, then following the Download page instructions, add the following parameters given below:

```
PHP composer-setup.php --install-dir=bin
--filename=composer
Now run PHP bin/composer to run Composer.
```

Globally

You can keep the Composer PHAR file anywhere in your system. You can access it globally if you place it in the same directory part of your PATH. You can make it executable and invoke it on UNIX systems without using the PHP interpreter directly.

By running the installer, you can run to move Composer. phar to a directory in your path using this line of code.

```
mv composer.phar /usr/local/bin/composer
```

If you install it only for your user and avoid requiring root permissions, you can use ~/.local/bin instead, which is available by default on some Linux distributions.

If the code fails due to permissions, you need to rerun it with sudo.

In some versions of macOS, the/user directory does not exist by default. If you receive the error "/user/local/bin/composer: No such file or directory," then you must create the directory on your own before proceeding with this command, mkdir -p /usr/local/bin.

For more information on changing your PATH, please read the other article and use your search engine of choice.

PHP Composer Installation on Linux/Unix/macOS

If you want to install the Composer, open your new project folder and enter the following command in the terminal or command prompt:

```
$ curl -s https://getcomposer.org/installer | PHP
```

The above command installs PHP composer is used for a single project, and now you will have a composer.phar file, which will be inside into your root directory of your PHP project. Move this "composer.phar" file to /usr/bin/directory to make Composer globally available in your system.

```
$ sudo mv composer.phar /usr/bin/composer
```

You can run the command as described below to ensure that the Composer is successfully installed. If it is fully installed, you will see a full list of composer commands in the output.

```
$ Composer
```

Package Installation Using Composer

Now it is time to explore a package in Packagist.org. Packagist is the preliminary package repository for PHP Composer. The Composer uses Packagist.org to search for packages as default. This is the place where you can publish your packages and examine to use other developers' packages.

It is a tool for composer dependency management in PHP that allows you to declare the libraries in your project, and it will manage, install, and update them for you.

The Composer is highly inspired by node npm (node package packager) and ruby bundler. Suppose you have any project that depends on various libraries and even some of those libraries depend on other libraries, then Composer enables you to declare the libraries you depend on.

It finds out which versions of which packages can and need to be installed and install them, and you can update all your dependencies in one command.

Now run Composer instead of PHP Composer.phar.

USING THE INSTALLER

This is the most comfortable way to set up Composer on your machine.

Now download and run Composer-Setup.exe setup, and it will install the latest Composer version and then set up your PATH so that you can call Composer from any directory in your command line.

Manual Installation

To change a directory on your PATH, run the installer following the Download page instructions to download Composer.phar.

Create a new composer.bat file alongside the Composer.phar:

- Using cmd.exe:

```
C:\bin> echo @php "%~dp0composer.phar"
%*>composer.bat
```

- Using PowerShell:

```
PS C:\bin> Set-Content composer.bat '@php
"%~dp0composer.phar" %*'
```

Add the folder path to your environment variable PATH, if it doesn't exist. For more information on changing your PATH variable, please see other data and use your search engine of choice.

Close your current terminal. Test usage with a new terminal:

```
C:\Users\PC>composer -V
```

The above command tells you the latest version installed in your system.

INSTALL PHP COMPOSER ON LINUX UBUNTU

Ubuntu runs many servers and websites in the world. And PHP is the most accustomed framework to build any website. So, installing a PHP composer on Linux Ubuntu can give you some extra time by reducing and automating the workload.

Installing the PHP composer on Ubuntu and other Debian distributions are pretty simple. You can install the PHP composer by using the package manager. Our Ubuntu system will install the tools such as PHP-GD, PHP-XML, PHP-CLI, and PHP-ZIP. You can run the following commands to install the PHP packages on your Debian system:

- sudo apt update
- sudo apt install php php-gd php-xml php-cli php-zip
- sudo apt install unzip curl

You can check the framework version to ensure that whether its dependencies are installed inside your system correctly or not.

Using the below command:

```
php -v
```

Now, run the following command of cURL to download the PHP composer tool on your Linux system. Then push the file into the /usr/local/bin/composer directory. If you cannot find a composer directory, you can make a directory by using the mkdir command.

Now, run the following change mode command to access the composer directory.

```
chmod +x /usr/local/bin/composer
```

Finally, now you can check the version of the PHP composer to check whether it is installed successfully on your Linux system or not.

Using the below command:

```
composer -v
```

PHP COMPOSER

We have installed the PHP composer inside our Linux system successfully. Suppose you want to install a spme PHP package dependency through the Composer; in this case, you make a directory or select other directories as the final destination folder, then run the following composer command in your terminal shell to install the PHP package dependencies.

```
mkdir shell && cd shell
composer install
```

Suppose you want to see the read-write logs of our PHP project. Then, we can run the following composer command to view the log files.

```
composer require psr/log
```

The PHP composer contains the PHP modules updated regularly, but it's also essential to update the composer tool regularly. Use the following command-line to update your PHP composer on Linux.

```
sudo composer self-update
```

We should know that two scripts are used to update and install the PHP composer. These are the composer.json and the composer.lock.

Explanation:

- The composer.json file is used to update all the previously installed package dependencies inside your system via the PHP composer.

- The composer.lock is used to install new package dependencies, modules, or packages on your PHP framework.

If you are a good PHP developer, you may use the Laravel framework inside your Linux system. It is a perfect tool to work with PHP. But occasionally, Laravel makes the Composer slower. You can bypass and avoid the Laravel vs. Composer conflict by running the following command-line in your Linux terminal shell using this command.

```
composer config --global repo.packagist composer
https://packagist.org
```

Requirements:

- Shell access to a running macOS

- PHP 5.3 or later version must be installed

INSTALL COMPOSER ON macOS

Download composer binary file from getcomposer.org website by running the following command. It will create a composer.phar file in the current directory.

```
curl -sS https://getcomposer.org/installer | php
```

Now, this Composer.phar file in the bin directory to make available anywhere in the system. Again, set the execute permission on the file that has changed the filename from Composer.phar to the Composer for manageable use.

```
mv composer.phar /usr/local/bin/composer
chmod +x /usr/local/bin/composer
```

Run composer command on the command line. This will provide you with composer version details and options available with the composer command.

UPGRADE PHP COMPOSER

The Composer provides a command-line option to upgrade itself (self-update). You can only run the below command from the terminal to upgrade compose on your macOS.

```
$ sudo composer self-update Basic introduction
```

We can install monolog/monolog, a logging library for our basic usage introduction if you have not yet, then install Composer.

This introduction assumes that you have performed installation of Composer locally using the below command.

`composer.json: Project setup`

All you need to start using Composer in your PHP project is a composer.json file. This file describes your project dependencies and contains other metadata as well. It should go in the top-most directory of your project/ VCS repository. You can run Composer anywhere, but if you want to publish a package to Packagist.org, you will have to find the file at the top of your VCS repository.

Understanding the Required Key

The thing you identify in composer.json is the required key that means you are telling Composer which packages your project depends on.

```
{
    "require": {
        "monolog/monolog": "2.2.*"
    }
}
```

Have a look at the above code requires taking an object that maps package names (e.g., monolog/monolog) to version constraints.

The Composer uses the above data to search for the set of files in package "repositories" that you register using the repositories key or in Packagist. org, in the default package repository.

Package Names

It consists of a vendor name and the project name. Frequently these will be identical, and the vendor name exists to prevent naming clashes with others.

For example, it allows two separate people to create the same library named JSON. One can be called igorw/JSON while the other should be seldaek/JSON.

Package Version Constraints

For example, we request the Monolog package with the version constraint 2.0.* (number can vary). This means any version in the 2.0 development branch is greater than or equal to 2.0 and less than 2.1 (≥ 2.0 < 2.1).

How Do We Update the Composer Itself?

Then if you want to update Composer, composer self-update and press Enter. That's all.

If you want the Composer back to the last version, then you can use the command as below,

```
composer self-update -rollback
```

Installing Dependencies

To install the dependencies for your project, you can run the following update command in the command prompt.

```
PHP composer.phar update
```

It will do two things given below.

It can resolve all dependencies listed in your composer.json file and register all packages with their exact versions to the Composer.lock file, locking means it closes the version of the project to those specific versions. It would be best to commit the Composer.lock file to your project repo so that all people working on the project are closed to identical versions of dependencies. This is the primary role of the update command.

It runs the install command implicitly. This will download all the dependencies files into the vendor directory in your PHP project. The vendor directory is the root location for all third-party. In the above example, you end up with the Monolog source files in vendor/monolog/monolog/. As Monolog depends on psr/log, that package files can also be found inside vendor/.

Committing Composer.lock File to Version Control

Committing files to version control is essential because it will cause anyone who sets up the project to use identical versions of the dependencies you are using.

Your CI server, production machines, or any other developers in your team, everything, and everyone run on the same dependencies, which mitigates bugs affecting some parts of the deployments even if you develop once in six months when reinstalling the project, you can feel much confident the dependencies installed are even working even if your dependencies have released many new versions since then.

Installing from the Composer.lock File

When there is a composer.lock file in the project folder already, it means either you ran the update command before, or someone else ran the command and committed the Composer.lock file to the project (which is good).

Either way, installing when a composer.lock file is present resolves and installs all dependencies you listed in composer.json.

Still, it uses the exact versions listed in Composer.lock to ensure that the package versions are consistent for all in your project. You will have all the dependencies by your composer.json file. Still, they may not all be at the latest available versions where some of the dependencies listed in the Composer.lock file may have released newer versions since the file was created. It ensures that your project doesn't break because of any unexpected changes in dependencies.

For fetching new differences from your VCS repository, it is recommended to you to run a Composer install to make sure whether the vendor directory is up in sync with your Composer.lock file or not.

```
PHP composer.phar install
```

Updating Dependencies to Their Latest Versions

The Composer.lock file stops you from automatically installing the latest versions of dependencies and to update the latest versions, use the update command. This fetches the latest matching versions according to your composer.json file and edits the lock file with the new versions.

The command is given below:

```
php composer.phar update
```

Remember, when executing an install command, the Composer shows a warning if the Composer.lock has not been updated. Since changes were made to the file composer.json, which might affect dependency.

If you want to install, upgrade or remove a single dependency, you can explicitly list it as an argument like this:

```
PHP composer.phar update monolog/monolog [...]
```

WHAT IS PACKAGIST?

Packagist.org is the central Composer repository. It is a package source that place, where you get packages from packagist, is the principal repository everyone uses. This means you can automatically need any available package without further specifying where Composer should look for the box.

Go to the Packagist.org official website, search and browse for packages.

Any open source project using Composer to publish their packages on Packagist, and this library does not need to be on Packagist used by Composer. Still, it enables adoption by other developers more quickly.

Platform Packages

The Composer has platform packages, which are virtual packages for things installed on the system but are not installable by the Composer – the PHP itself with its extensions and some system libraries.

PHP represents the PHP version, allowing to apply some constraints, e.g., To require a 64bit version of PHP, you need the PHP-64bit package.

The hhvm represents the version of the HHVM runtime that allows you to apply a constraint.

ext-<name> allows you to need PHP extensions that includes core extensions. The versioning can be quite inconsistent here, so it is often a good to set the constraint to * (will select all). For example of an extension package name is ext-gd.

lib-<name> allows conditions to be made on other versions of libraries used by PHP. The following are available: xsl, OpenSSL, curl, iconv, ICU, libxml, pcre, uuid.

You can use the show –platform to get a list of your locally available platform packages.

AUTOLOADING

Why Do We Need Autoloading?

When you create any PHP applications, you may use third-party libraries. If you would like to use these libraries in the project, you need to include libraries in source files using require () or include () statements.

These require () or include () functions are sufficient as long as you develop small applications. But as your PHP application grows, the list of required or included statements gets longer, which is a bit annoying, difficult to maintain. The other main problem is that you load the entire libraries in the application, including some of the parts you are not even using. This leads to a heavier memory for your application.

It would be ideal for loading classes only when needed to overcome this problem. That's where autoloading comes in.

When you use a class in your project, the autoloader checks if it is already loaded, and if it is not, then the autoloader loads the important class into memory then the class is loaded on the fly. This is called autoloading. When using autoloading, you do not need to manually include all the library files. You need to have the autoloader file, which contains the logic of autoloading, and the necessary classes will be included dynamically.

How Autoloading Works without Composer

It implements autoloading in PHP without Composer. The spl_autoload_register() function makes this possible. This function allows you to register functions that are put into a queue to be triggered consecutively when PHP tries to load classes that are not loaded yet.

```php
<?php
function custom_autoloader_function ($class) {
   include 'lib/' . $class . '.php';
}
 spl_autoload_register('custom_autoloader_function ');
$objFooBar = new ClassName();
?>
```

Our custom autoloader uses the spl_autoload_register() function. Next, when you instantiate the ClassNameclass, and it's not yet available, PHP will execute all the registered autoloader functions sequentially. And thus, the custom_autoloader_function function is called. It includes the necessary class file, and finally, the object is instantiated. We are assuming the ClassNameclass is defined in the lib/main.php file.

Without autoloading, you need to use the required or include a statement to include the ClassNameclass file. The autoloader implementation is quite simple in the above example, but you could build on this by registering multiple autoloaders for different classes.

How Autoloading Works with Composer

First, you need to install Composer on your system. There are different methods you can choose to install autoloading with Composer.

Composer gives you four different methods for autoloading files:

- file autoloading

- class-map autoloading

- PSR-0 autoloading

- PSR-4 autoloading

PSR-4 is the recommended way of autoloading, and in this section, we will briefly discuss the other three options.

Before we go ahead, you need to perform where you want to use Composer autoloading.

- Defining the composer.json file in the root project or library. It should have directives based on autoloading.

- Run the Composer dump-autoload command to generate the necessary files autoloading.

- Include the required 'vendor/autoload.php' statement at the top of the file where you want to use autoloading.

Autoloading: The Files Directive

File autoloading works to include or require statements that allow you to load entire source files. All the source files referenced will be loaded every time your application runs. This is valuable for loading source files that do not use classes.

If you want to use autoloading, then provide a list of files in the directive of the composer.json file, as displayed in the following snippet code.

```
{
    "autoload": {
        "files": ["lib/index.php", "lib/home.php"]
    }
}
```

We can also provide a list of files in the directive that we want to autoload with the Composer. After creating the composer.json file in your root folder, you need to run the Composer dump-autoload command to generate the autoloader files. These will be made under the vendor directory. Then, you need to include the required 'vendor/autoload.php' statement at the top of the file where you want to load autoload files with Composer, as shown in the following example.

```
<?php
require 'vendor/autoload.php'; //file name in the vendor
```

```
// The code uses things declared in the "lib/index.
php" or "lib/home.php" file
?>
```

The statement of requiring 'vendor/autoload.php' makes sure that the necessary files are loaded dynamically.

Autoloading: The class-map Directive

This autoloading is an enhanced version of autoloading. You need to give a list of directories, and the Composer will scan all the files in those directories. The Composer will make a list of classes contained in the file for individual files, and whenever one of those classes is needed, the composers will autoload the related file.

Let's have a quick revise the composer.json file to demonstrate the class-map autoloader.

```
{
    "autoload": {
        "classmap": ["lib"]
    }
}
```

Now, run the Composer dump-autoload command, and the Composer reads the files in the lib directory to create a map of classes that can be autoloaded.

Autoloading: PSR-0

The PHP-FIG group recommends PSR-0 for autoloading. In the PSR-0 standard, you can use namespaces to define your libraries. The entry qualified class name reflects the\<Vendor Name>\(<Namespace>\)*<Class Name> structure. Also, your class must save in files that follow the same directory structure as the namespaces.

Let's have a look at the following composer.json file.

```
{
    "autoload": {
        "psr-0": {
            "folder\\Library": "src"
        }
    }
}
```

In PSR-0 autoloading, it needs to map namespaces to directories. In the example, we tell the Composer that anything starting with the Folder\ Library namespace should be available in the src\folder\Library directory.

```php
<?php
namespace Folder\Library;
 class ClassName
{
    //...
}
?>
```

As you can see, this class is defined in the folder Folder\Library namespace. Also, you can file the name corresponds to the class name. Let's quickly see how you could autoload the ClassNameclass.

```php
<?PHP
require 'vendor/autoload.php';
   $obj = new Folder\Library\ClassName();
?>
```

LIBRARIES

Here in this section, we will tell you how to make your library installable through Composer.

Every project is a package.

When you have a composer.json in a directory, that directory is a package. When you add a requirement to a project, you make a package that depends on other packages. The difference between your project and a library is that your project is a package without a name.

For those libraries that specify autoload information, the composer can generate a folder vendor/autoload.php file. You can include the file and start using the libraries' classes without any extra work.

To make the package installable, give it a name and do this by adding the name property in composer.json:

```json
{
    "name": "acme/hello-php",
    "require": {
        "monolog/monolog": "1.0.*"
    }
}
```

Here, the project name is acme/hello-PHP, where acme is the vendor name and supplying a vendor name is mandatory.

Library Versioning

In most cases, you will be maintaining your library using some version control systems like git, svn, hg, or fossil. In these cases, Composer assumes versions from your VCS, and you should not specify a version in your composer.json file.

If you are holding packages by hand, i.e., without a VCS, you will need to specify the version explicitly by adding a version in your composer.json file:

```
{
    "version": "1.0.0"
}
```

Built-in PHP libraries are introduced in the market to reduce developers' load while coding the project effectively. Various developmental functions are configured in the project easily using these libraries, allowing developers to focus on the other complex operations.

The library functions such as the array_push part of the PHP library can be accessed and used by anyone. However, you can also compose your function and utilize that in your code.

Here we have top PHP Libraries are given below:

- Symfony Console Component

- Symfony Finder Component

- Psr/log

- Monolog

- Guzzle

- Assert

- Symfony/Translation

- PHPUnit

- PHP-code-coverage

- Swiftmailer

- Email-validator
- PHP dotenv
- Symfony Filesystem Component
- Twig
- Faker
- AWS SDK for PHP
- PHPseclib
- Laravel Tinker
- Predis
- PHP AMQP Library
- Laravel-Permission Library
- Twill Library
- OAuth 2.0
- Laravel Backup
- PHP Rector
- Lighthouse
- Laravel Admin LTE
- Swagger PHP Library
- Laravel/Passport MongoDB
- Stripe-PHP
- Omnipay
- Laravel Cashier
- Sylius
- Laravel Aimeos
- Space Image Optimizer
- Elastica

- Intervention/Image

- Minify

- Swap

- Tcpdf

VCS VERSIONING

The Composer uses your VCS's branch and tag features to resolve the version constraints you specify in your required field to specific sets of files. When determining valid available versions, the Composer looks at all of your tags and branches and translates their names into an internal list of options that it then matches against the version constraint you provided.

Read the versions article for additionally on how the Composer treats tags and branches and resolves package version constraints.

Lock File

You can commit the Composer.lock file if you want for your library. It can help your team to test against identical dependency versions continuously. However, this lock file will not affect other projects that depend on it. It only affects the main project.

If you don't want to commit the lock file and use git, add it to the .gitignore.

Publishing to a VCS

Your library is composer-installable once you have a VCS repository with a composer.json file. In this example, we will create the acme/hello-world library on GitHub under github.com/username/hello-world.

To test installing the acme/hello-PHP package, create a new project locally and call it acme/blog. This blog depends on acme/hello-PHP, which depends on monolog/monolog.

Example:

```
{
    "name": "acme/blog",
    "require": {
        "acme/hello-php": "dev-master"
    }
}
```

The name is not needed since we do not want to publish the blog as a library. It is added here just to clarify which composer.json is being described.

Command-Line Interface

You have learned how to use the command-line interface to do some things. This section will have all the available commands and to get help from the command-line, call Composer or composer list to see the complete list of commands, then help combined with any of those that can give you more information.

The Composer uses Symfony/console, and you can call commands by short name if it's not ambiguous.

```
PHP composer.phar dump
```

GLOBAL OPTIONS

There are the following options available with every command:

- **--verbose (-v):** It increases the verbosity of messages.

- **--help (-h):** It displays helpful information.

- **--quiet (-q):** It does not output any message.

- **--no-interaction (-n):** It does not ask any interactive questions.

- **--no-plugins:** It disables plugins.

- **--no-cache:** It disables the use of the cache directory.

- **--working-dir (-d):** If specified, use the given directory as the working directory.

- **--profile:** It displays timing and memory usage information.

- **--ANSI:** It forces ANSI output.

- **--no-ansi:** It disables ANSI output.

- **--version (-V):** It displays this application version.

There are three process Exit Codes in PHP composer:

0: OK
1: Generic/unknown error code
2: Dependency solving error code

Now we are going to discuss some browse packages in PHP Composer:

- init
- install / i
- update / u
- require
- remove
- reinstall
- check-platform-reqs
- global
- search
- show
- outdated
- browse / home
- suggests
- fund
- depends (why)
- prohibits (why-not)
- validate
- status
- self-update (selfupdate)
- create-project
- dump-autoload (dumpautoload)
- clear-cache / clear cache / cc
- licenses
- run-script
- exec

- diagnose

- archive

- help

- Command-line completion

Explanation:

- **install / i:** This command reads the composer.json file from the current directory, resolves the dependencies, and installs it into the vendor.

  ```
  php composer.phar install
  ```

  If there is a composer.lock file in the current directory, it will use the identical versions instead of resolving them. This ensures that everyone using the library will get similar versions of the dependencies.

  If there is no composer.lock file, the Composer will create one after dependency resolution.

- **update / u:** To update the Composer.lock file, you must use the update command and this command is also used as an upgrade as it does.

- **php composer.phar update:** If you want to update only few packages, you can list them as such:

  PHP composer.phar update vendor/package vendor/package2

  There are various options available given below:

  - --prefer-install

  - --dry-run

  - --dev

  - --no-dev

  - --no-install

  - --lock

  - --with

  - --no-autoloader

  - --no-scripts

- --no-progress

- --with-dependencies

- --with-all-dependencies

- --optimize-autoloader

- --classmap-authoritative

- --apcu-autoloader

- --apcu-autoloader-prefix

- --ignore-platform-reqs

- --ignore-platform-req

- --prefer-stable

- --prefer-lowest

- --interactive

- --root-reqs

- **require:** This command is used to add new packages to the composer.json file from the current directory. If no file exists, one will be created on the fly.

  ```
  PHP composer.phar require
  ```

  There are various options available given below:

  - --prefer-install

  - --dry-run

  - --dev

  - --no-dev

  - --no-install

  - --lock

  - --with

  - --no-autoloader

  - --no-scripts

- --no-progress
- --with-dependencies
- --with-all-dependencies
- --optimize-autoloader
- --classmap-authoritative
- --apcu-autoloader
- --apcu-autoloader-prefix
- --ignore-platform-reqs
- --ignore-platform-req
- --prefer-stable
- --prefer-lowest
- --optimize-autoloader
- --classmap-authoritative
- --apcu-autoloader
- --apcu-autoloader-prefix

- **reinstall:** This command installs packages by name, uninstalls them, and reinstalls them. It lets you do a clean install of a package if you messed with its files or wish to change the installation type using –prefer-install.

  ```
  PHP composer.phar reinstall acme/foo acme/bar
  ```

  - --dev
  - --no-dev
  - --no-install
  - --lock
  - --with
  - --no-autoloader
  - --no-scripts

- --no-progress

- --with-dependencies

- --with-all-dependencies

- --optimize-autoloader

- --classmap-authoritative

- --apcu-autoloader

- --apcu-autoloader-prefix

- **check-platform-reqs:** This command check-platform-reqs checks that your PHP and extensions versions match the platform requirements of the installed packages and is used to verify that a production server has all the extensions needed to run a project after installing it.

  Unlike update/install, this command will ignore config.platform settings and check the actual platform packages to ensure you have the required platform dependencies.

- **global:** This command allows you to run commands like install, remove, require, or update.

  This is only a helper to manage a project stored in a location that can hold CLI tools or Composer plugins that you want to have available everywhere.

  This can be used to install CLI utilities globally. Here is an example:

```
PHP composer.phar global require friendsofphp/
PHP-cs-fixer
```

If you update the binary, later on, you can run a global update:

```
PHP composer.phar global update
```

- **search:** This command allows searching through the current project's package repositories. Usually, this will be a packagist. You can pass the terms you want to search using the command prompt.

```
php composer.phar search monolog
```

You can search for more terms, just bypassing multiple arguments. Options:

- **--only-name (-N):** It searches only in package names.

- **--only-vendor (-O):** It searches only for vendor/organization names, returns only "vendor" as a result.

- **--type (-t):** It searches for a specific package type.

- **--format (-f):** It lets you pick between text (default) or JSON output format. Note that in the JSON, only the name and description keys are guaranteed to be present. The rest (URL, repository, downloads) are available for Packagist.org search results, and different repositories may return more or fewer data.

- **show:** To list all available packages, you can use the show command.

```
PHP composer.phar show
```

You can also pass the package version, which tells you the details of that specific version.

```
PHP composer.phar show monolog/monolog 1.0.*
```

Options:

- --all
- --installed
- --locked
- --platform
- --available
- --self
- --name-only
- --path
- --tree
- --latest
- --outdated
- --no-dev
- --minor-only
- --direct

- --strict

- --format

- --ignore-platform-reqs

- --ignore-platform-req

- **outdated:** This command shows a list of installed packages that have updates available, including their current and latest versions. This is +an alias for composer show -lo.

  The color coding is as such:

  - **green (=):** The dependency is in the latest version and is up to date.

  - **yellow (~):** The dependency has a new version available that includes backward compatibility breaks according to semver, so upgrade when you can, but it may involve work.

  - **red (!):** The dependency has a new version that is semver-compatible, and you should upgrade it.

- **browse/home:** The browse opens a package repository URL or homepage in your browser.

  Options:

  - **--homepage (-H):** It opens the homepage instead of the repository URL.

  - **--show (-s):** It only shows the homepage or repository URL.

- **suggests:** It lists all packages suggested by currently installed packages. You can pass one or multiple package names in the format of vendor/package to limit the output.

  - Use the –by-package or –by-suggestion flags to merge the output by the package presenting the suggestions.

  - Use – It lists the suggested package names.

- **fund:** It discovers how to help fund the maintenance of your dependencies. This lists all funding links from the installed dependencies. Use –format=json to get machine-readable output.

  Options:

  - **--format (-f):** It lets you pick between text (default) or JSON output format.

- **validate:** You must run the validate command before committing your composer.json file and tag a release and it will check if your composer.json is valid.

  Using this command given below,

  ```
  php composer.phar validate
  ```

- **status:** If you need to modify the code of your dependencies installed from the source, the status command allows you to check if you have local changes in any of them.

  ```
  PHP composer.phar status
  ```

- **self-update (selfupdate):** To update the Composer itself to the latest version, run the self-update command. It will replace your Composer. phar with the latest version using the below command.

  ```
  PHP composer.phar self-update
  ```

- **config:** This command allows others to edit Composer config settings and repositories in either the local composer.json file or the global config.json file.

  Additionally it lets you edit most properties in the local composer. json.

  ```
  PHP composer.phar config -list
  ```

CREATE A PROJECT USING THE COMPOSER

You can create new projects from an existing package using Composer. This is similar to doing a git clone/svn checkout followed by a composer install of the vendors.

There are various applications for this:

- You can deploy your application packages.

- You can also check out any package and start developing on patches.

- The projects with multiple developers can use this feature to bootstrap the initial development application.

dump-autoload (dumpautoload)

If you would like to update the autoloader because of new classes in a classmap package, you can use dump-autoload to do that without going through an install or update.

Additionally, it can dump an optimized autoloader that converts PSR-0/4 packages into classmap for performance reasons. The autoloader can take up a substantial portion of every request's time in large applications with many classes. Using classmaps for everything is less convenient in development, but using this option, you can still use PSR-0/4 for convenience and classmaps for performance.

BENEFITS OF USING COMPOSER

There are other locations where Composer will help you to improve your workflow. Here are the most common benefits:

- The quickly integrate libraries for your SaaS like a pusher, algolia, aws, opentok, Twilio, stripe, and many others get the package name and version, add them to your composer.json file, and run the install command.

- It can use ready-made packages that solve everyday problems. Do you need a routing package? Search for routing on packagist and get started right away. Do you need to handle uploaded files? Search for upload on packagist and get started right away.

- You can customize your composer workflow with Composer scripts. You can run your scripts before/after composer install, before/after composer update, etc.

CHAPTER SUMMARY

Composer can help developers in managing the dependencies of PHP projects. The project can easily integrate and manage open source packages in a single place.

It can also resolve dependencies on a per-project basis. Therefore, the developers can control some of the packages for each project and keep the project size in check.

Here in this entire chapter, you have learned how to install and use Composer effectively. To summarize, let's review all the steps once again:

- Install Composer on shared hosting or different operating systems, Linux, macOS, or Windows systems.

- It generates and understands the composer.json file.

- It uses Autoload script to load dependencies into your PHP file.

- Update your project dependencies.

- I hope you will clear your doubts and get a solid foundation to create unique projects with PHP by following our guide.

In this chapter, we have covered the dependency manager, PHP composer, installation on various operating systems locally as well as globally, as well as packagist, autoloading, and VCS versioning.

CHAPTER 10

WEB Services

IN THIS CHAPTER

➤ Introduction to web services

➤ Types of web services

➤ API vs. web services

➤ SOAP (Simple Object Access Protocol)

➤ WSDL (Web Services Description Language)

➤ REST (REpresentational State Transfer)

➤ SOAP vs. REST web services

In the previous chapter, we have covered the dependency manager, PHP composer, installation on various operating systems, and other important related topics.

But here in this chapter, you will learn Web services basics. Nowadays, the term "web services" references Amazon Web Services or Google's Web service, Google Cloud Platform.

However, web service testing and processes are still complicated despite technological advancements. They depend on systems to manage applications. The minor variances can result in multifaceted workflows when moving data between servers and the cloud, which can throw a wrench into your ecosystem and application integration strategy.

DOI: 10.1201/9781003308669-10

Web developers integrate the advanced functions and features into their apps, allowing for better customization and flexibility using APIs. The benefits of well-built web APIs increase the efficiency and practicality of services and apps. The goal is to offer an experience and result in an understanding for users and customers.

So here we have a brief discussion on the web services.

WHAT IS WEB SERVICE?

Web service is a standardized medium to communication between the client and server applications on the WWW, i.e., the World Wide Web. A web service is a software module designed to perform a particular set of tasks.

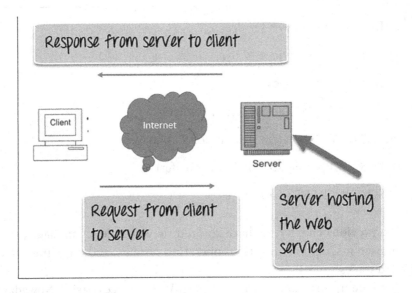

Web services.

It includes any software, application, or cloud technology that provides standardized web protocols such as HTTP or HTTPS to interoperate, communicate, and exchange data messaging – usually XML stands for Extensible Markup Language, throughout the Internet.

A web service has these essential functions:

- Its services are available over the Internet or Intranet networks.

- It standardizes XML messaging system.

- A web service is independent of a single operating system or programming language.

- It is self-describing via standard XML language.

- It is discoverable through a simple location method.

Web services in cloud computing can be searched for over the network and invoked accordingly.

When invoked, the web service would provide the functionality to the client, which invokes that web service.

A web service supports multiple applications such as HTML, XML, WSDL, SOAP, and other open standards. XML tags the data, SOAP transfers the message, and WSDL describes the service's accessibility.

Here's an example of how it works: a web service works between two sets of java, .net, or PHP apps, providing a method for these applications to communicate over a network. For instance, on one side, a java app interacts with the java, .net, and PHP apps on the other end by way of the web service communicating an independent language.

Web services offer additional benefits over business operations and help IT and web architects simplify the connectivity by minimizing development time. With this simplified infrastructure, company executives begin to see higher ROI. In a B2B operation where both understand how the process works, web services provide efficient technology distribution throughout an entire network.

DIFFERENT TYPES OF WEB SERVICES

Main types of web services are:

- XML-RPC

- UDDI

- SOAP

- REST

XML-RPC or Remote Procedure Call is the most fundamental XML protocol to exchange data between various devices on a network. It uses HTTP to quickly and easily transfer data and other information from client to server.

UDDI

Universal Description, Discovery, and Integration (UDDI) stand an XML-based standard for detailing, publishing, and discovering web services. It is an Internet registry for businesses around the world. Its goal is to streamline digital transactions and e-commerce among company systems.

SOAP

It will describe an XML-based web service protocol to exchange data and documents over HTTP or SMTP or Simple Mail Transfer Protocol. It allows independent processes operating on disparate systems to communicate using XML.

REST

It will also describe in full detail later in the blog, providing communication and connectivity between devices and the Internet for API-based tasks. Most RESTful services use HTTP as the supporting protocol.

Here are some known web services that use markup languages.

The lists of web templates are as follows:

- JSON-RPC
- JSON-WSP
- Web Services Description Language (WSDL)
- Web Services Conversation Language (WSCL)
- Web Services Flow Language (WSFL)
- Web Services Metadata Exchange (WS-MetadataExchange)
- XML Interface for Network Services (XINS)

COMPONENTS OF WEB SERVICES

The web services platform is XML + HTTP. All the standard web services use the following components:

- SOAP stands for Simple Object Access Protocol)
- UDDI stands for the Universal Description Discovery and Integration
- WSDL stands for Web Services Description Language

HOW DOES A WEB SERVICE WORK?

It enables communication among different applications using open standards such as HTML, XML, WSDL, and SOAP. A web service takes the help of the following:

- XML to tag the data

- SOAP to transfer a message

- WSDL to describe the availability of service

API VS. WEB SERVICES

Web services and APIs are usually mistaken for each other, which isn't all that surprising since there is some distinct common ground.

Most web services provide an API, which is used to retrieve data with its set of commands and functions. Here is an example: Twitter delivers an API that authorizes a developer to access tweets from a server and then collects data in JSON format.

Here are things to keep in mind. All web services can be APIs, but not all APIs can be web services. Now, if that syllogism makes your head spin, maybe these distinctions will clear up the API vs. web services confusion.

Differences between APIs and Web Services:

- APIs can host within an app or IIS, but a web service can only be hosted.

- Web services are not open source and are used to understand JSON (JavaScript Object Notation) or XML, whereas APIs are open-source and only used for XML.

- API is a lightweight architecture. But Web services are not lightweight. They need SOAP to send and receive network data.

- APIs can use any form of communication, but a Web service only uses SOAP, REST, and XML-RPC.

- APIs support URL, request/response headers, caching, versioning, content formats. Web services only support HTTP.

WHY DO YOU NEED A WEB SERVICE?

Modern-day business applications use a variety of programming platforms to develop web-based applications. Some applications may be formed in Java, others in .Net, while others in Angular JS, Node.js, etc.

These applications need some communication to happen between them. They are built using different development languages, and it is challenging to ensure good contact between applications.

Here the web services provide a platform that allows multiple applications built on various languages to have the ability to communicate with each other.

SIMPLE OBJECT ACCESS PROTOCOL (SOAP) 1.1

SOAP is a beautiful technology that can help you in developing great applications. In this tutorial, we will investigate the use of SOAP in PHP.

Unless or until you have been living in a cave somewhere without Internet access for the last few years, you have undoubtedly heard of XML, SOAP, and Multi-Tiered Application Programming. Like many programmers, including myself, you were pretty taken aback by these ideas and technologies. You may have gone so far as to dismiss them as irrelevant to your skillset. It's time to wake up and realize they're here to stay... and for a good reason!

XML and SOAP, and in turn Multi-Tiered Programming are technologies that can take you from being a run-of-the-mill code hacker to a professional application developer that builds cool things that work and which other people can work on. These technologies enable you to build applications that separate data from presentation, keep things organized and allow your application to scale as your needs and user base increases.

Today we will learn a Web Service using SOAP. In doing so, I hope that you will become familiar with the technology to start incorporating it into your future applications.

It stands for Simple Object Access Protocol, a network platform used in a web service to exchange or communicate data between two different machines on a network. It uses the XML data format to transfer messages over the HTTP protocol. SOAP can allow the user request to interact with other programming languages in Web services. This provides a way to communicate between applications running on different platforms (operating systems), with programming languages and technologies used in web service.

It provides you a simple, lightweight mechanism for exchanging structured, typed information between peers in a decentralized and distributed environment using XML. It does not define application semantics such as a programming model or implementation-specific semantics; instead, it represents a simple mechanism for expressing application semantics by providing a modular packaging model and encoding tools for encoding data within modules. This allows SOAP to be used in various systems ranging from messaging systems to RPC.

Characteristics of SOAP

The SOAP message consists of an envelope, header, and body element.

- It is an independent platform and language.

- It is a method of communicating through the Internet.

- It is used to send a message across the Internet and exchange documents.

- It can use on any platform and can support multi-languages.

- It sends messages via the HTTP protocol using the XML format.

SOAP consists of three parts:

- Its envelope construct defines an overall framework for expressing what is in a message, who should deal with it, and optional or mandatory.

- Its encoding rules define a serialization mechanism that can exchange instances of application-defined datatypes.

- Its RPC representation defines a convention representing remote procedure calls and responses.

However, these parts are represented together as part of SOAP web services, and they are functionally orthogonal. The envelope and its encoding rules are defined in different namespaces to promote simplicity through modularity, and in addition to the SOAP envelope, the SOAP encoding rules, and the SOAP RPC conventions, this specification defines two protocol bindings that describe how a message can be carried out in HTTP messages with or without the Extension Framework.

Design Goals

A primary goal for SOAP is simplicity and extensibility. It means that several features from traditional messaging systems and distributed object systems are not part of the core SOAP. Such features include:

- Distributed garbage collection

- Boxcarring or batching of messages

- Objects-by-reference which requires distributed garbage collection

- Activation which requires objects-by-reference

The SOAP Message Exchange Model

It is a fundamentally one-way transmission from a sender to a receiver, but as illustrated above, SOAP messages are often combined to implement patterns such as to request/response.

- Its implementations can optimize to exploit the unique characteristics of particular network systems. For example, the HTTP binding provides SOAP response messages as HTTP responses, using the same connection as the inbound request.

- The protocol to which SOAP is bound and messages are routed along is called "message path," which allows for processing at one or more intermediate nodes and the ultimate destination.

- Its application receiving a SOAP message must process that message by performing the actions in the order listed below.

- It should identify all parts of the SOAP message intended for that application.

- It should verify that all mandatory parts identified in step 1 are supported by the application for this message and process them accordingly.

- If the SOAP application is not the desired message destination, remove all parts specified in step 1 before forwarding the message.

It processes a message or a part of a message requires that the SOAP processor understands, among other things, the exchange pattern being used (one way, request/response, multicast, etc.), the role of the recipient in that pattern, the employment (if any) of RPC mechanisms such as the one documented, the representation or encoding of data as well as the other semantics necessary for the correct processing.

While the attributes such as the SOAP encodingStyle attribute can describe certain aspects of a message, this specification does not mandate a particular means by which the recipient makes such determinations in general. For example, specific applications will understand that one particular <getStockPrice> element signals an RPC request using the conventions. In contrast, another application may infer that all traffic directed to it is encoded as one-way messages.

SOAP Building Block

The block describes what XML data is sent to the web service and client application. The following figure represents the SOAP building block.

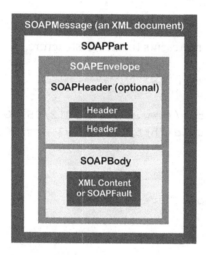

SOAP building block.

- **SOAP Envelope:** It is an important element of the XML documents. The envelope is used to define the start and end of the SOAP message, and it contains the details of the SOAP message.

- **SOAP Body:** It contains request and response information in the XML format and defines the content of the message sent between the client and the webserver.

- **SOAP Fault:** It holds the status of SOAP messages and errors. It is an optional element used to display an error message that occurs during a message's transmission.

- **SOAP Envelope:** It is used to define the start and end of the message and contains the details of the SOAP message.

The sub-elements of the Fault element are given below:

Element	Description
<faultcode>	It is used to detect the fault code in the SOAP message.
<faultactor>	An optional element in SOAP Fault that indicates the fault.
<faultstring>	It is used to offer a human-readable explanation of an error that occurred during message processing.
<detail>	It is used to hold the application-specific status error of the Body element.

SOAP Structure

The following code represents the SOAP structure.

```
<?xml version="1.0"?>
<SOAP:Envelope
xmlns:SOAP="http://www.w3.org/2012/05/SOAP-envelope/"
SOAP:encodingStyle="http://www.w3.org/2003/05/
SOAP-encoding">

<SOAP:Header>
//Write your code here
</SOAP:Header>

<SOAP:Body>
//Write your code here
  <SOAP:Fault>
  //Write your code here
  </SOAP:Fault>
</SOAP:Body>
</SOAP:Envelope>
```

Examples of SOAP Messages

In the given example, a TradePrice SOAP request is sent to a stock quote service, and it takes a string parameter, ticker symbol, and returns a float in the SOAP response. The envelope is the topmost element of the XML document representing the SOAP message. The XML namespaces are used to disambiguate identifiers from application-specific identifiers. The XML payload format in SOAP is entirely independent of the payload being carried in HTTP.

POST/StockQuote HTTP/1.1

Host: www.stockquoteserver.com

Content-Type: text/xml; charset="utf-8"
Content-Length: nnnn
SOAPAction: "Some-URI"

```
<SOAP-ENV:Envelope
  xmlns:SOAP-ENV="http://schema.xmlsoap.org/soap/
envelope/"
  SOAP-ENV:encodingStyle="http://schema.xmlsoap.org/
soap/encoding/">
  <SOAP-ENV:Body>
      <m:GetLastTradePrice xmlns:m="Some-URI">
          <symbol>DIST</symbol>
      </m:TradePrice>
  </SOAP-ENV:Body>
</SOAP-ENV:Envelope>
```

Relation to XML

All the messages are encoded using XML.

An application SHOULD include the proper namespace on all elements and attributes defined by SOAP in messages. An application MUST process namespaces in messages that it receives. It MUST discard messages with incorrect namespaces, and it MAY process SOAP messages without SOAP namespaces as though they had the correct SOAP namespaces.

SOAP defines two namespaces:

- The SOAP envelope has the namespace identifier.

- The SOAP serialization has the namespace identifier.

A message NOT contains a Document Type Declaration, but the message MUST NOT contain Processing Instructions.

It uses the local, unqualified "id" attribute of type "ID" to specify the unique identifier of an encoded element. It uses the local, unqualified attribute "href" of type "URI-reference" to determine a reference to that value, in a manner conforming to the XML Specification XML Schema Specification and XML Linking Language Specification.

The SOAP mustUnderstand attribute and actor attributes; it is generally permissible to have attributes and their values appear in XML instances or schemas with equal effect.

SOAP Envelope

A message (SOAP) is an XML document consisting of a mandatory SOAP envelope, an optionally SOAP header, and a mandatory SOAP body. The XML document is referred to as a SOAP message for the rest of this specification. A SOAP message contains the following:

- It is the top element of the XML document representing the message.

- The header is a method for adding features to a SOAP message decentralized without prior agreement between the communicating parties.

- A SOAP defines a few attributes that indicate who should deal with an element whether it is optional or mandatory.

- The Body is a container for important information intended for the ultimate recipient of the message. SOAP defines one element for the Body; the Fault element used for reporting errors.

SOAP Header

SOAP provides a mechanism for extending a message decentralized and modular without previous knowledge between the communicating parties. Extensions can be implemented as header entries are authentication, transaction management, payment, etc.

The Header element is encoded as the immediate child element of the SOAP Envelope XML element. All primary child elements of the Header element are called header entries.

SOAP Body

The SOAP Body element provides a mechanism for exchanging mandatory information intended for the ultimate recipient of the message. Its uses of the Body element include RPC calls and error reporting.

The Body element is encoded as the SOAP Envelope XML element's immediate child element. If a Header element is present and then the Body element MUST be immediately follow the Header element. Otherwise, it MUST be the primary child element of the Envelope element.

All primary child elements of the Body element are called body entries, and each body entry is encoded as an independent element within the SOAP Body element.

Relationship between SOAP Header and SOAP Body

The Soap Header and Soap Body are represented as independent elements, and they are related to each other. The following is the connection between a body entry and a header entry.

- A body entry is logically equal to a header entry meant for the default actor and with a value of "1" in the SOAP mustUnderstand property.

- By omitting the actor property, the default actor is provided.

SOAP Fault Codes

The values of faultcode defined in this section MUST be used in the faultcode element when we describe the faults defined by this specification. The namespace identifier for these SOAP faultcode values is "http://schemas.xmlsoap.org/soap/envelope/." This space is recommended to specify methods defined outside of the present specification.

The faultcode values are defined below:

The processing found an invalid namespace for the element.

mustUnderstand

A child element of the SOAP Header that was neither understood nor obeyed by the processing party contained a SOAP mustUnderstand attribute with a value of "1".

Client

It indicates that the message was incorrectly formed or did not contain the appropriate information to succeed. For instance, the message lacks the proper authentication or payment information. It is an indication that the message should not be resent without change.

Server

It indicates that the message could not be processed for reasons not directly attributable to the directive's contents but rather to its processing. For example, the processing includes communicating with an upstream processor, which did not respond.

The encoding style is based on a simple system that generalizes the standard features in type systems in programming languages, databases, and semi-structured data. This type either is a simple scalar type or is a compound type constructed as a composite of several parts, each with a type.

This defines rules for the serialization of a graph of typed objects. It operates on two levels. First, it is given a schema in any notation consistent with the type system described; a schema for an XML grammar may be constructed. Second, an XML instance may be built given a type-system schema and a particular graph of values conforming to that schema. In reverse, a copy of the actual graph may be constructed given an XML instance produced by these rules and the original schema.

WEB SERVICES DESCRIPTION LANGUAGE (WSDL)

What Is WSDL PHP?

Web Services Description Language (WSDL) PHP is an XML file that describes a web service's interface. We used the WSDL file published by the Kansas Department of Revenue. We observe the parameters in this WSDL and write the PHP script we used SOAP (nusoap).

Features of WSDL

- WSDL is the language that UDDI uses. An XML-based protocol for information exchange in decentralized and distributed environments.

- Its definitions describe how to access a web service and its operations and define how to interface with XML-based services.

- It is an integral part of UDDI, an XML-based worldwide business registry.

- It is pronounced as 'wiz-dull' and spelled as 'W-S-D-L.'

Is WSDL a Web Service?

It is an XML notation for describing a web service. It tells a client how to compose a web service request and describes its interface.

It breaks down into three specific, identifiable elements combined or reused once defined.

The three significant elements of WSDL defined separately are:

- Types
- Operations
- Binding

A WSDL document has various elements, whereas they are contained within these three main elements, which can be developed as separate documents. They can combine or reuse to form complete WSDL files.

The WSDL Document Structure

The structure of a WSDL looks like this:

```
<definitions>
    <types>
        here definition of types........
    </types>

    <message>
        here definition of a message....
    </message>

    <portType>
        <operation>
          here  definition of a operation.......
        </operation>
    </portType>

    <binding>
      here  definition of a binding....
    </binding>

    <service>
        here definition of a service....
    </service>
</definitions>
```

A WSDL document can contain other elements, like extension elements and a service element, making it possible to group the definitions of several web services in one single WSDL document.

How Do I Find the WSDL for a Web Service?

Steps to find WSDL document:

- Open your Web Service class, in this case, SOAP Tutorial. SOAP Service, in Studio.

- On the Studio menu bar, click View -> Web Page. This opens the Catalog Page in a browser.

- Click the Service Description link. This opens the WSDL in a browser.

How to Know if I Have a PHP SOAP Extension?

SOAP is a PHP extension, so if it's correctly installed, it will appear in phpinfo().

REST

A web service is a client, and a server application used to communicate over the World Wide Web's via Hypertext Transfer Protocol (HTTP). According to the WWW Consortium, the web services offer a common interoperation between software applications running on various platforms and frameworks.

What Is REST Architecture?

REST stands for REpresentational State Transfer. REST is a web standards-based architecture and uses HTTP Protocol. It revolves around resources where every component is a resource and is accessed by a common interface using HTTP standard methods. Roy Fielding first introduced REST in 2000.

A REST Server is simply provides access to resources in REST architecture, and a REST client accesses and modifies the resources as per needs. Here each resource is defined by URIs of global IDs. REST uses various kinds of representations to represent a resource like text, JSON, XML. JSON is the most popular one.

HTTP Methods

Four HTTP methods are commonly used in REST-based architecture:

- **GET:** It provides read-only access to a resource.

- **POST:** It is used to create a new resource.

- **DELETE:** It is used to remove a resource.

- **PUT:** It is used to update a current existing resource or create a new one.

Introduction to RESTful Web Services

A web service is a collection of available protocols and standards used for exchanging data between applications or systems. Software applications can be written in various programming languages, and run on multiple platforms can use web services to swap data over computer networks like the Internet, like inter-process communication on a single computer. This interoperability is due to open standards.

Web services based on REST Architecture are called RESTful web services and use HTTP methods to implement the concept of REST architecture. It usually defines a Uniform Resource Identifier (URI) a service, and provides resource representation such as JSON and set of HTTP Methods.

Difference between SOAP and REST Web Services

SOAP	REST
SOAP is a protocol.	REST is an architectural style.
SOAP stands for Simple Object Access Protocol.	REST stands for REpresentational State Transfer.
SOAP cannot use as REST because it is a protocol.	REST can use SOAP web services because it holds a concept and can use any protocol like HTTP, SOAP.
SOAP can use services interfaces to expose the business logic.	REST can use URI to expose business logic.
JAX-WS is fundamentally the java API for SOAP web services	JAX-RS is the Java API for RESTful web services.
SOAP defines standards to be strictly followed.	REST does not define too many standards like SOAP.
SOAP may require more bandwidth and resource than REST.	REST requires less bandwidth and resources than SOAP.
SOAP defines its own security.	RESTful web services inherit security measures from the underlying transport.
SOAP permits XML data format only.	REST permits different data formats such as Plain text, HTML, XML, JSON, etc.
SOAP is less preferred than REST.	REST is more preferred than SOAP.

Advantages of RESTful Web Services

- **Fast:** It is fast because there is no strict specification like SOAP. It consumes less bandwidth and resources.

- **Language and platform independent:** It can be written in any programming language and executed on any platform.

- **Use SOAP:** It can use SOAP web services as the implementation.

- **Permits different data formats:** It permits other data formats such as Plain Text, HTML, XML, and JSON.

CHAPTER SUMMARY

In this chapter, we have discussed the basics of web services with their types. We compare API and web services, and have full-fledged discussion on topics like Simple Object Access Protocol (SOAP), Web Services Description Language (WSDL), REpresentational State Transfer (REST), and we address SOAP and REST web services.

CHAPTER 11

Using PHP-based CMSs

IN THIS CHAPTER

> Introduction CMS

> Various CMS

> WordPress

> Jamal

> Magento

> Drupal

In the previous chapter, we have covered the basics of web services with its types. Other topics like Simple Object Access Protocol (SOAP), Web Services Description Language (WSDL), and REpresentational State Transfer (REST) were also discussed.

CMS is short for Content Management System. There are various kinds of CMSs available, and they all exist to make creating websites easier for people who do not want to learn the programming language. Some of these systems are made for customers with at least some understanding of code, but the majority are pitched at website owners who want to get their sites built fast and maintenance to be easy. There are so many choices, and this chapter explores a few criteria to keep in mind when choosing between the different PHP CMS platforms available.

DOI: 10.1201/9781003308669-11

WHAT IS A CMS?

It is an application designed to make the website accessible to add multiple features and manage whatever content you want to show with your site.

Webpages are put together by developers using various programming languages and technologies like PHP, ASP, HTML, JavaScript, and CSS. A CMS is a platform that uses languages like these, but the website creator doesn't necessarily need to see them or understand them because there is an interface that simplifies all of the stuff going on. If you are a new and want to build a blog or a shop for your own, a CMS will let you do that just by dragging and dropping the various elements into place.

CMS is abbreviated as Content Management System, a Graphic User Interface (GUI) software application that interacts with the website database to read and write the information. There are various kinds of CMS options available to run a blog or a website. Some are WordPress, Drupal, Wix, Joomla, Magento (e-commerce CMS), etc.

TYPES OF CMS

CMSs are categorized into two, based on their functional operation as The Enterprise Content Management (ECM) system and the Web Content Management (WCM) system are significant classifications. Both the CMS are similar compared to the operation of digital assets. They include two components such as:

- The Content Management Application (CMA) is used to control the functions such as writing, modifying, editing, and removing the content from the database.

- The Content Delivery Application (CDA) is used to serve the process of publishing the content across the web.

FEATURES OF CMS

The critical reason for the launch of the CMA is to make the setting more reliable and easy to access. The world is moving faster, so a developer should not waste time typing the same codes, repeating, writing, reading, fetching, and getting the information.

The primary functions of the CMS are often classified as indexing, search, retrieval, formatting, storing, and publishing.

Some of the features of CMS are as follows:

- The indexing features allow the user to write information and store it in the database and allow the same user to search by attributes whenever required.

- Formatting features help format the content using the WYSIWYG editor to turn the document into HTML, PHP, and PDF files.

- The revision control allows you to edit, modify, and update the information anytime when you want. It also tracks the changes made to the files.

- The publishing function allows creating, modifying, and using the existing templates to publish the information on the web.

WHAT ROLE DOES A CMS PLAY IN A BUSINESS?

A CMS can help build your business ahead if you can source, implement, and use the suitable CMS options and manage it properly.

A CMS can play a significant role in reducing the costs of maintaining your website. You do not need to hire staff to manage the updates to your site. Even the non-technical staff can handle all the necessary elements of your website building, though they may need a little training in the essential functions of building and updating a site. The simple and functional CMS helps you avoid appointing webmasters and developers with high remuneration requirements.

CMS also helps properly integrate other elements like asset management and customer relationship sections of your website. You can also use dynamic marketing techniques for sales management and user satisfaction. Other roles that a CMS can play include optimizing your website for a multitude of search engines and mobile-friendliness.

The most critical aspect is to enhance the functionality of your website. Some of the advantages of implementing the CMS solution are as follows:

- It works as a primarily located control system for your website.

- You can perform various activities like updating the content, implementing essential SEO functions, or even media content.

- All you can do without the need for technical knowledge.

- It needs a lesser number of employees in IT. It can go a long way in improving your budgeting.

- The CMS aids in reducing the costs to a particular level.

- It can update the data on a website with a CMS implementation that should be straightforward to work with.

- The process involved the concept and functionality of pretty user-friendly.

- CMS offers you extended security support. The owners have complete control over what pages they want to make public or private.

- The CMS implementation is simple and more manageable and helps deploy your site.

- The various plug-ins are supported on a CMS platform.

- Its tools offer you an excellent option for providing community support and help channels.

THE DISADVANTAGES OF CMS

Just as a CMS tool offers you the advantages we have outlined here, it also comes with a few limitations and disadvantages. Some of these limitations are as follows:

- Its solutions can be a little heavy on computer resources. Also, make your system go slow or crawl.

- You need to update your software from time to time.

- Its updates can be a huge issue at times. If you have anything incompatible with the update, you may find the site go haywire.

- Such situations warrant the services of an expert.

- If your aim of starting a website or blog is to share your views and not necessarily for money-making or turning it into a business, it will incur huge expenses.

- Some CMS solutions may need exceptional system resources and require you to upgrade your devices to handle your website or blog.

VARIOUS CMS

Some CMS platforms are free, whereas others charge you per month. But even with the free ones, you will probably have to part with some cash for the add-ons and templates.

So, keep all of these points we've mentioned in mind, and you should be able to start tracking down the perfect PHP-based CMS for your needs. Here is the list of some CMS:

- WordPress

- Joomla

- Drupal

- OctoberCMS

- OpenCart

- ExpressionEngine

- PyroCMS

- Magento

- Craft CMS

- TYPO3

WordPress

It has become the well-known and most widely used open-source PHP CMSs, which can accommodate lots of apps and is flexible enough to handle a wide range of different scenarios. It provides the foundation for a primary blog as it is a large e-commerce store. You only have to look at the 75 million currently active websites that rely on it to confirm how universally popular it is.

Wordpress CMS.

It is a free and open-source written using PHP, MySQL language. All you have to do is purchase a domain name from Bluehost, Godaddy, or any other domain provider. Then, buy any reliable hosting of your choice that fits within your budget. I recommend buying cPanel shared hosting from Bluehost, Godaddy, or cloud hosting from Cloudways to practice if you are a beginner.

It is an open-source platform and benefited from the ongoing attention of thousands of developers. The reasons for its rapid evolution and why it is the preferred choice of many web application developers and offers you the widest selection of additional widgets, themes, and plug-ins.

It also ships with integrated SEO tools to optimize search engine visibility, which is why developers rate it so very highly.

Before installing WordPress, make sure you should have the following:

- FTP access to your web hosting account

- FTP client

- Web browser

- A web hosting account with the requirements such as PHP version 7 or greater, MySQL version 5.6 or greater, or MariaDB version 10.0 or greater.

Step-by-Step Instructions on How to Install WordPress:

1. **Download WordPress and Upload it:** Download the ZIP file of WordPress from the official WordPress website to your computer, then extract it and upload all files from the inside of the "WordPress" folder to the root folder of your domain, and it is usually called public_html. Upload all files using an FTP client.

2. **Create a Database:** Some of the hosting providers already have a database created but not, in this case, so you will need to create one. If your web host uses cPanel, navigate the Databases section and click the "MySQL Databases" icon. Then create a new database.

3. **Create a Database User:** After creating a database, you will need to create a user for it. So make a new user. After this, add the user to the database, i.e., choose All Privileges options.

   Then write down the following details in the next step. You need to know the hostname, database name, username, and password.

4. **Run the Install:** Navigate to the domain name or to the subdomain into which you uploaded the WordPress files in your web browser.

    Then, choose your language and click Continue.

    Now you add the following details:

- Database Name

- Username

- Password

- Database Host

- Table Prefix

The database host is "localhost," but some web hosts can differ.

We recommend changing this to something different than wp_ for security purposes. You can use, e.g., x3a_. Lastly, click "Submit."

Then, you will see "Run the install" as below. Click on it.

5. **Finish the Installation:** Fill in the following details such as,

- Site Title

- Username

- Password

- Your Email

Then, click "Install WordPress." After this, you should log into your WordPress admin panel.

What Are WordPress Hooks?

WordPress hook allows you to manipulate a procedure without modifying the file on WordPress core. A hook can be applied to action (action hook) and filter (filter hook).

Hooks are essential for any WordPress user. It can help you create some functions or edit the default settings of themes or plug-ins.

A hook is a term that refers to places where you can add your code or change what WordPress is doing or out-putting by default.

Two types of hooks exist in WordPress are:

- **Actions:** An Action is a hook triggered when WordPress is running and lets you take action and include things like creating a widget when WordPress is initializing.

- **Filters:** A Filter allows getting and modifying WordPress data before sending it to the database or the browser. Some filters would include customizing how sections are displayed or adding custom code to the end of a blog post.

Purpose of Hooks

The primary purpose of hooks is to run a function automatically. In addition, this technique also can modify, extend, or limit the functionality of a theme or plug-in.

Here an example of a hook in WordPress:

```
function mytheme_script()
{wp_enqueue_script( 'myCustomJs', 'Custom.js', false
);}
add_action( 'wp_enqueue_scripts', 'mytheme_enqueue_
script' );
```

The above example shows that the hook connects the mytheme_script-function with the wp_enqueue_scripts action. Hook triggers a new action on your site. Thus, it is called an action hook.

How to Use WordPress Hooks

Using hooks does require a bit of knowledge about HTML and PHP. However, creating both action and filter hooks might not be as difficult if you are a beginner.

You only need to go to the post page, then switch to the text editor. You can paste the hooks you have copied from other sites or create yourself when you are there.

Creating an Action Hook

It would be best to activate the add_action () function in the WordPress plug-in to add an action hook. And this function can start by writing the patterns below in your functions.php file.

```
add_action('function name target_hook', 'The_name_of_
function_you_want_to_use', 'priority_scale').
```

A lower preference value means that the function will be run earlier, while the higher one will be later. The scale will show the output in a series of the functions installed using the target_hooks.

The default value of priority_scale is 10. You can arrange the scale according to the number of target_hooks.

Here is an example of a hook:

```php
<?php
add_action( 'wp_print_footerscripts', 'hostinger_
custom_footerscripts' );
function webhost_custom_footerscripts(){
?>
<script>//fill the footer scripts right here</script>
<?php
}
?>
```

The patterns in the above example are:

- <?PHP is where you keep the hook

- add_action is a command for creating the action_hook

- wp_print_footerscripts is the target_hook that you link to a new function

- Hostinger_custom_footerscripts is the function installed and linked to the target_hook

- <script> defines the text you want to show on the target_hook

Details:

- It supports over 68 languages

- WordPress accounts for 76.4% of the CMS market

- The Plug-ins have been downloaded 1.48 billion times

- WordPress powers many government websites around the world

Pros:

- It is an accessible platform

- The most extensive plug-in and theme directories

- It is a very secure platform

- It is integrated SEO features

- It is the availability of WordPress Toolkit extension for the Plesk hosting platform

Cons:

- The themes and plug-ins can require annoyingly frequent updates

- It is open source can mean 'more open to hackers'

- Its customization requires a deep level of understanding

Joomla

It is an open-source Content Management System (CMS) tool. Powerful online applications and websites are built using Joomla. Clients can easily manage their websites with a minimal amount of instructions. It is highly extensible. It runs off PHP or MySQL and is used to create, maintain a structured, flexible portal, add or edit content, and change the site's look and feel. PHP scripting is used and persists most of its data/information in the MySQL database.

Joomla CMS.

History

It is based on Mambo CMS, developed by an Australian company in 2001 and initially released on August 17, 2005. The official version of Joomla 1.0 was released on September 22, 2005.

What Is Joomla in PHP?

It is an open-source CMS used in PHP to publish web content. It allows the user to manage the content of the web pages with ease.

Advantages:

- It is an open-source platform, available for free, and compatible with all browsers.

- Joomla is designed to be easy to install and set up even if you're not an advanced user.

- Since Joomla is so easy to use, you can quickly build sites for your clients as a web designer or developer. With minimal instructions to the clients, clients can easily manage their sites independently.

- It is straightforward to edit the content as it uses the WYSIWYG editor.

- It ensures the safety of data content and doesn't allow anyone to edit the data.

- The templates are very flexible to use, and media files can be uploaded easily in the article editor tool.

- It provides an easy menu creation tool.

Disadvantages:

- It gives compatibility problems while installing several modules, extensions, and plug-ins simultaneously.

- Plug-ins and modules are not available in Joomla.

- Development is too challenging to handle when you want to change the layout.

- Joomla is not much SEO-friendly and makes the website heavy to load and run.

- Joomla! Templates usually contain PHP statements. Understanding at least a little of the language is necessary to create or customize templates. This chunk will describe how to use each section of PHP in the context of a Joomla! Template. For instance, a simple explanation of the PHP if-then-else syntax.

The resource to learn PHP is probably hands-on experience, and Joomla can provide that to you thanks to its native PHP code. Joomla is easy to install with the community's help and takes a little of your time.

Pros:

- It has an intuitive UI

- It is a highly adaptable front-end

- It regularly makes security updates

- Well-suited to blogs and dynamic web apps

Cons:

- It is not as SEO-enabled as some PHP CMSs

- It is difficult for non-developers to add custom designs

- There are not many modules for sale

- Some plug-ins are not completely compatible without modification

How to Download and Install Joomla:

- **Download the Joomla Installation Package before installation:** You need to download its installation package from the application's official site; otherwise, if you download the Joomla package from somewhere else rather than from the official site, if you want to begin a Joomla establishment on a web server.

- **Transfer the Joomla files to your server:** FTP transfers the documents and envelopes to the web server and moves the Joomla establishment documents. For nitty-gritty data, the best way to share documents is through FTP.

- **Make a MySQL database:** Now, you make a MySQL database and relegate a client. When you make your database and user in MYSQL, ensure you record the name, username of the database.

Magento 2.

Magento 2 is the most used CMS to create online stores worldwide. Its robust, scalable architecture and compatibility with the latest technology, such as PHP 7, means a faster load than Magento 1. A Magento version 2 allows the user to update the e-commerce website automatically.

Magento 2 CMS.

History

It is an open-source e-commerce platform developed by Roy Rubin and Yoav Kutner underneath Varien Inc. Its first was released on March 31, 2007. It is a useful software for online business and is currently the largest e-commerce platform globally. Magento 2 is straightforward, versatile, and quick to use.

What Is e-commerce?

E-commerce was first introduced in 1960 through EDI and VAN. It means purchasing, selling goods, services over the Internet, transferring money and data to execute these transactions. It is also called Electronic Commerce or Internet Commerce.

Why Use Magento 2?

- It is compatible with technology like PHP 7, which means a faster load time than Magento 1.

- It handles approximately 10 million page views in a single hour.

- It is a multi-store and multi-language tool and provides an easy admin panel, which is very handy for customization, product creation, filtering data, and navigation.

- It provides the easy ability to set up different websites using a subset of the catalog and the design variation.

- With its open-source nature, you can design your e-commerce store precisely like what you want, without any compromise, and allow searching and sorting the product in various ways.

- It enables several integrated payment gateway methods such as Paypal, Google Checkouts, Braintree, etc.

- WordPress is also good, but it cannot develop business websites. Even WordPress provides plug-ins for e-commerce, but Magento is specifically built for e-commerce.

Features of Magento 2:

- Open and flexible architecture
- Enhanced business agility and productivity
- Faster load time
- Secure payment gateways
- Migration tool
- High performance
- Scalability
- Testing the frameworks
- Catalog management
- Fully SEO centered
- Tools for advertising and marketing

Magento 2 has a Model View ViewModel architecture. The MVVM architecture provides a more robust separation between the Model and View layer, closely related to the Model View Controller (MVC).

Magento 2 is divided into four layers, according to the official documentation.

- Presentation Layer
- Service Layer

- Domain Layer

- Persistence Layer

Installation

This chapter provides a step-by-step procedure for Magento installation. Before installing Magento, you require the following system requirements.

System Requirements for Magento:

- Database – MySQL 5.1 +

- Web Server:

  - Apache 2.x

  - Nginx 1.7.x

- Operating System – Cross-platform

- Browser Support – Internet Explorer 7, Firefox, Google chrome

- SSL (Secure Socket Layer) – A valid security certificate is required for HTTPS

- PHP Compatibility – PHP 5.4 or later

Download Magento:

1. Visit the official documentation of the Magento using this link, https://www.magentocommerce.com/products/downloads/magento/, and you will get to see the new screen.

2. Click on the dropdown menu, and the archive file is available in .zip, .tar.gz, and .tar.bz2 for downloading.

3. Extract the Magento web files from the archive on your computer and upload them into your web server or localhost.

4. Extract the Magento web files from the archive on your computer and upload them into your web server or localhost.

5. Open your browser and navigate your Magento file path (e.g., http://localhost/magento) to start your Magento installation.

6. Click on the Continue button and get the Validation for Magento Downloader screen as shown in the following screen. Here, enter the database details to check for InnoDB support for Magento. Otherwise, click on the Continue button to proceed to the next step.

7. Next, you will get the Magento Connect Manager Deployment screen.

8. It gives protocol names (HTTP or FTP) and stability versions such as stable, beta, alpha, and deployment types. Select appropriate options and click on the Continue button, and it starts the downloading process for Magento.

9. The installation Wizard screen pops up, and check the I agree to the above terms and conditions checkbox and click on the Continue button.

10. Next, you will get the screen for selecting the Locale, Time Zone, and Currency.

11. The screen that pops up is the Configuration screen and now fills the database information such as Type, Host, Name, User Name, and Password. If you don't want to validate the Base URL, you can check the Skip Base URL validation before the Next Step checkbox and click on the Continue button.

12. Go to the Create Admin Account.

13. Now, enter your details such as First Name, Last Name, and Email and the Login Information such as Username, Password, and Confirm Password for admin to use in the back-end. Need not worry about the Encryption Key field, as Magento will generate a key on the next page. Now, enter the details and click on the Continue button.

14. Now, copy the encryption key, which will encrypt passwords, credit cards, and other confidential information. Then you can select the front-end or back-end of the new Magento website.

15. After installation of Magento, click on the Go to Back-end button to log in to the admin panel.

16. You will get the Admin panel as you successfully log in.

Drupal

It is a free and open-source (CMS) that allows organizing, managing, and publishing your content. It is built on PHP-based environments. It is carried out under GNU, i.e., General Public License, which means anyone can download and share it with others. It is used on million sites such as WhiteHouse.gov, World Economic Forum, Stanford University, Examiner. com, and many more.

Drupal CMS.

History

Dries Buytaert developed the standard release of Drupal core in January 2001. It is considered a leading CMS in a variety of industries.

Features:

- It is an open-source software hence requires no licensing costs and makes it easy to create and manage your site, containing the content on informational sites, social media sites, member sites, intranets, and web applications.

- It translates anything in the system with built-in user interfaces and connects your website to other sites and services using feeds, search engine connection capabilities, etc.

- It designs a highly flexible and creative website with adequate display quality, thus increasing the number of visitors to the site and can publish your content on social media such as Twitter, Facebook, and other social mediums.

- It provides more customizable themes, including several base themes used to design your themes for developing web applications.

Advantages:

- It is a more flexible CMS that allows handling content types, including video, text, blog, menu handling, real-time statistics, etc.

- It provides several templates for developing web applications.

- Drupal is easy to manage or create a blog or website. It helps to organize, structure, find, and reuse content.

- It provides exciting themes and templates which give your website an attractive look.

- It has over 7000 plug-ins to boost your website.

Disadvantages:

- It has not a user-friendly interface but requires advanced knowledge and a few basic things to install and modify.

- Its performance is low compared to other CMS. The website built using Drupal will generate big server loads and will never open with a slow Internet connection.

Download Drupal
Steps to download Drupal:

- By using your web browser, navigate to http://drupal.org/project/drupal.

- Click the appropriate version "tar.gz" or "zip" file link of Drupal you want to download.

CHAPTER SUMMARY

In this chapter, we have learned the basics of PHP CMS, and its features, which also define that what the role of CMS in your business is. We have covered various CMSs such as WordPress, Drupal, Magneto, Joomla in brief, including their features, installation, and advantages and disadvantages.

Appraisal

People learn PHP for many reasons. Each programming language has a bit of a learning curve, and one can get bogged down in theory, which can make learning the language unappealing because the task ahead seems exceptionally unpleasant. You may want to build a simple blog or something as advanced as a massive online e-commerce site with thousands of products for sale or education purposes. But it is tough to know where to start getting the needed knowledge about how the language works as a whole.

But if you are looking for a way to get into it fast to make your dreams a reality, then you have come to the right place! This book gives a bit of clearance, and its main aim is to get you through the starting point of your journey to Core PHP and make you clear in Advanced! It only does by telling you the most critical part you need to know to get started quickly for the extreme beginner, in either PHP or MySQL, so you get to doing useful stuff as soon as possible.

This is not a complete guide to PHP that covers all the aspects, but it is the crash course that gives you some practical guidance on how to do cool stuff with PHP and MySQL on their own and together. They both can also get some pretty advanced things, but with the knowledge in this book, you should be able to get those guidelines up and running as you handle the more advanced topics.

A bit of knowledge of HTML and CSS will be required because PHP is just a language used to make web pages and its final result on HTML page and all the styling done on the CSS file. We will cover all the basics of PHP and MySQL and finally, put it all together and build a simple website, for example, where you will be able to store a record of your favorite artists using the dynamic way.

Developing a website is a priority for your business to have a presence on the Internet. Design and development are foundational steps for any website. It is commonly used for website and web application development.

DOI: 10.1201/9781003308669-12

PHP is a general-purpose, server-side scripting language designed to make static and dynamic pages and applications. It is considered a web-development option that is secure, fast, and reliable and offers lots more advantages that make it accessible to many people. We should think about what has made PHP – one of the most widely used programming languages in the web industry.

Then we have covered the basic introduction of PHP that covers the fundamentals of using the PHP programming language. Here you will learn basic PHP syntax and program structure. Next, you know to use the expression, variables, data types, operators, and conditionals. Further, we have covered the control statement concept in PHP, for example, for beginners. Arrays and Loops show you how to use the flow control structures.

We will specifically cover loops and arrays in this chapter. Functions and Classes teach you to identify how to define and call functions. We will also cover how to create classes and how to use the classes and functions together. Some data operations teach you how to handle input from users and print outcomes back to them, handle errors gracefully, and learn the basics of using the MySQL database. Moreover, it will teach you to apply OOP concepts in a framework. We will cover error reporting using the library and learn how to handle those errors using exceptional handling. We will also cover how to manage and structure our application in a framework. Building a PHP Framework, teaches you to build an MVC framework from scratch. Starting from an empty directory, we will create an entire working framework as a starting point for more complex applications.

Further, we have covered building a Contacts Management System, which teaches you to make a contacts CRUD (Create, Read, Update, and Delete) section, which will have a view page to view an individual contact. Besides all these concepts, the main topic of the content management system (CMS) is also described here in this chapter. CMS like WordPress, Drupal, Magento, and Joomla explained briefly.

The basics are all you need to get in this book just by reading it, and it is all you need for understanding the PHP concept. This book gets you up to speed by starting with basic concepts, such as variables, data types, arrays, loops, functions, and OOPS. It then progresses to more advanced concepts, such as OOPS building your frameworks and creating your app. The book has been designed to reduce the gap between learning and implementation. It provides a lot of actual business case scenarios, which will help you understand the concepts and start writing PHP programs as soon as they complete the book.

This book will teach you to install and configure PHP and MySQL with both performance and security in mind and highlight some of the new functionality available in PHP 8 and new data types supported by the current version of MySQL.

Every user has specific reasons for using PHP to build their dream web application, although one could argue that such motives tend to fall into four key categories: practicality, power, possibility, and price.

Bibliography

Abstract classes and methods in PHP | PHPenthusiast. (n.d.). Abstract Classes and Methods in PHP | PHPenthusiast; phpenthusiast.com. Retrieved July 11, 2022, from https://phpenthusiast.com/object-oriented-php-tutorials/abstract-classes-and-methods

API vs Web Service: What's the Difference? (2020, February 9). Guru99; www.guru99.com. https://www.guru99.com/api-vs-web-service-difference.html

Ashwani, K. (2021, May 10). *What is PHP? and How PHP works?* www.devopsschool.com. https://www.devopsschool.com/blog/what-is-php-and-how-php-works/.

Bashir, A. (2019, October 14). *OOP in PHP – Inheritance | Encapsulation | Abstraction | Polymorphism.* Coding Infinite; codinginfinite.com. https://codinginfinite.com/oop-php-inheritance-encapsulation-abstraction-polymorphism/

Chapter 4: The if/else (if) statement and Nested statements. (n.d.). Chapter 4: The If/Else (If) Statement and Nested Statements; eecs.oregonstate.edu. Retrieved July 11, 2022, from https://eecs.oregonstate.edu/ecampus-video/CS161/template/chapter_4/ifelse.html

Chief, E. in. (2021, June 25). *PHP Arithmetic Operators.* PHP Tutorial; www.phptutorial.net. https://www.phptutorial.net/php-tutorial/php-arithmetic-operators/

Chief, E. in. (2021, July 12). *PHP Polymorphism Explained Clearly By Examples.* PHP Tutorial; www.phptutorial.net. https://www.phptutorial.net/php-oop/php-polymorphism/

Chief, E. in. (2021, November 25). *PHP Constants.* PHP Tutorial; www.phptutorial.net. https://www.phptutorial.net/php-tutorial/php-constants/

Chinnathambi, K. (n.d.). *Conditional Statements: If, Else, and Switch.* Kirupa.Com; www.kirupa.com. Retrieved July 11, 2022, from https://www.kirupa.com/html5/conditional_statements_if_else_switch_javascript.htm

CSS Introduction. (n.d.). CSS Introduction; www.w3schools.com. Retrieved July 11, 2022, from https://www.w3schools.com/css/css_intro.asp

Difference Between PHP 5 and 7 – InterviewBit. (2021, October 31). InterviewBit; www.interviewbit.com. https://www.interviewbit.com/blog/difference-between-php-5-and-7/

Difference between while and do-while: Explained with Examples. (2020, April 26). Guru99; www.guru99.com. https://www.guru99.com/while-vs-do-while.html

Do You Know the Trick for Using HTML and PHP on the Same Page? (2019, July 17). ThoughtCo; www.thoughtco.com. https://www.thoughtco.com/php-with-html-2693952

Error handling in PHP – GeeksforGeeks. (2018, October 30). GeeksforGeeks; www.geeksforgeeks.org. https://www.geeksforgeeks.org/error-handling-in-php/

Explain Encapsulation in PHP. (n.d.). Explain Encapsulation in PHP.; www.tutorialspoint.com. Retrieved July 11, 2022, from https://www.tutorialspoint.com/explain-encapsulation-in-php#:~:text=Encapsulation%20is%20a%20protection%20mechanism,code%20more%20secure%20and%20robust.

Explain Polymorphism in PHP. (n.d.). Explain Polymorphism in PHP.; www.tutorialspoint.com. Retrieved July 11, 2022, from https://www.tutorialspoint.com/explain-polymorphism-in-php#:~:text=Polymorphism%20is%20essentially%20an%20OOP,used%20in%20the%20same%20way.

Expressions and Operators (Programming PHP). (n.d.). Expressions and Operators (Programming PHP); docstore.mik.ua. Retrieved July 11, 2022, from https://docstore.mik.ua/orelly/weblinux2/php/ch02_04.htm

Functions — reusable blocks of code – Learn web development | MDN. (2022, July 10). Functions — Reusable Blocks of Code – Learn Web Development | MDN; developer.mozilla.org. https://developer.mozilla.org/en-US/docs/Learn/JavaScript/Building_blocks/Functions

Gabil, D. (n.d.). *PHP Command Line, Interactive Shell/Mode.* ScriptVerse; scriptverse.academy. Retrieved July 11, 2022, from https://scriptverse.academy/tutorials/php-command-line.html

Getting Started with PHP Composer for DependencyManagement. (n.d.). Getting Started with PHP Composer for DependencyManagement; www.w3schools.in. Retrieved July 11, 2022, from https://www.w3schools.in/php/php-composer

Getting Started with PHP Templating — Smashing Magazine. (2011, October 17). Smashing Magazine; www.smashingmagazine.com. https://www.smashingmagazine.com/2011/10/getting-started-with-php-templating/

How to pass PHP Variables by reference? – GeeksforGeeks. (2018, December 20). GeeksforGeeks; www.geeksforgeeks.org. https://www.geeksforgeeks.org/how-to-pass-php-variables-by-reference/#:~:text=Pass%20by%20reference%3A%20When%20variables,are%20defined%20by%20same%20reference.

How to use Global Variables in JavaScript? (n.d.). How to Use Global Variables in JavaScript?; www.tutorialspoint.com. Retrieved July 11, 2022, from https://www.tutorialspoint.com/how-to-use-global-variables-in-javascript

HTML Block and Inline Elements. (n.d.). HTML Block and Inline Elements; www.w3schools.com. Retrieved July 11, 2022, from https://www.w3schools.com/html/html_blocks.asp

HTTP – HyperText Transfer Protocol – javatpoint. (n.d.). Www.Javatpoint.Com; www.javatpoint.com. Retrieved July 11, 2022, from https://www.javatpoint.com/computer-network-http

https://www.educba.com/introduction-to-php/?source=leftnav

https://www.educba.com/php-versions/

Hudson, P. (n.d.). *Escape sequences – Hacking with PHP – Practical PHP.* Escape Sequences – Hacking with PHP – Practical PHP; www.hackingwithphp. com. Retrieved July 11, 2022, from http://www.hackingwithphp.com/2/6/2/ escape-sequences

Hypertext Transfer Protocol – Wikipedia. (1991, January 1). Hypertext Transfer Protocol – Wikipedia; en.wikipedia.org. https://en.wikipedia.org/wiki/ Hypertext_Transfer_Protocol#:~:text=The%20Hypertext%20Transfer%20 Protocol%20(HTTP,%2C%20collaborative%2C%20hypermedia%20 information%20systems.

Introduction – Composer. (n.d.). Introduction – Composer; getcomposer.org. Retrieved July 11, 2022, from https://getcomposer.org/doc/00-intro.md

Introduction to Content Management System (CMS). (n.d.). Introduction to Content Management System (CMS); www.w3schools.in. Retrieved July 11, 2022, from https://www.w3schools.in/wordpress/introduction-to-content-management-system-cms#:~:text=Content%20Management%20System%20 (CMS)%20can,%2C%20WordPress%2C%20TYPO3%2C%20etc.

Introduction to OOPS in PHP | Studytonight. (n.d.). Introduction to OOPS in PHP | Studytonight; www.studytonight.com. Retrieved July 11, 2022, from https://www.studytonight.com/php/php-object-oriented-programming

Jowett, Tony Harris, Rick Hurst, Chris Lacher, M. K. (n.d.). *Data Types, Arrays and Strings.* Data Types, Arrays and Strings; www.cs.fsu.edu. Retrieved July 11, 2022, from https://www.cs.fsu.edu/~cop3014p/lectures/ch9/index.html

Juviler, J. (n.d.). *Static vs. Dynamic Websites: Here's the Difference.* Static vs. Dynamic Websites: Here's the Difference; blog.hubspot.com. Retrieved July 11, 2022, from https://blog.hubspot.com/website/static-vs-dynamic-website#:~:text=Static%20 vs.-,Dynamic%20Website,different%20information%20to%20different%20 visitors.

lvalue and rvalue in C language – GeeksforGeeks. (2017, September 27). GeeksforGeeks; www.geeksforgeeks.org. https://www.geeksforgeeks.org/ lvalue-and-rvalue-in-c-language/

MySQL – Introduction. (n.d.). MySQL – Introduction; www.tutorialspoint.com. Retrieved July 11, 2022, from https://www.tutorialspoint.com/mysql/ mysql-introduction.htm

Object Oriented Programming in PHP. (n.d.). Object Oriented Programming in PHP; www.tutorialspoint.com. Retrieved July 11, 2022, from https://www. tutorialspoint.com/php/php_object_oriented.htm

Operators | Functions and Operators | User Guide | Support | Epi Info™ | CDC. (2021, September 16). Operators | Functions and Operators | User Guide | Support | Epi Info™ | CDC; www.cdc.gov. https://www.cdc.gov/epiinfo/user-guide/functions-and-operators/operators.html#:~:text=Comparison%20 Operators%20are%20used%20to,two%20values%2C%20true%20or%20false.

@phppot. (n.d.). *PHP Escape Sequences – Phppot.* Phppot; phppot.com. Retrieved July 11, 2022, from https://phppot.com/php/php-escape-sequences/

PHP – Error & Exception Handling. (n.d.). PHP – Error & Exception Handling; www.tutorialspoint.com. Retrieved July 11, 2022, from https://www.tutori-alspoint.com/php/php_error_handling.htm

PHP – Function Handling. (n.d.). PHP – Function Handling; www.tutorialspoint. com. Retrieved July 11, 2022, from https://www.tutorialspoint.com/php/ php_function_handling_functions.htm

PHP – Functions. (n.d.). PHP – Functions; www.tutorialspoint.com. Retrieved July 11, 2022, from https://www.tutorialspoint.com/php/php_functions. htm

PHP&CaseSensitivity.(2015,October22).StackOverflow;stackoverflow.com.https:// stackoverflow.com/questions/33273941/php-case-sensitivity#:~:text=In%20 PHP%2C%20variable%20and%20constant,while%20function%20 names%20are%20not.

PHP | Bitwise Operators – GeeksforGeeks. (2018, January 4). GeeksforGeeks; www. geeksforgeeks.org. https://www.geeksforgeeks.org/php-bitwise-operators/

PHP | Encapsulation – GeeksforGeeks. (2019, October 9). GeeksforGeeks; www. geeksforgeeks.org. https://www.geeksforgeeks.org/php-encapsulation/

PHP 5 vs PHP 7 – GeeksforGeeks. (2016, May 5). GeeksforGeeks; www.geeksfor-geeks.org. https://www.geeksforgeeks.org/php-5-vs-php-7/

PHP 7 features & improvements. (2015, December 3). Thijs Feryn; feryn.eu. https://feryn.eu/blog/php-7-is-now-available-new-features-improvements/

PHP Array Functions. (n.d.). PHP Array Functions; www.w3schools.com. Retrieved July 11, 2022, from https://www.w3schools.com/php/php_ref_ array.asp

PHP Arrays. (n.d.). PHP Arrays; www.w3schools.com. Retrieved July 11, 2022, from https://www.w3schools.com/php/php_arrays.asp#:~:text=In%20PHP% 2C%20there%20are%20three,containing%20one%20or%20more%20 arrays

PHP Break and Continue. (n.d.). PHP Break and Continue; www.w3schools.com. Retrieved July 11, 2022, from https://www.w3schools.com/php/php_loop-ing_break.asp

PHP Break and Continue. (n.d.). PHP Break and Continue; www.w3schools.com. Retrieved July 11, 2022, from https://www.w3schools.com/php/php_loop-ing_break.asp

PHP Built-in Functions. (n.d.). PHP Built-in Functions; technosmarter.com. Retrieved July 11, 2022, from https://technosmarter.com/php/PHP-built-in-functions.html

PHP callable Keyword. (n.d.). PHP Callable Keyword; www.w3schools.com. Retrieved July 11, 2022, from https://www.w3schools.com/php/keyword_ callable.asp#:~:text=The%20callable%20keyword%20is%20used,the%20 name%20of%20a%20function

PHP Constructor and Destructor | Studytonight. (n.d.). PHP Constructor and Destructor | Studytonight; www.studytonight.com. Retrieved July 11, 2022, from https://www.studytonight.com/php/php-constructor-and-destructor

PHP Constructors and Destructors. (n.d.). PHP Constructors and Destructors; www.tutorialspoint.com. Retrieved July 11, 2022, from https://www.tutori-alspoint.com/php-constructors-and-destructors

PHP Data Types – Booleans – w3resource. (n.d.). W3resource; www.w3resource. com. Retrieved July 11, 2022, from https://www.w3resource.com/php/data-types/booleans.php

PHP Date/Time Functions. (n.d.). PHP Date/Time Functions; www.w3schools. com. Retrieved July 11, 2022, from https://www.w3schools.com/php/php_ ref_date.asp

PHP declare Keyword. (n.d.). PHP Declare Keyword; www.w3schools.com. Retrieved July 11, 2022, from https://www.w3schools.com/php/keyword_ declare.asp

PHP Echo and Print Statements. (n.d.). PHP Echo and Print Statements; www. w3schools.com. Retrieved July 11, 2022, from https://www.w3schools.com/ php/php_echo_print.asp

PHP Error Functions. (n.d.). PHP Error Functions; www.w3schools.com. Retrieved July 11, 2022, from https://www.w3schools.com/php/php_ref_error.asp

PHP Error Handling and Logging – Tutorial Republic. (n.d.). PHP Error Handling and Logging – Tutorial Republic; www.tutorialrepublic.com. Retrieved July 11, 2022, from https://www.tutorialrepublic.com/php-tutorial/php-error-handling.php

PHP Errors: 4 Different Types (Warning, Parse, Fatal, and Notice Error). (2019, August 6). Knowledge Base by phoenixNAP; phoenixnap.com. https:// phoenixnap.com/kb/php-error-types

PHP File() Function: File_exists, Fopen, Fwrite, Fclose, Fgets, copy, unlink. (2020, February 29). Guru99; www.guru99.com. https://www.guru99.com/php-file-processing.html

PHP Filesystem Functions. (n.d.). PHP Filesystem Functions; www.w3schools. com. Retrieved July 11, 2022, from https://www.w3schools.com/php/php_ ref_filesystem.asp

PHP Function: How to Define? Built in | String | User Defined. (2020, February 14). Guru99; www.guru99.com. https://www.guru99.com/functions-in-php.html

PHP Function: How to Define? Built in | String | User Defined. (2020, February 14). Guru99; www.guru99.com. https://www.guru99.com/functions-in-php .html#:~:text=A%20Function%20in%20PHP%20is,operation%20 without%20returning%20any%20value.

PHP HTTP – javatpoint. (n.d.). Www.Javatpoint.Com; www.javatpoint.com. Retrieved July 11, 2022, from https://www.javatpoint.com/php-http

PHP if...else...elseif Statements. (n.d.). PHP If...Else...Elseif Statements; www.w3schools.com. Retrieved July 11, 2022, from https://www. w3schools.com/php/php_if_else.asp#:~:text=PHP%20Conditional%20 Statements&text=if%20statement%20%2D%20executes%20some%20 code,for%20more%20than%20two%20conditions

PHP Keywords & Identifiers Tutorial | KoderHQ. (n.d.). PHP Keywords & Identifiers Tutorial | KoderHQ; www.koderhq.com. Retrieved July 11, 2022, from https://www.koderhq.com/tutorial/php/keywords-identifiers/

PHP Math Functions. (n.d.). PHP Math Functions; www.w3schools.com. Retrieved July 11, 2022, from https://www.w3schools.com/php/php_ref_math.asp

PHP Object Oriented Programming (OOPs) concept Tutorial with Example. (2020, March 25). Guru99; www.guru99.com. https://www.guru99.com/object-oriented-programming.html

PHP OOP Abstract Classes. (n.d.). PHP OOP Abstract Classes; www.w3schools.com. Retrieved July 11, 2022, from https://www.w3schools.com/php/php_oop_classes_abstract.asp

PHP OOP Classes and Objects. (n.d.). PHP OOP Classes and Objects; www.w3schools.com. Retrieved July 11, 2022, from https://www.w3schools.com/php/php_oop_classes_objects.asp#:~:text=A%20class%20is%20a%20template,is%20an%20instance%20of%20class.

PHP OOP Intro. (n.d.). PHP OOP Intro; www.w3schools.com. Retrieved July 11, 2022, from https://www.w3schools.com/php/php_oop_what_is.asp

PHP OOP: Object-Oriented Programming Concepts in PHP. (n.d.). PHP OOP: Object-Oriented Programming Concepts in PHP; www.valuebound.com. Retrieved July 11, 2022, from https://www.valuebound.com/resources/blog/object-oriented-programming-concepts-php-part-1

PHP Regular Expressions. (n.d.). PHP Regular Expressions; www.w3schools.com. Retrieved July 11, 2022, from https://www.w3schools.com/php/php_regex.asp

PHP return Keyword. (n.d.). PHP Return Keyword; www.w3schools.com. Retrieved July 11, 2022, from https://www.w3schools.com/php/keyword_return.asp

PHP String Functions Complete Reference – GeeksforGeeks. (2019, June 18). GeeksforGeeks; www.geeksforgeeks.org. https://www.geeksforgeeks.org/php-string-functions-complete-reference/

PHP String Functions. (n.d.). PHP String Functions; www.w3schools.com. Retrieved July 11, 2022, from https://www.w3schools.com/php/php_ref_string.asp

PHP Syntax. (n.d.). PHP Syntax; www.w3schools.com. Retrieved July 11, 2022, from https://www.w3schools.com/php/php_syntax.asp

PHP Tutorial: Get started with PHP from scratch. (n.d.). Educative: Interactive Courses for Software Developers; www.educative.io. Retrieved July 11, 2022, from https://www.educative.io/blog/php-tutorial-from-scratch

PHP Type Casting and Conversion of an Object to an Object of other class – javatpoint. (n.d.). Www.Javatpoint.Com; www.javatpoint.com. Retrieved July 11,2022,fromhttps://www.javatpoint.com/php-type-casting-and-conversion-of-an-object-to-an-object-of-other-class

PHP type hinting | PHPenthusiast. (n.d.). PHP Type Hinting | PHPenthusiast; phpenthusiast.com. Retrieved July 11, 2022, from https://phpenthusiast.com/object-oriented-php-tutorials/type-hinting

PHP type hinting | PHPenthusiast. (n.d.). PHP Type Hinting | PHPenthusiast; phpenthusiast.com. Retrieved July 11, 2022, from https://phpenthusiast.com/object-oriented-php-tutorials/type-hinting#:~:text=PHP5%20does%20not%20support%20type,boolean%20(true%20or%20false).

PHP User-defined functions. (n.d.). PHP User-Defined Functions; www.tutorialspoint.com. Retrieved July 11, 2022, from https://www.tutorialspoint.com/php-user-defined-functions

PHP Variable Length Argument Function – javatpoint. (n.d.). Www.Javatpoint. Com; www.javatpoint.com. Retrieved July 11, 2022, from https://www. javatpoint.com/php-variable-length-argument-function

PHP Variable Scope – javatpoint. (n.d.). Www.Javatpoint.Com; www.javatpoint.com. Retrieved July 11, 2022, from https://www.javatpoint.com/php-variable-scope

PHP Variables Scope. (n.d.). PHP Variables Scope; www.w3schools.com. Retrieved July 11, 2022, from https://www.w3schools.com/php/php_variables_scope.asp

PHP: Alternative syntax for control structures – Manual. (n.d.). PHP: Alternative Syntax for Control Structures – Manual; www.php.net. Retrieved July 11, 2022, from https://www.php.net/manual/en/control-structures.alternative-syntax.php

PHP: Anonymous functions – Manual. (n.d.). PHP: Anonymous Functions – Manual; www.php.net. Retrieved July 11, 2022, from https://www.php.net/manual/en/functions.anonymous.php

PHP: array – Manual. (n.d.). PHP: Array – Manual; www.php.net. Retrieved July 11, 2022, from https://www.php.net/manual/en/function.array.php

PHP: Array Operators – Manual. (n.d.). PHP: Array Operators – Manual; www.php.net. Retrieved July 11, 2022, from https://www.php.net/manual/en/language.operators.array.php

PHP: Assignment Operators – Manual. (n.d.). PHP: Assignment Operators – Manual; www.php.net. Retrieved July 11, 2022, from https://www.php.net/manual/en/language.operators.assignment.php

PHP: Basics – Manual. (n.d.). PHP: Basics – Manual; www.php.net. Retrieved July 11, 2022, from https://www.php.net/manual/en/language.variables.basics.php

PHP: Class Abstraction – Manual. (n.d.). PHP: Class Abstraction – Manual; www.php.net. Retrieved July 11, 2022, from https://www.php.net/manual/en/language.oop5.abstract.php

PHP: Comparison Operators – Manual. (n.d.). PHP: Comparison Operators – Manual; www.php.net. Retrieved July 11, 2022, from https://www.php.net/manual/en/language.operators.comparison.php

PHP: Constructors and Destructors – Manual. (n.d.). PHP: Constructors and Destructors – Manual; www.php.net. Retrieved July 11, 2022, from https://www.php.net/manual/en/language.oop5.decon.php

PHP: Expressions – Manual. (n.d.). PHP: Expressions – Manual; www.php.net. Retrieved July 11, 2022, from https://www.php.net/manual/en/language.expressions.php

PHP: Floating point numbers – Manual. (n.d.). PHP: Floating Point Numbers – Manual; www.php.net. Retrieved July 11, 2022, from https://www.php.net/manual/en/language.types.float.php

PHP: foreach – Manual. (n.d.). PHP: Foreach – Manual; www.php.net. Retrieved July 11, 2022, from https://www.php.net/manual/en/control-structures.foreach.php

PHP: Function arguments – Manual. (n.d.). PHP: Function Arguments – Manual; www.php.net. Retrieved July 11, 2022, from https://www.php.net/manual/en/functions.arguments.php

PHP: goto – Manual. (n.d.). PHP: Goto – Manual; www.php.net. Retrieved July 11, 2022, from https://www.php.net/manual/en/control-structures.goto.php

PHP: History of PHP – Manual. (n.d.). PHP: History of PHP – Manual; www.php. net. Retrieved July 11, 2022, from https://www.php.net/manual/en/history. php.php

PHP: if – Manual. (n.d.). PHP: If – Manual; www.php.net. Retrieved July 11, 2022, from https://www.php.net/manual/en/control-structures.if.php

PHP: Introduction – Manual. (n.d.). PHP: Introduction – Manual; www.php.net. Retrieved July 11, 2022, from https://www.php.net/manual/en/language. types.intro.php

PHP: List of Keywords – Manual. (n.d.). PHP: List of Keywords – Manual; www. php.net. Retrieved July 11, 2022, from https://www.php.net/manual/en/ reserved.keywords.php

PHP: match – Manual. (n.d.). PHP: Match – Manual; www.php.net. Retrieved July 11, 2022, from https://www.php.net/manual/en/control-structures. match.php

PHP: mysqli::__construct – Manual. (n.d.). PHP: Mysqli::__construct – Manual; www.php.net. Retrieved July 11, 2022, from https://www.php.net/manual/en/mysqli.construct.php

PHP: Namespaces overview – Manual. (n.d.). PHP: Namespaces Overview – Manual; www.php.net. Retrieved July 11, 2022, from https://www.php.net/manual/en/language.namespaces.rationale.php

PHP: Passing by Reference – Manual. (n.d.). PHP: Passing by Reference – Manual; www.php.net. Retrieved July 11, 2022, from https://www.php.net/manual/en/language.references.pass.php

PHP: Predefined Variables – Manual. (n.d.). PHP: Predefined Variables – Manual; www.php.net. Retrieved July 11, 2022, from https://www.php.net/manual/en/reserved.variables.php

PHP: print_r – Manual. (n.d.). PHP: Print_r – Manual; www.php.net. Retrieved July 11, 2022, from https://www.php.net/manual/en/function.print-r.php

PHP: require – Manual. (n.d.). PHP: Require – Manual; www.php.net. Retrieved July 11, 2022, from https://www.php.net/manual/en/function.require.php

PHP: Strings – Manual. (n.d.). PHP: Strings – Manual; www.php.net. Retrieved July 11, 2022, from https://www.php.net/manual/en/language.types.string. php

PHP: String Operators – Manual. (n.d.). PHP: String Operators – Manual; www.php.net. Retrieved July 11, 2022, from https://www.php.net/manual/en/language.operators.string.php#:~:text=String%20Operators%20%C2%B6&text=The%20first%20is%20the%20concatenation,argument%20on%20the%20left%20side.

PHP: Variable functions – Manual. (n.d.). PHP: Variable Functions – Manual; www.php.net. Retrieved July 11, 2022, from https://www.php.net/manual/en/functions.variable-functions.php

PHP: Variable scope – Manual. (n.d.). PHP: Variable Scope – Manual; www.php.net. Retrieved July 11, 2022, from https://www.php.net/manual/en/language .variables.scope.php

PHP: Variables From External Sources – Manual. (n.d.). PHP: Variables From External Sources – Manual; www.php.net. Retrieved July 11, 2022, from https://www.php.net/manual/en/language.variables.external.php

Polymorphism in PHP – javatpoint. (n.d.). Www.Javatpoint.Com; www.javatpoint.com. Retrieved July 11, 2022, from https://www.javatpoint.com/polymorphism-in-php

Pros and cons of PHP programming language that every developer must know | TechGig. (2021, March 22). TechGig; content.techgig.com. https://content.techgig.com/pros-and-cons-of-php-programming-language-that-every-developer-must-know/articleshow/81637605.cms

Python Global, Local and Nonlocal variables (With Examples). (n.d.). Python Global, Local and Nonlocal Variables (With Examples); www.programiz.com. Retrieved July 11, 2022, from https://www.programiz.com/python-programming/global-local-nonlocal-variables

8 Reasons Why PHP Is Still So Important for Web Development. (2022, April 29). 8 Reasons Why PHP Is Still So Important for Web Development; www.jobsity.com. https://www.jobsity.com/blog/8-reasons-why-php-is-still-so-important-for-web-development

Regular expression – Wikipedia. (2016, October 31). Regular Expression – Wikipedia; en.wikipedia.org. https://en.wikipedia.org/wiki/Regular_expression

Regular Expression (Regex) Tutorial. (n.d.). Regular Expression (Regex) Tutorial; www3.ntu.edu.sg. Retrieved July 11, 2022, from https://www3.ntu.edu.sg/home/ehchua/programming/howto/Regexe.html

Regular Expressions Cookbook, 2nd Edition. (n.d.). O'Reilly Online Learning; www.oreilly.com. Retrieved July 11, 2022, from https://www.oreilly.com/library/view/regular-expressions-cookbook/9781449327453/ch04s01.html

Regular Expressions in PHP – Tutorial Republic. (n.d.). Regular Expressions in PHP – Tutorial Republic; www.tutorialrepublic.com. Retrieved July 11, 2022, from https://www.tutorialrepublic.com/php-tutorial/php-regular-expressions.php

RESTful Web Services – Introduction. (n.d.). RESTful Web Services – Introduction; www.tutorialspoint.com. Retrieved July 11, 2022, from https://www.tutorialspoint.com/restful/restful_introduction.htm#

RESTful Web Services. (n.d.). RESTful Web Services; www.w3schools.in. Retrieved July 11, 2022, from https://www.w3schools.in/restful-web-services/intro

Sá, J. de. (n.d.). *PHP The Ultimate Step by Step guide for beginners on how to learn PHP and MYSQL programming in just 6 hours – PDF Room – Lógica I – 8*. Passei Direto; www.passeidireto.com. Retrieved July 11, 2022, from https://www.passeidireto.com/arquivo/92560233/php-the-ultimate-step-by-step-guide-for-beginners-on-how-to-learn-php-and-mysql-/8

Sarosa, A. (2018, November 15). *What Is HTML? Hypertext Markup Language Basics for Beginners*. Hostinger Tutorials; www.hostinger.in. https://www.hostinger.in/tutorials/what-is-html#:~:text=HTML%20(stands%20for%20Hypertext%20Markup,and%20structure%20of%20a%20document.

Scope of Variables. (n.d.). Scope of Variables; www.cpp.edu. Retrieved July 11, 2022, from https://www.cpp.edu/~elab/ECE114/Scope%20of%20Variables. html

Simple Object Access Protocol (SOAP) 1.1. (n.d.). Simple Object Access Protocol (SOAP) 1.1; www.w3.org. Retrieved July 11, 2022, from https://www.w3.org/ TR/2000/NOTE-SOAP-20000508/

SOAP Web Services Tutorial: What is SOAP Protocol? EXAMPLE. (2020, January 15). Guru99; www.guru99.com. https://www.guru99.com/soap-simple-object-access-protocol.html

Soni, S. (2018, December 4). *Object-Oriented PHP With Classes and Objects.* Code Envato Tuts+; code.tutsplus.com. https://code.tutsplus.com/tutorials/ basics-of-object-oriented-programming-in-php–cms-31910

Soni, S. (2020, November 24). *How to Use PHP in HTML.* Code Envato Tuts+; code.tutsplus.com. https://code.tutsplus.com/tutorials/how-to-use-php-in-html-code–cms-34378

Soni, S. (2020, October 26). *PHP Control Structures and Loops: if, else, for, foreach, while, and More.* Code Envato Tuts+; code.tutsplus.com. https://code.tutsplus.com/tutorials/php-control-structures-and-loops–cms-31999

Staff, E. (2013, June 28). *What is HTTP, Structure of HTTP Request and Response? – WebNots.* WebNots; www.webnots.com. https://www.webnots. com/what-is-http/

Static Variables in C – GeeksforGeeks. (2015, July 3). GeeksforGeeks; www.geeksforgeeks.org. https://www.geeksforgeeks.org/static-variables-in-c/

$this keyword in PHP – GeeksforGeeks. (2020, July 8). GeeksforGeeks; www. geeksforgeeks.org. https://www.geeksforgeeks.org/this-keyword-in-php/

Top 10 PHP CMS Platforms For Developers in 2021. (2021, April 7). Plesk; www.plesk.com. https://www.plesk.com/blog/various/top-10-php-cms-platforms-for-developers-in-2020/

Type Conversion: Convert variable data type in PHP – BrainBell. (n.d.). Type Conversion: Convert Variable Data Type in PHP – BrainBell; brainbell.com. Retrieved July 11, 2022, from https://brainbell.com/php/type-conversion.html

Understanding the PHP Data Types – Tutorial Republic. (n.d.). Understanding the PHP Data Types – Tutorial Republic; www.tutorialrepublic.com. Retrieved July 11, 2022, from https://www.tutorialrepublic.com/php-tutorial/php-data-types.php#:~:text=The%20values%20assigned%20to%20a,%2C%20Object%2C%20resource%20and%20NULL.

Use of FLAG in programming – GeeksforGeeks. (2018, December 4). GeeksforGeeks; www.geeksforgeeks.org. https://www.geeksforgeeks.org/ use-of-flag-in-programming/

Vijay, K. (2020, May 20). *Control Statements In PHP.* Control Statements In PHP; www.c-sharpcorner.com. https://www.c-sharpcorner.com/article/control-statements-in-php/#:~:text=Introduction,until%20the%20condition%20 is%20satisfied.

Web technology for developers | MDN. (2022, May 30). Web Technology for Developers | MDN; developer.mozilla.org. https://developer.mozilla.org/ en-US/docs/Web

What are String Functions in PHP | Importance of String Functions. (2021, May 10). Simplilearn.Com; www.simplilearn.com. https://www.simplilearn .com/tutorials/php-tutorial/string-funtions-in-php

What are String Functions in PHP | Importance of String Functions. (2021, May 10). Simplilearn.Com; www.simplilearn.com. https://www.simplilearn.com/ tutorials/php-tutorial/string-funtions-in-php#:~:text=According%20to%20 string%20functions%20in,is%20returned%20by%20this%20function.

What are Web Services? – GeeksforGeeks. (2021, July 11). GeeksforGeeks; www. geeksforgeeks.org.https://www.geeksforgeeks.org/what-are-web-services/#: ~:text=On%20the%20World%20Wide%20Web,and%20invoked%20 over%20the%20network.

What are Web Services? Architecture, Types, Example. (2020, January 10). Guru99; www.guru99.com. https://www.guru99.com/web-service-architecture.html

What Is a Content Management System (CMS)? (2022, June 16). Kinsta®; kinsta. com. https://kinsta.com/knowledgebase/content-management-system/

What is a relational database? (n.d.). What Is a Relational Database | Oracle India; www.oracle.com. Retrieved July 11, 2022, from https://www.oracle.com/in/ database/what-is-a-relational-database/

What is a URL (Uniform Resource Locator)? Definition from SearchNetworking. (2021, September 1). SearchNetworking; www.techtarget.com. https://www. techtarget.com/searchnetworking/definition/URL

What is a Web Server and How Does it Work? (2020, July 1). WhatIs.Com; www. techtarget.com. https://www.techtarget.com/whatis/definition/Web-server

What is CSS? – Learn web development | MDN. (2022, May 30). What Is CSS? – Learn Web Development | MDN; developer.mozilla.org. https://developer. mozilla.org/en-US/docs/Learn/CSS/First_steps/What_is_CSS

What is Object-Oriented Programming (OOP)? (2021, July 1). SearchAppArchitecture; www.techtarget.com. https://www.techtarget.com/ searchapparchitecture/definition/object-oriented-programming-OOP

What Is Ternary Operator in PHP: Syntax, Advantages & More | Simplilearn. (2022, January 3). Simplilearn.Com; www.simplilearn.com. https://www.simplilearn. com/tutorials/php-tutorial/ternary-operator-in-php?source=frs_category

What is the difference between a language construct and a "built-in" function in PHP ? – GeeksforGeeks. (2019, February 26). GeeksforGeeks; www.geeksfor-geeks.org. https://www.geeksforgeeks.org/what-is-the-difference-between-a-language-construct-and-a-built-in-function-in-php/

Why PHP is Good Choice for Web Development. (n.d.). Why PHP Is Good Choice for Web Development; www.tekshapers.com. Retrieved July 11, 2022, from https://www.tekshapers.com/blog/Why-PHP-is-Good-Choice-for-Web-Development

Why should we learn PHP in 2020? (n.d.). Quora; www.quora.com. Retrieved July 11, 2022, from https://www.quora.com/Why-should-we-learn-PHP-in-2020

Working with PHP Operators – Tutorial Republic. (n.d.). Working with PHP Operators – Tutorial Republic; www.tutorialrepublic.com. Retrieved July 11, 2022, from https://www.tutorialrepublic.com/php-tutorial/php-operators.php

Index